Barriers to Asset Recovery

Barriers to Asset Recovery

Kevin M. Stephenson
Larissa Gray
Ric Power
Jean-Pierre Brun
Gabriele Dunker
Melissa Panjer

StAR Stolen Asset Recovery Initiative
The World Bank • UNODC

ISBN: 978-0-8213-8660-6
eISBN: 978-0-8213-8661-3
DOI: 10.1596/978-0-8213-8660-6

Cover photo: Istockphoto

Library of Congress Cataloging-in-Publication Data
Stephenson, Kevin, 1962-
    Barriers to asset recovery : an analysis of the key barriers and recommendations for action / Kevin Stephenson, Larissa Gray, Ric Power.
        p. cm.
    Includes bibliographical references and index.
    ISBN 978-0-8213-8660-6 — ISBN 978-0-8213-8661-3 (electronic)
    1. Forfeiture—Criminal provisions. 2. Searches and seizures. I. Gray, Larissa. II. Power, Ric. III. Title.
    K5107.S74 2011
    345'.0773—dc22

                                                                                    2011010618

Contents

Acknowledgments

This study is the result of special collaborative efforts from colleagues around the world. Their time and expertise were invaluable in identifying barriers to asset recovery and developing recommendations to overcome these barriers.

This publication was written by Mr. Kevin M. Stephenson (team leader, Financial Market Integrity Unit, World Bank), Ms. Larissa Gray (Financial Market Integrity Unit, World Bank), Mr. Ric Power (United Nations Office on Drugs and Crime [UNODC]), Mr. Jean-Pierre Brun (Financial Market Integrity Unit, World Bank), Ms. Gabriele Dunker (project consultant), and Ms. Melissa Panjer (project consultant).

The authors are especially grateful to Mr. Adrian Fozzard (Coordinator, Stolen Asset Recovery [StAR] Initiative), Mr. Dimitri Vlassis (Chief of the Corruption and Economic Crime Section - UNODC) and Mr. Jean Pesme (Manager, Financial Market Integrity Unit, Financial and Private Sector Development Network) for their ongoing support and guidance on the project.

As part of the drafting and consultation process, practitioners' workshops were held in Vienna, Austria (May 2009), Casablanca, Morocco (August 2009), Buenos Aires, Argentina (August 2009), and Lausanne, Switzerland (May 2010). Also, country visits were conducted in Cayman Islands, Italy, Japan, and Singapore with some practitioners that were unable to attend the aforementioned workshops. Practitioners brought experience conducting criminal confiscation, non-conviction based confiscation, civil actions, investigations, asset tracing, international cooperation and asset management—from both civil and common law jurisdictions, and from both developed and developing countries. The following list is by name followed by the country or organization with which that person is affiliated. This does not mean that this person's participation necessarily represented the views of the countries mentioned. The people participating in one or more of these workshops or country visits were Yves Aeschlimann (Switzerland), Oscar Alberto Del Rio (Colombia), Jorge Alberto Lara Rivera (Mexico), Georgis Taylor Alexander (Saint Lucia), Simon Alexis (Trinidad), Jose Amarilla (Paraguay), Maria Araujo (Brazil), Luis Arocena (Argentina), William Bailhache (Jersey), Gary Balch (United Kingdom), Jaime S. Bautista (Philippines), Kennedy Bosire (Kenya), Robert Broekhuijsen (Netherlands), Katia Bucaino (Italy), Rachmat Budiman (Indonesia), Ian Bulmer (Canada), Lindsey Cacho (Cayman Islands), Ricardo Cespedes (República Bolivariana de Venezuela), Zephyerine A.T. Charles (Grenada), Leong Kok

Cheong (Singapore), Jean-Sebastien Conty (France), Mohammed Dauda (Nigeria), Maxence Delorme (France), Jean-Pierre Mvondo Evezo'o (Cameroon), Mario Gara (Italy), Pascal Gossin (Switzerland), Adrian Fajardo (Mexico), Ahmed Yassine Foukara (Morocco), Vernon Francois (Saint Lucia), Clara Garrido (Colombia), Rudolph Gordon (Cayman Islands), Yoshinobu Goto (Japan), Soh Kee Hean (Singapore), Hay Hung Chun (Singapore), Koji Hayashi (Japan), Edward Hoseah (Tanzania), Henderson Hunte (Cayman Islands), Takeshi Hiramatsu (Japan), Karen Hughes (St. Kitts and Nevis), Giovanni Ilacqua (Italy),Toshifumi Ishida (Japan), Lawrence Iwodi (Nigeria), Shoichi Izawa (Japan), Elena Jacob (Cayman Islands), Stephanie Jeavons (United Kingdom), Mathew Joseph (Singapore), Miguel Jurado Fabara (Ecuador), Vitaliy Kasko (Ukraine), Jumpei Kawahara (Japan), Shuhei Kojima (Japan), Yoshiyuki Komiya (Japan), Bibiana Lee (Singapore), Chua Jia Leng (Singapore), Fernanda Lima (Brazil), Raymond Lockiby (Grenada), Marko Magdic (Chile), Nahid Mahtab (Bangladesh), Jennifer Marie (Singapore), Claudio Mascotto (Switzerland), John Masters (Cayman Islands), Takashi Miura (Japan), Winston Cheng Howe Ming (Singapore), Abdul Mobin (Bangladesh), Ruth Molina (Guatemala), Yoshinori Momonoi (Japan), Enrico Monfrini (Switzerland), Shoko Moriya (Japan), Holly Morton (United Kingdom), Charles Moynot (France), Elnur Musayev (Azerbaijan), Cahyo Rahadian Muzhar (Indonesia), Maxwell Nkole (Zambia), Jean Fils Kleber Ntamack (Cameroon), Mirza Nurhidayat (Indonesia), Arif Havas Oegroseno (Indonesia), Patricia O'Reilly (Argentina), Juan Pavia Cardell (Spain), Dr. Ricardo Perez Blanco (Uruguay), Justice Jean Permanand (Trinidad), Pedro Pereira (Basel Institute on Governance), Amelia Julia Principe Trujillo (Peru), Frederic Raffray (Guernsey), Renato Righetti (Italy), Nuhu Ribadu (Nigeria), Indra Rosandry (Indonesia), LaTeisha Sandy (St. Vincent and the Grenadines), Jean-Bernard Schmid (Switzerland), Maria Schnebli (Switzerland), Michael Scully (Singapore), Shunsuke Shirakawa (Japan), Gavin Shiu (Hong Kong SAR, China), Salim Succar (Haiti), Romina Tello Cortez (Argentina), Takahiro "Taka" Tsuda (Japan), Akinori Tsuruya (Japan), Ronald Viquez Solis (Costa Rica), Naotsugu Umeda (Japan), Valerie Tay Mei Ing (Singapore), Carmen Visuetti (Panama), Masaki Wada (Japan), Gerhard Wahle (Germany), Dr. Robert Wallner (Liechtenstein), Gary Walters (United Kingdom), Wayne Patrick Walsh (Hong Kong SAR, China), Paul Whatmore (United Kingdom), Marilyn Williams (Belize), Simon Williams (Canada), Valentin Zellweger (Switzerland), and Dr. Fausto Zuccarelli (Italy).

The team benefited from many insightful comments during the peer review process, which was co-chaired by Mr. Jean Pesme and Mr. Adrian Fozzard. The peer reviewers were Mr. Luis Urrutia Corral (Head of FIU, Ministry of Finance and Public Credit, Mexico), Mr. Agustin Flah (Legal Department, World Bank), Mr. Giovanni Gallo (UNODC), Ms. Jeanne Hauch (Integrity Operations, World Bank), Mr. Mutembo Nchito (MNB Legal Practitioners, Zambia), Ms. Heba Shams (Special Assistant, Office of the Managing Director, World Bank), and Mr. Simon Whitfield (Anti-Corruption Team, United Kingdom Department for International Development). The team also appreciated the advice of the Honorable Barry O'Keefe (retired Chief Judge of the Commercial Division and an Additional Judge of Appeal of the Supreme Court of New South Wales, Australia) and Mr. Stephen Zimmermann (Director, Integrity Operations, World Bank) during the concept note phase of the project.

The team also appreciated the comments on the checklists and other matters related to this study by Timothy Le Cocq (Jersey), Samuel Bulgin (Cayman Islands), Jack de Kluiver (United States), John Roth (United States), Andrea Tisi (United States), Robert Leventhal (United States), Tim Steele (StAR), and Jean Weld (United States).

A special thanks also to Ms. Thelma Ayamel, Ms. Maria Orellano, and Ms. Jocelyn Taylor for administrative support, in particular arranging the logistics of the workshops in Vienna, Casablanca, and Lausanne; and to Miguel Nicolas de la Riva for his support in the administration of the project. Also, special thanks to Mr. Valentin Zellweger (Switzerland), Mr. Pierre-Yves Morier (Switzerland), and Ms. Meret Adam (Switzerland) for their cooperation and collaboration while incorporating the Lausanne workshop into the Lausanne process (Lausanne V).

Kevin M. Stephenson
Task Team Leader
Financial Market Integrity Unit
World Bank

Abbreviations

ARINSA	Asset Recovery Inter-Agency Network for Southern Africa
AML	anti-money laundering
CARIN	Camden Asset Recovery Inter-Agency Network
CFT	combating the financing of terrorism
DEA	U.S. Drug Enforcement Administration
EU	European Union
FATF	Financial Action Task Force on Money Laundering
FBI	U.S. Federal Bureau of Investigation
FIU	financial intelligence unit
IBERRED	Red Iberoamericana de Cooperación Juridica Internacional
ICAR	International Centre for Asset Recovery
ICE	U.S. Immigration and Customs Enforcement
IMoLIN	International Money Laundering Information Network
INTERPOL	International Criminal Police Organization
IRS	U.S. Internal Revenue Service
MLA	mutual legal assistance
MLAT	mutual legal assistance treaty
MOU	memorandum of understanding
NCB	non-conviction based
OECD	Organisation for Economic Co-operation and Development
PEP	politically exposed person
SAR	special administrative region (of China)
StAR	Stolen Asset Recovery Initiative
UNCAC	United Nations Convention against Corruption
UNODC	United Nations Office on Drugs and Crime
UNTOC	United Nations Convention against Transnational Organized Crime

Executive Summary

Theft of public assets from developing countries is an immense problem with a staggering development impact. These thefts divert valuable public resources from addressing the abject poverty and fragile infrastructure often present in these countries. Although the exact magnitude of the proceeds of corruption circulating in the global economy is impossible to ascertain, estimates demonstrate the severity and scale of the problem. An estimated $20 to $40 billion is lost to developing countries each year through corruption.[5] What this estimate does not capture are the societal costs of corruption and the devastating impact of such crimes on victim countries. Theft of assets by corrupt officials, often at the highest levels of government, weakens confidence in public institutions, damages the private investment climate, and divests needed funding available for core investment in such poverty alleviation measures as public health, education, and infrastructure.[6]

The Stolen Asset Recovery Initiative (StAR) estimates that only $5 billion in stolen assets has been repatriated over the past 15 years. The huge gap between even the lowest estimates of assets stolen and those repatriated demonstrates the importance of forcefully addressing the barriers to asset recovery. International cooperation is essential. Barriers to asset recovery have been discussed in previous works, and the United Nations Convention against Corruption (UNCAC) was to be the solution to many of these barriers.[7] Yet the lengthy process for asset recovery, the low level of activity, and the difficulties reported by practitioners suggest that many barriers are still firmly in place.

This study, prepared by the StAR Initiative, builds on the experience of dozens of practitioners around the world who have hands-on experience in asset recovery and on independent analyses by staff. More than 50 practitioners with day-to-day experience in asset recovery, both from requesting jurisdictions and from the requested jurisdictions, were consulted through a series of workshops, country visits, and a thorough review of the findings of the study before publication.

---

5. United Nations Office on Drugs and Crime (UNODC) and the World Bank, "Stolen Asset Recovery (StAR) Initiative: Challenges, Opportunities, and Action Plan" (Washington, DC: World Bank 2007), p. 10, citing Raymond Baker, *Capitalism's Achilles Heel: Dirty Money and How to Renew the Free-Market System* (Hoboken, NJ: John Wiley & Sons, Inc., 2005).

6. UNODC and World Bank, "Stolen Asset Recovery (StAR) Initiative: Challenges, Opportunities, and Action Plan," p. 9.

7. See for example, "Report of the Commonwealth Working Group on Asset Repatriation" (London: Commonwealth Secretariat, Marlboro House, August 2005.

This study is for policy makers. Its key objective is to mobilize policy makers on the existing difficulties in stolen asset recovery actions and convince them to take action on the featured recommendations. Such action would enhance the capacity of practitioners to successfully recover stolen assets. We also recommend that practitioners should make more use of the existing tools, as outlined in the Operational Recommendations of this study.

Because asset recovery is about collective action, we also believe that other critical constituencies—such as the Group of 20, the UNCAC Asset Recovery Working Group, the Financial Action Task Force on Money Laundering, financial institutions, developmental agencies, and civil society—can all take actions that could assist in diminishing the barriers to assets recovery. Also, civil society could use this study to derive a checklist for measuring states' progress in addressing and overcoming the barriers to asset recovery.

Both UNCAC and the United Nations Convention on Transnational Organized Crime (UNTOC) are essential to collective action to recover the proceeds of corruption and stolen assets. Ratification and full implementation of these two conventions is a necessary step forward. It is, however, not sufficient nor a panacea, because several of the barriers identified cannot be overcome through the conventions per se.

We have identified various obstacles to asset recovery under three distinct headings of general barriers and institutional issues, legal barriers and requirements that delay assistance, and operational barriers and communication issues.

First, the general, or institutional, barriers include issues related to the overall context in which asset recovery takes place. Throughout the study, "lack of political will" was cited as a key impediment to the recovery of the proceeds of corruption. The project team defined this phrase to mean a lack of a comprehensive, sustained, and concerted policy or strategy to identify asset recovery as a priority and to ensure alignment of objectives, tools, and resources to this end. The general barriers also include the lack of adherence to and enforcement of anti-money laundering (AML) measures as a means to prevent and detect the proceeds of corruption in the first place.

The cornerstone of any country's successful and lasting policy and practice on the recovery of stolen assets is the adoption of a clear, comprehensive, sustained, and concerted policy and strategy. Beyond publicly showing commitment by policy makers, such a strategy is necessary to define goals and targets, to identify all available tools (laws and regulations as well as processes), to mobilize the needed expertise and resources, and to make stakeholders accountable. Such a strategy should build on a proactive, responsive, spontaneous, and transparent policy and practice toward asset recovery—where, for example, a refusal for mutual legal assistance in asset recovery cases cannot rely on opaque arguments, such as "economic interest."

Part of this strategy should also build on more forceful implementation of anti-money laundering measures, many of which are not properly observed or enforced. We call on financial institutions and their supervisors to be more diligent and proactive when dealing with politically exposed persons (PEPs) in the first place.

Most of the legal barriers are onerous requirements to the provision of mutual legal assistance (MLA); excessive banking secrecy; lack of non-conviction based asset confiscation procedures; and overly burdensome procedural and evidentiary laws, including the need to disclose information to asset holders during investigations. Removing the legal barriers is obviously essential. Absent a clear and sound legal framework, asset recovery becomes, in a best-case scenario, arduous and, in a worst-case scenario, impossible.

The essence of the recommendations to effectively address legal barriers is to adopt a more flexible and proactive approach to dual criminality (criminalization of the offense in both jurisdictions) and reciprocity; to protect the integrity of investigations by not informing the asset holder in cases where investigative and asset preservation measures are involved, provided that sufficient protections of due process rights are present; to take steps to limit the grounds for MLA refusal, including by extending statutes of limitations; and to stop automatic denial of MLA for reasons of economic interest. In addition, this report strongly recommends a systematic lifting of bank secrecy in international cases involving all UNCAC and UNTOC offenses. Finally, legislation allowing non-conviction based confiscation should be adopted and implemented.

Even with a sound legal framework, asset recovery is stymied by operational barriers—impediments involving processes and communication between parties. Communication issues dominate: difficulties in identifying focal points to make MLA requests, challenges in maintaining contacts and coordinating asset recovery actions, delays in processing and responding to MLA requests, and deficiencies in the drafting of the requests all impede the provision of assistance. Other important operational barriers include difficulties in identifying owners of bank accounts because of the lack of a national bank registry, as well as failure to manage and preserve assets that have been restrained during the recovery process before a formal confiscation occurs. Establishing a national bank registry of account holder information is a powerful tool to facilitate the tracing of assets and to accelerate and assist international cooperation. Setting up credible and effective asset management measures, aimed at preventing the depletion of restrained or seized assets, are strong incentives to improved asset recovery.

To foster trust and communication among practitioners, and bolster their expertise, this study recommends significant efforts to train investigators, investigative magistrates, prosecutors, and judges on the international standards, on the various tools available for asset recovery, and on the experience to be gained from actual cases. In addition, we recommend that jurisdictions significantly improve, and have more recourse to, the procedural tools allowing international cooperation before a formal MLA request is made—both to streamline the exchange of information and to improve the quality of the assistance.

International asset recovery is a complex legal issue, and its practice is further complicated by its reliance on international cooperation at every stage of the process. This complexity makes it even more difficult to mobilize attention and efforts to overcome the barriers identified in this study. We have identified key recommendations that, if implemented, will provide practitioners with the tools needed to improve effectiveness in asset recovery cases. We hope that monitoring progress in their implementation will lead to an increased number of successful asset recovery cases—which is the ultimate acid test.

Principal Recommendations

The study sets out many recommendations to help overcome the barriers to stolen asset recovery; it is important to highlight those recommendations that policy makers and practitioners should prioritize. Each principal recommendation identified in this section contains a brief statement of the issues it addresses, followed by a succinct policy or operational recommendation.

These principal recommendations were chosen because they are considered the most important to implement if efforts to improve stolen asset recovery worldwide are to succeed. In many cases, they relate to more than one of the barriers identified in this study or to the more significant obstacles to asset recovery. If properly implemented, these recommendations will thus secure the greatest progress in asset recovery.

Recommendations

Recommendation 1

Adopt and Implement Comprehensive Strategic Plans Targeting Stolen Asset Recovery and Provide Sufficient Resources and Training *(Provide Practitioners the Framework and the Tools).*
Many jurisdictions do not sufficiently prioritize asset recovery cases or devote sufficient resources to them, resulting in a lack of competent practitioners, expertise, and necessary tools. Ultimately, these jurisdictions lack true commitment and do not mobilize effectively the tools to recover stolen assets (Barrier 2). Moreover, responsible authorities lack the expertise and experience necessary for drafting proper MLA requests or using international conventions and other tools to cooperate in international asset recovery cases (Barriers 1, 3, and 8).

Recovery efforts have been most successful when jurisdictions develop and implement effective strategic plans to improve on the recovery of the proceeds of corruption. Such plans should establish reporting mechanisms so that progress can be tracked and results monitored. In addition, jurisdictions should prioritize training of the competent authorities in asset recovery matters, including training on relevant domestic laws and international conventions and standards; jurisdictions should establish specialized investigative or prosecution teams; and jurisdictions should also ensure that financial investigators, prosecutors, judges, and other responsible authorities have the proper resources.

Clear accountability for results will help create incentives for specialized teams to be proactive in pursuing the proceeds of corruption.

Recommendation 2

Adopt Policies and Operational Procedures to Cultivate Mutual Trust and Improve Communication *(Build Trusting Relationships).*
A lack of trust between jurisdictions may inhibit or delay the provision of MLA, particularly in urgent matters or where jurisdictions have significantly different legal, political, or judicial systems. Without trust, jurisdictions are hesitant to share intelligence data; to assist in gathering evidence; or to freeze, seize, confiscate, or repatriate assets (Barriers 2 and 7). Moreover, MLA requests may be denied if they are inappropriate, unclear, unfocused, or contain irrelevant information. Furthermore, international cooperation is hindered by insufficient information about informal assistance, applicable laws, procedures, evidentiary standards, MLA requirements, and the status of requests (Barriers 4, 23 and 24).

Improved communication and mentoring of the relevant authorities in originating jurisdictions will improve the quality of requests and the chance of successfully identifying and recovering stolen assets. Jurisdictions should adopt policies and procedures that cultivate trust and improve communication, such as:

- legislation allowing for the spontaneous sharing of information with another jurisdiction;
- policies that facilitate personal contacts between competent authorities through, for example, the provision of liaison magistrates, financial intelligence units, liaison officers, customs and police attachés, and financial support for the placement of liaison officers or attachés in other jurisdictions;
- communication strategies whereby developed countries provide technical support and other assistance on communication issues faced by developing jurisdictions;
- policies encouraging participation at relevant international and bilateral meetings and in practitioner networks, including regional asset recovery networks; and
- plans which identify the primary and secondary focal points within the central authority and other relevant competent authorities as initial contact points for informal and formal MLA.

Jurisdictions should adopt policies and procedures that improve the sharing of information between authorities that request MLA assistance (originating authorities) and those receiving such requests (requested authorities), including information on the status of requests. This information should be comprehensive, easy to obtain, and publicly available on a government Web site. Examples of information to be made available include

- MLA laws and relevant statutory provisions, regulations, and tools available in the jurisdiction;
- explanatory guidelines and sample requests for assistance;
- types of investigative techniques permitted or disallowed;
- burden and standard-of-proof requirements;
- information that can be provided without the need for a formal MLA request;
- reports on the status of MLA requests; and
- reasons for rejection of MLA request.

Recommendation 3

Introduce Legislative Reforms that Support Authorities' Capacity to Restrain and Confiscate Stolen Assets *(Think outside the Box).*
In most jurisdictions, a criminal conviction must be obtained before stolen assets can be confiscated. Convictions can be especially problematic if corrupt officials prevent or delay criminal investigations (Barrier 15). In addition, to freeze, seize, or confiscate assets, many jurisdictions require that the prosecution establish a link between the offense and the assets. As stolen assets are frequently commingled with legitimate assets, meeting the criminal standard of proof in showing this link is often difficult (Barriers 13 and 14).

To assist authorities in overcoming these problems, jurisdictions should introduce and employ legislative reforms that

- lower the burden of proof for confiscation of proceeds of crime in cases involving UNCAC and UNTOC offenses;
- shift the burden of proof to the alleged offender to show that the assets in fact stem from a legitimate source, when the prosecution has provided credible evidence that assets cannot stem from a legitimate source;
- permit confiscation without a conviction or a finding of guilt;
- allow for direct and indirect enforcement of foreign non-conviction based asset confiscation orders; and,
- allow for substitute- or equivalent-value restraint and confiscation of legitimate assets of the same value as the stolen assets.

Recommendation 4

Effectively Apply Anti-Money Laundering Measures *(Make Better Use of Existing Tools).*
Jurisdictions that fail to effectively implement anti-money laundering measures make it easy for corrupt politically exposed persons and other corrupt officials to move stolen

assets into financial centres. If preventive measures, including customer due diligence and suspicious transaction reporting requirements, are properly implemented and enforced, authorities and financial institutions can better intercept and prevent stolen assets from being placed in their financial institutions (Barrier 4).

To strengthen preventive measures, jurisdictions should

- fully implement the anti-money laundering measures set out in international conventions and standards (including UNCAC and the Financial Action Task Force on Money Laundering recommendations); and
- adopt the StAR Initiative recommendations on politically exposed persons, urging financial institutions to
  - ○ apply enhanced due diligence to all PEPs, foreign and domestic;
  - ○ require a declaration of beneficial ownership;
  - ○ request asset and income disclosure forms;
  - ○ conduct a periodic review of PEP customers; and
  - ○ avoid setting "one size fits all" limits on the time a PEP remains a PEP.

Recommendation 5

Provide a Sound Legal Basis for a Wide Range of Types of Mutual Legal Assistance *(Where There is Political Will, There is a Legal Way).*
Jurisdictions require a legal basis to provide MLA, whether through international conventions, domestic legislation, bilateral mutual legal assistance agreements, or an assurance of reciprocity. Most MLA laws and bilateral MLA agreements permit requested states to refuse to provide the assistance in certain circumstances. If the grounds for refusal are not properly defined or are too broad, they are an obstacle to asset recovery (Barrier 22).

To overcome these barriers, jurisdictions should ensure that MLA laws give the authorities the widest range of mutual legal assistance in criminal matters, including all types of assistance as set out under UNCAC and UNTOC. Jurisdictions should also limit and clearly define the grounds for refusal of MLA. In particular, jurisdictions should

- limit grounds for refusal to those set out in UNCAC and UNTOC;
- avoid mandatory grounds for refusal; and
- provide assistance without requiring criminalization of the offense in both jurisdictions (dual criminality) or reciprocity, particularly in cases involving investigative, seizure, and restraint orders; or allow use of a conduct-based approach to determine whether dual criminality exists.

Recommendation 6

Allow for the Rapid Tracing and Temporary Freezing or Seizing of Assets before Receiving a Formal MLA Request *(Freeze, before Assets Disperse).*

Delays in executing a freezing or seizing request can result in the transfer of stolen assets. Current MLA processes are not sufficiently agile to prevent the removal of the target assets, especially in common law countries that require a judicial order to trace or temporarily freeze or seize assets (Barrier 10). Excessive banking secrecy laws prevent disclosure of account information that would help to identify the accounts that hold those assets. Obtaining the necessary property descriptions is often difficult without information from government registries (Barrier 12). In making MLA requests, identifying the property in question or locating foreign bank accounts holding the stolen assets can be very difficult (Barriers 27 and 28).

To overcome these problems, jurisdictions should enact legislation or implement policies that assist in identifying stolen assets within their jurisdiction, including policies that

- limit and precisely define the types of information that are protected by banking secrecy;
- create more permissive criteria, allowing access to information needed by investigators; and,
- permit certain information to be provided without a formal MLA request, including land records, registered company documents, and director and shareholder information.

Jurisdictions also need to adopt tools that will facilitate the identification and freezing of assets. For the identification of assets, jurisdictions should implement and maintain publicly available registries that are accessible to other jurisdictions without a formal MLA request. Such registries include company registries, land registries and registries of nonprofit organizations. In addition, jurisdictions should establish a national bank registry that maintains account identification information, including the names of beneficial owner(s) and holders of powers of attorney.

For the freezing of assets, there are a number of tools that can help overcome current delays, such as temporary administrative freezes (lasting at least 72 hours), and giving freezing authority to an investigating magistrate, prosecutor, or other competent authority. For jurisdictions that do not permit investigating magistrates or prosecutors to implement a freeze, allow an automatic freeze upon the filing of charges or an arrest.

Recommendation 7

Encourage, Pursue, and Maintain all Methods of Informal Assistance before Initiation of a Formal MLA Request *(First Step, Talk to Colleagues).*
A formal, written request for MLA may not be required at all stages of an investigation or during the collection of information and intelligence. Informal assistance is provided

through channels other than a formal MLA request.[8] Although informal assistance is generally quicker and can assist originating jurisdictions in developing a strategy and foundation for an eventual formal MLA request, informal channels are rarely used to their full potential (Barrier 6).

Originating jurisdictions should pursue all paths of informal assistance both before and during the making of a formal MLA request, while respecting confidentiality agreements. Requested jurisdictions should be prepared to provide informal assistance and to encourage communication outside the formal process at all stages of assistance. Examples of informal assistance include direct communication between financial intelligence units, police, prosecutors, and investigating magistrates.

Recommendation 8

Experienced Asset Recovery Jurisdictions Should Mentor and Train Practitioners in Less Experienced Jurisdictions *(Lend a Helping Hand)*.
Practitioners in many jurisdictions do not have sufficient experience or knowledge about asset recovery to permit them to prepare clear and focused MLA requests that are appropriate to the particular case. Poorly drafted and inappropriate requests will likely be refused by the requested jurisdiction (Barrier 24).

To improve the quality of requests, experienced jurisdictions should

- provide assistance and training through the placement of liaison magistrates, prosecutors, attachés, or legal mentors in lower-capacity jurisdictions;
- provide financial support to developing countries for embedding liaison officers from the originating jurisdiction in the relevant authorities of the requested jurisdiction; and
- nurture capacity in developing countries by integrating asset recovery assistance into technical assistance programs.

---

8. Although less formal in the sense that fewer procedural requirements are associated with it, informal assistance should not be construed to include any illegal means or "backroom dealing."

The Problem and a Path to a Solution

Theft of public assets from developing countries is an immense problem with a staggering development impact. These kinds of thefts mean valuable public resources are diverted from addressing the abject poverty and fragile infrastructure so prevalent in these countries. The international community cannot stand idly by and allow corrupt leaders to engage in such criminal conduct with impunity or to enjoy their ill-gotten wealth.

Although the exact magnitude of the proceeds of corruption circulating in the global economy is impossible to ascertain, estimates demonstrate the severity and scale of the problem. The proceeds of crime, corruption, and tax evasion are estimated to represent between $1 trillion and $1.6 trillion annually, with half coming from developing countries.[5] These estimates do not capture the societal costs of corruption and the devastating impact of such crimes on victim countries. Theft of assets by corrupt officials weakens confidence in public institutions, damages the private investment climate, and reduces the funds available for core investment in public health, education, and other poverty alleviation measures.[6]

Given the billions of dollars stolen by political leaders and other high-ranking officials in developing jurisdictions, the World Bank and the United Nations Office on Drugs and Crime (UNODC) initiated the Stolen Asset Recovery (StAR) Initiative in 2007 to assist countries with recovering and returning these stolen assets to victim jurisdictions. StAR is focused on instances where corrupt leaders, other officials, and their close associates are responsible for stealing millions, if not billions, of dollars. This grand corruption typically derives from acts of theft, embezzlement, bribery, and other criminal conduct. Although the StAR Initiative is not aimed at petty and mild corruption, it recognizes that some of the recommendations discussed in this study can help practitioners be more effective in investigating and prosecuting all types of corruption.

Officials with StAR estimate that only $5 billion in stolen assets has been repatriated over the past 15 years. The huge gap between even the lowest estimates of assets stolen

5. United Nations Office on Drugs and Crime, "Stolen Asset Recovery (StAR) Initiative: Challenges, Opportunities, and Action Plan" (Washington, DC: World Bank 2007), citing Raymond Baker, *Capitalism's Achilles Heel: Dirty Money and How to Renew the Free-Market System* (Hoboken, NJ: John Wiley & Sons, Inc., 2005).
6. UNODC and World Bank, "Stolen Asset Recovery (StAR) Initiative: Challenges, Opportunities, and Action Plan," p. 9.

and those repatriated demonstrates the significant difficulties jurisdictions face in achieving justice for victims of corruption. Upon closer examination, it is clear that these difficulties involve preventing assets from leaving victim jurisdictions; preventing stolen assets from entering financial centers; and identifying and tracing assets. Another major difficulty is achieving international cooperation on the many facets of identifying and recovering stolen assets. Politically exposed persons (PEPs), or those people who hold prominent public office, other officials, and close associates, typically have easy access to gatekeepers, such as financial institutions, services, and other professionals, that help them to disguise the sources of the stolen assets and the identities of those who benefit from them. Ineffective anti-money laundering regimes and weak enforcement of preventive measures allows corrupt PEPs and their gatekeepers to launder proceeds of corruption and move them from victim jurisdictions to traditional financial centers.

Once the assets have left the victim jurisdiction, they can be difficult to locate and recover before they are moved to yet another jurisdiction or dissipated. Unique skill, capacity, resources, and timely and effective international cooperation and coordination are required to identify, trace, restrain, confiscate, and eventually repatriate these assets. The current environment makes the successful recovery of stolen assets very difficult. Even with effective, prompt, and cooperative assistance between jurisdictions, differences across jurisdictions in the evidence required, the burden of proof, notification requirements, and banking secrecy are just some of the obstacles that practitioners in the field find challenging. Addressing these barriers and implementing the recommendations contained within this study are important steps for jurisdictions to take if billions of stolen dollars are to be returned to the victim jurisdictions and used to combat poverty and promote the rule of law.

In recent years the recovery of stolen assets has received significant attention from the international community. The United Nations Convention against Corruption (UNCAC), with 140 signatory governments and 147 other signatory jurisdictions, is the first global instrument to enshrine the recovery of stolen assets in international law.[7] It requires States parties to assist states that have been victims of corruption by freezing, confiscating, and returning any proceeds of corruption deposited in their jurisdictions. UNCAC also provides a legal basis for addressing key challenges associated with asset recovery, such as the conduct of international investigations and differences in common and civil law traditions, confiscation procedures, and dual criminality (the requirement that the corruption be recognized as a criminal offense in both jurisdictions). UNCAC also establishes the return of assets as a fundamental principle and requires States parties to give each other the widest measure of cooperation and assistance in this regard.[8]

The United Nations Convention against Transnational Organized Crime (UNTOC) is another useful tool in fighting corruption. UNTOC, which entered into force on

---

7. The number of signatories as of September 1, 2010. UNCAC was adopted by the United Nations General Assembly by resolution 58/4 on October 31, 2003, and entered into force on December 14, 2005.
8. UNCAC, Article 51.

September 29, 2003, is the main international instrument specifically aimed at combating international criminal organizations that are also involved in the theft and laundering of public assets. Among other things, UNTOC requires States parties to adopt comprehensive systems for providing each other mutual legal assistance (MLA) and cooperation among law enforcement agencies.

In addition, the Financial Action Task Force on Money Laundering (FATF), an intergovernmental body established in 1989 to promote and develop national and international policies to combat money laundering, has developed a set of internationally endorsed recommendations for implementing effective anti-money laundering measures. Although the FATF recommendations do not have the force of an internationally binding convention, many countries have committed politically to implementing them. Recognizing that many countries are not fully complying with these recommendations, however, FATF recently released a report on best practices for confiscation (FATF recommendations 3 and 38) with targeted and practical recommendations to improve on the identification, tracing, and evaluation of property that may be subject to confiscation.

Despite the many steps taken by governments, civil society, and the private sector to put these commitments into action, there are still significant barriers to asset recovery. In light of these practical challenges, the StAR Initiative launched this study in 2009, aiming to identify and analyze barriers that impede the recovery of stolen assets. Asset recovery and mutual legal assistance are essential elements in international efforts to combat corruption but are still often misunderstood. Some of the issues addressed by this study have been discussed in previous works[9] and are subject to UN conventions; however, practitioners indicated that, while UNCAC's focus on corruption and its attempt to address prevention, criminalization, international cooperation, and asset recovery are excellent, they nevertheless rely primarily on bilateral treaties and their domestic legal framework for day-to-day international cooperation and asset recovery efforts. Practitioners added that bilateral treaties are often more explicit than UNCAC on how two states will cooperate with each other; moreover, domestic legal frameworks are typically both more explicit and more familiar to the practitioner. MLA generally begins with a request for legal assistance from another jurisdiction and often involves, in the context of stolen asset recovery, requests to trace, freeze, or confiscate the proceeds and instrumentalities of crime. Even practitioners working in the area continue to encounter challenges stemming from the lack of information about the MLA processes and procedures in different jurisdictions. Unreliable information, as well as excessive or unrealized expectations, also hampers effective international cooperation. The purposes of this study, then, are to promote asset recovery by identifying actual barriers that impede countries from cooperating to recover stolen assets, to analyze briefly the impact of these barriers on attempts to recover assets, and to put forward recommendations that will overcome or bring down these obstacles.

---

9. See, for example, http://www.coe.int/t/dghl/monitoring/moneyval/Web.../FATF_BPR3&38.pdf; http://www.u4.no/themes/uncac/report.cfm; and http://www.assetrecovery.org.

The study was originally intended to focus on barriers in sixteen financial centers to try to assist the developing world with the problem of asset recovery.[10] This approach recognized that victim states in the developing world traditionally request assistance from these jurisdictions to recover plundered assets and that these financial centers must play an active and supportive role to assist developing countries if asset recovery is to succeed.

The study has shown, however, that these financial centers are increasingly appealing to other financial centers or even victim states for the information and evidence necessary to take action against corruption in their own jurisdictions. As a result, this study acknowledges that many of the barriers to asset recovery exist in both traditional "requested" jurisdictions (financial centers that typically receive requests for MLA) and traditional "originating" jurisdictions (victim jurisdictions that seek MLA).

Based on their experience, all practitioners participating in the study said that financial centers should not be the sole focus of the report's recommendations. They said it was also important that the report provide assistance to the developing world in the form of specific recommendations on how to overcome the obstacles they face in asset recovery. The project team agrees with this approach, which more broadly reflects the stolen asset recovery landscape. Moreover, looking at the issue from both sides offers a better chance to overcome the real impediments to asset recovery. As a result, the study has evolved from identifying barriers to asset recovery in financial centers to a more comprehensive analysis of all obstacles in all jurisdictions, whether victim state or financial center, originating or requested jurisdiction.

Methodology

To ensure a practical focus, StAR consulted with a group of stolen asset recovery practitioners working in the developed world (the traditional financial centers) and the developing world (typically the victim jurisdictions) to assist the study team in identifying the barriers to asset recovery and evaluating the recommendations for overcoming these hurdles. These practitioners, who came from both common law and civil law jurisdictions, represented expertise in different phases of the asset recovery process and included law enforcement officers, officials in foreign ministries, prosecutors, private lawyers, and investigating magistrates.[11] The study team conducted four workshops: the first was

---

10. The sixteen financial centers are Canada; Cayman Islands; France; Germany; Guernsey; Hong Kong SAR, China; Italy; Japan; Jersey; Liechtenstein; Singapore; Spain; Switzerland; the United Arab Emirates; the United Kingdom; and the United States. Nine of the sixteen financial centers originally included in the study have ratified UNCAC. (Please note that Hong Kong SAR, China, is not a party to the Convention; although China is. As with other conventions, China applies UNCAC to Hong Kong SAR, China, pursuant to an internal mechanism under the Basic Law.)

11. Practitioners from Argentina; Azerbaijan; Bangladesh; Belize; Brazil; Cameroon; Canada; the Cayman Islands; Chile; Colombia; Costa Rica; Ecuador; France; Germany; Guatemala; Guernsey; Haiti; Hong Kong SAR, China; Indonesia; Jersey; Kenya; Liechtenstein; Mexico; the Netherlands; Nigeria; the Philippines; Singapore; St. Kitts and Nevis; St. Lucia; Switzerland; Tanzania; Trinidad and Tobago; the United Kingdom; the United States; Uruguay; and Zambia attended one or more workshops or participated in a country visit

attended by practitioners from the traditional financial centers,[12] followed by two regional meetings for practitioners in countries that historically submitted MLA requests,[13] and a final workshop bringing together practitioners from both receiving and originating jurisdictions.[14] In addition, members of the team conducted country visits to some financial centers that were unable to participate in workshops, meeting with the competent practitioners to discuss the study and the impediments they encountered during the course of their work.[15] The expertise, practical experience, and candid discussions of more than 50 practitioners formed the backbone of the study. Independent research also helped form the basis for the analysis and recommendations, particularly with respect to the checklists that provide details on asset recovery provisions in certain jurisdictions (see appendix B).

In an effort to provide a conducive atmosphere for candid discussion, all of the workshops and country visits proceeded on the understanding that no particular jurisdiction would be singled out for having a particular barrier to asset recovery. Although examples were sometimes discussed in more detail in the analytical and drafting process, the report has been written without reference to specific jurisdictions. While this approach eliminates a degree of particularity and specificity, the purpose of this study was to draw on the expertise and knowledge of practitioners all over the world, not to single out any particular jurisdiction. The team thanks all practitioners who participated in the study for their willingness to share their knowledge and expertise and to devote time and energy to this project. In general, there is consensus on almost all of the barriers and recommendations included in this paper. Where consensus is lacking, the report's authors attempt to acknowledge and identify all perspectives on the issues raised.

The StAR Secretariat also thanks the Swiss government for its assistance in cohosting the final workshop as part of the ongoing Swiss government's initiative relating to asset recovery, known as the Lausanne Process.

The Lausanne Process

Assets of illicit origin held by corrupt officials not only affect developing economies, they also threaten the integrity of international financial centers. Faced with a series of complex cases involving stolen assets placed in Swiss banks, the Swiss government

---

from members of the team responsible for preparing the study. One country initially identified by the project team in the concept note declined to participate.

12. Practitioners were from France; Germany; Guernsey; Hong Kong SAR, China; Jersey; Liechtenstein; Switzerland; the United Kingdom; and the United States.

13. Practitioners were from Argentina, Azerbaijan, Bangladesh, Belize, Bolivia, Brazil, Cameroon, Chile, Colombia, Costa Rica, Ecuador, Grenada, Guatemala, Haiti, Indonesia, Mexico, Morocco, Nigeria, Panama, Paraguay, Peru, the Philippines, St. Kitts and Nevis, St. Lucia, St. Vincent and the Grenadines, Tanzania, and Trinidad and Tobago.

14. Practitioners were from Azerbaijan, Bangladesh, Brazil, Cameroon, Canada, the Cayman Islands, Chile, France, Guernsey, Haiti, Indonesia, Kenya, Liechtenstein, Mexico, Nigeria, the Philippines, St. Kitts and Nevis, Spain, Switzerland, Tanzania, the United Kingdom, and Zambia.

15. Country visits were conducted in the Cayman Islands, Italy, Japan, and Singapore.

decided to find new and pragmatic solutions to return the assets to their countries of origin. Given the absence of any forum at the international level dedicated to discussing the legal and political aspects of asset recovery, Switzerland started the process of the Lausanne seminars.

In January 2001, the Swiss government invited officials and experts from different financial centers to the first Lausanne seminar to discuss issues related to illicit assets of corrupt officials. Practitioners brainstormed innovative ways to solve issues related to recovering stolen assets. The meeting also showed the importance of direct contacts between the main actors in asset recovery cases as well as the relevance of establishing trusting personal relationships. A follow-up seminar organized in November 2001 proved to be an important gathering in the context of the negotiations of the United Nations Convention against Corruption, which had just begun. Eventually, UNCAC Article 57 would become the first legal provision on the international level making the return and disposal of recovered assets an obligation for States parties.

In October 2006, *Lausanne III* brought together for the first time experts from so-called victim, or originating, states; that is, states who lost funds through corruption and were therefore in the position of *requesting* mutual legal assistance, and receiving, or requested, states, from which mutual legal cooperation is usually *requested*. Representatives of the World Bank and the United Nations also attended the discussions focused on the implementation of Article 57. Several high-profile cases, including those of Ferdinand Marcos of the Philippines, General Sani Abacha of Nigeria, Jean Claude Duvalier of Haiti, Sese Seko Mobutu of the Democratic Republic of Congo, and Vladimiro Montesinos of Peru provided enough experience to allow for constructive discussions of the main practical and legal obstacles encountered when recovering stolen assets.[16] The participants generally agreed that a strong partnership and active mutual cooperation between originating and requested states are prerequisites for successful asset recovery.

Lausanne IV, held in May 2008, focused on concrete examples of successful and unsuccessful asset recovery. Representatives involved in specific cases highlighted the obstacles they had encountered. The discussion of specific proceedings from the opposing perspectives of originating and requested states deepened the understanding of existing barriers. The participants also reiterated the importance of political will of both parties, of direct contacts between the key practitioners working on asset recovery, and of the necessity for clear and sustained communication to overcome differences between legal systems—in particular common and civil law jurisdictions—to avoid frustrations caused by mistaken perceptions or inflated expectations.

Because both Switzerland, on the basis of the Lausanne process, and StAR emphasize the joint responsibility of originating and requested states in solving asset recovery

---

16. For information on Abacha, Duvalier, Mobutu, and Montesinos, see, respectively, http://www.asset recovery.org/kc; http://online.wsj.com/article/SB10001424052748703954804575380942951459772.html; http://www.baselgovernance.org/fileadmin/docs/.../asset-tracing_web-version.pdf; and http://www.gwu .edu/~nsarchiv/NSAEBB/NSAEBB37.

cases, they decided to join forces to co-organize the final workshop in the preparation of this StAR study, which was aimed at identifying and analyzing barriers that impede the recovery of stolen assets. That workshop became *Lausanne V* (April 29–30, 2010) in the Lausanne process.

Almost 10 years ago, the first Lausanne seminar provided one of the first global forums to discuss issues related to asset recovery. By initiating this process, Switzerland's objectives were to start a discussion on the international level, to provide a platform to informally share experiences, and to develop trust and networking opportunities among practitioners and experts. Over time, a certain "Spirit of Lausanne" developed that stands for candid exchanges and the clear political will to develop and promote the asset recovery agenda.

How to Use This Study

This study identifies barriers to asset recovery and offers recommendations for policy, procedural, and legislative reform that, if enacted, will provide investigators and legal practitioners with the necessary tools to effectively manage asset recovery cases.[17] The report also includes practical recommendations, directed toward managers and practitioners, to improve communications and understanding of differences in the legal systems of originating and requested jurisdictions.

Policy makers and standard setters may use the recommendations and good practices to inform efforts at legislative reform and to allocate adequate resources for agencies and practitioners. The study, particularly its principal recommendations, will be most effective if it is incorporated as part of a sustained policy initiative, forming one piece of an integrated strategy that is targeted more generally at reducing corruption and that has clearly defined objectives and dedicated resources. These policy strategies have been most successful when adopted and promoted by high-level officeholders who publicly promote them as a national strategy. Public statements by these officials help demonstrate commitment and encourage accountability, particularly where an active element of civil society is engaged with the issues.

The principal recommendations are formulated so that jurisdictions may use them as benchmarks to assess the achievement of their strategic and policy goals. In addition, parties to UNCAC may find the study useful as part of the upcoming review in 2015 to consider the degree of success in implementation of UNCAC. In some cases, the study notes departures by State parties in transposing UNCAC into domestic law, and in others, it notes failures in the practical implementation and use of the convention.

A secondary purpose of this paper is to expose practitioners in all jurisdictions to problems encountered by their foreign and domestic colleagues when dealing with asset

---

17. Generally, this analysis and recommendations relate only to the proceeds of corruption-related offenses and attempts to recover and return those assets to victim jurisdictions. However, this report refers to "proceeds of crime" where a broader reference is more appropriate.

recovery cases and to introduce solutions to these problems that will lead to more successful asset recovery operations. The study, particularly its operational and good practice recommendations, can also be used in developing training and education programs for practitioners. This study is available online on the StAR Web site (http://www.world bank.org/star) to help to highlight these barriers and raise public awareness of the issues. Civil society organizations and individuals may find the study valuable for obtaining a better understanding of the status of international asset recovery and as a tool to evaluate asset recovery within their jurisdiction, including efforts (or a lack of effort) at reducing the barriers identified by the study.

Although the number of barriers and recommendations may seem overwhelming, many changes are relatively straightforward and, once implemented, will have a significant positive effect on improving stolen asset recovery. In many cases, the framework already exists in international instruments and standards such as UNCAC, UNTOC, and the FATF recommendations, but practical implementation and operational changes are required to give full effect in practice to these standards.

Following this introduction, the report is organized into three major sections. The first sets out general barriers and institutional issues that touch on many different barriers and have a general effect on the problem. The second then focuses on legal barriers and requirements that delay or otherwise impede assistance with stolen asset recovery. The third section is more practical, dealing with operational and communication issues that practitioners in the area face. The study also contains an appendix containing brief detailed checklists for all 14 financial centers that were part of its original focus. The project team made sustained efforts to engage with these jurisdictions to ensure that the checklists were accurate. Unfortunately, not all jurisdictions fully engaged with the project team. Nevertheless, these checklists contain information about the MLA legal framework, MLA general procedures, and specifics about asset recovery efforts, including tracing, freezing, restraint or seizure, and confiscation in that jurisdiction.

Many of the recommendations found in this study are linked to existing international standards found either in UN conventions or within the FATF recommendations. Some recommendations are made to support better implementation of these already-existing standards, such as better execution of anti-money laundering measures. Some of the recommendations are asking for new international standards to be considered, such as the establishment of national bank registries to retain account identification information, including beneficial owners and powers of attorney; introduction of tools that allow—before receipt of formal MLA request—a temporary administrative freeze of assets for at least 72 hours, a freeze by a competent authority, or an automatic freeze upon imposition of charges or arrest; new legislative reforms that support authorities' capacity to restrain and confiscate stolen assets; new legislation or policies that allow foreign competent authorities access to certain information without requiring a formal MLA request; a requirement that jurisdictions provide certain information about MLA issues online; and a requirement that jurisdictions implement and maintain publicly available company and land registries as well as registries of nonprofit organizations.

General Barriers and Institutional Issues

Barrier 1: Lack of Trust

A relationship of trust between parties is important to ensure successful and proactive international cooperation for all of the asset recovery stages, whether it is for collecting and sharing intelligence data, gathering evidence for use in an investigation or prosecution, or the freezing, seizure, confiscation, and repatriation of the proceeds of corruption.[18] Lack of trust can cause delays or even refusal to provide assistance to originating jurisdictions seeking to recover stolen assets. In cases involving urgent matters or where the jurisdictions have very different legal, political, or judicial systems, a lack of trust can be particularly problematic.

A report published by the European Commission on August 23, 2010, shows how a lack of trust can impede efforts at asset recovery, even where countries have previously agreed to cooperate. According to the report, half of the European Union's (EU) member countries have yet to put rules in place seeking confiscation of criminal assets located in other countries, despite EU rules permitting member countries to do so since 2006 (Council Framework Decision 2006/783/JHA90).[19] The report states that "poor implementation and red tape, which often reflect a lack of trust in other [countries'] justice systems, still make it hard to attack criminal assets." As a result, the report said, the assets of a criminal organization prosecuted in one EU country will be safe if located in another EU country. The report recommends that "EU rules ... allow justice authorities to ask their counterparts in other Member States to enforce confiscation orders."[20]

Viviane Reding, vice president of the EU Commission for Justice, Fundamental Rights, and Citizenship, stated in a press release "in a time of economic crisis, it is unfortunate that EU Member States are letting billions of euro worth of convicted criminals' assets slip through the net. This happens even though governments agreed on confiscation

---

18. The importance of trust has also been repeatedly recognized by the Conference of the States Parties to UNCAC and its Open-ended Intergovernmental Working Group on Asset Recovery and by the Lausanne process. See Resolution 1/4, Resolution 2/3, and Resolution 3/3, all found online at http://www.unodc.org/unodc/en/treaties/CAC/working-group2.html.

19. "European Commission Calls on 14 EU Member States to Make Sure Cross-Border Crime Doesn't Pay," press release IP/10/1063, August 23, 2010, http://europa.eu/rapid/pressReleasesAction. Under EU rules, one EU country can send a confiscation order to the country where the subject of the order lives or has property or income. That country directly carries out the confiscation, under its own national rules, without any further formality.

20. Ibid.

measures four years ago." Reding stressed that "in future, we must have clearer rules, more consistent application and enforcement and—above all—trust between justice systems. In the meantime, I call on Member States to put the anti-crime rules in place so that the justice authorities can work together and effectively attack criminals' ill-gotten gains."[21]

In international asset recovery cases, success frequently depends on the capacity of the competent authorities to take urgent investigative or provisional measures to secure evidence or assets, including searches or seizures, arrests, monitoring orders, other investigative techniques, and freezing of assets.[22] In a world where funds deposited into bank accounts can be easily transferred electronically, even short delays can be the difference between a successful and a failed recovery. To address this issue, some jurisdictions have the capacity, through their financial intelligence units (FIUs) or other agencies, to temporarily freeze assets for a maximum of 72 hours as an emergency measure based on telephone and fax information, if originating authorities undertake to send an official follow-up request in a timely manner. If assistance is to be provided in such circumstances, authorities in requested jurisdictions need to be confident that their counterparts are committed to timely provision of all necessary documentation to justify their requests, that information provided will not be misused, and that their own requests for additional information will be answered. Similarly, jurisdictions may provide information under the condition that it not be used to prosecute other offenses or to start other criminal or administrative proceedings.[23] Requested jurisdictions sometimes hesitate or refuse to provide this information if they have concerns that originating authorities will fail to live up to their undertaking. If originating jurisdictions do not keep their promises to requested jurisdictions, then certain mutual legal assistance (MLA) channels, especially informal and expedient assistance, will be stymied and possibly denied in the future, because of lack of trust in the relationship. Practitioners indicated that such swift assistance might also be refused if, in the past, information was leaked to the media or improperly used in abusive proceedings to discredit a political personality.

Lack of trust can also be a barrier to mutual legal assistance when the process involves jurisdictions with significantly different political, judicial, or legal systems. A requested country that takes action to exercise what it considers to be due process requirements, domestic legal frameworks of general application, or human rights guarantees may be seen by the originating jurisdiction as unduly blocking cooperation. For example, requested authorities may hesitate or refuse to provide assistance if they are not certain that the originating jurisdiction will provide defendants with guarantees of due process. Extraditions have been refused or delayed because requested authorities considered that defendants could be mistreated or abused by their counterparts in the originating jurisdiction.[24] In other cases, requested jurisdictions granted political asylum to defendants

---

21. Ibid.
22. As prescribed by UNCAC, Article 54(2).
23. As prescribed by UNCAC, Article 46(5).
24. Under the *aut dedere, aut judicare* principle (the obligation under public international law to extradite or prosecute for serious international crimes), if a country chooses not to extradite for reasons other than

suspected of embezzlement in the originating jurisdiction. Similarly, requested jurisdictions may hesitate or refuse to provide MLA when requests are made by law enforcement or anticorruption agencies that the requested jurisdiction does not recognize as having the authority to request assistance. Refusal to conduct investigations on behalf of originating jurisdictions may also be linked to the perception that their legal frameworks provide for disproportionate penalties such as the death penalty.

Where lack of cooperation is caused by differences in the legal, political, and judicial systems between the jurisdictions, requested jurisdictions should foster trust by fairly evaluating each MLA request and communicating with the originating jurisdiction to attempt to best coordinate their efforts. Early and clear communication between both jurisdictions can significantly ease the challenges of differences between systems because the context of each case can guide the specific legislative, legal, and political differences that must be addressed for MLA to move forward. Reviews of draft MLA requests by appropriate practitioners in the requested jurisdiction before its submission can help to alleviate potential problems.

Any concern that due process may not have been provided by the originating jurisdiction should be looked at by the courts in the requested jurisdiction. Due process rights are certainly important, and failure to provide due process is a valid reason for rejecting an MLA request. However, requested jurisdictions should closely examine the circumstances of each case before determining, on specific and articulable grounds, that due process was not provided (see Barrier 22). Good communication between the two jurisdictions may permit at least partial MLA to proceed. To further foster trust, requested jurisdictions should make every attempt to avoid refusing MLA solely because of differences in the legal and judicial system, except where precise and strong domestic legal grounds require such a refusal. If such a refusal is required, the originating jurisdiction should be informed and given an opportunity to show there is no such reason to deny the request, as required by UNCAC.[25]

Building trust may be particularly difficult where no previous relationship exists. Practitioners suggested that requested and originating jurisdictions trying to work together for the first time should try to facilitate personal contacts between the authorities of both jurisdictions and make consistent efforts to move the case forward, actions that will help to develop a trusting relationship. Establishing and maintaining personal contacts has its own challenges, including identifying the appropriate contact and effective approaches to securing cooperation (see Barrier 21). Additional impediments for developing countries include lack of access to telephones for international calling, lack of IT equipment with Internet access, and a lack of resources to attend conferences that facilitate networking. Once established, contact can prove ineffective if one of the parties moves on to another role in the organization or leaves government service.

---

those accepted by international customary law, then it must begin a domestic prosecution. Such decisions, nevertheless, must be transparent, and full disclosure of the reasons must be made available to the requesting country.
25. UNCAC, Article 46(26).

Experts in the field also highlighted the value of maintaining contacts at the institutional level. The development and maintenance of meaningful agency-to-agency contacts can serve as the basis for strong professional relationships between relevant agencies and help sustain the relationship when key personnel move on to other jobs. Once initial contact is made, arrangements should be put in place to ensure communication on a regular basis. Where one jurisdiction is a developing country and the other not, the developed-country jurisdiction could initiate the communication at regular intervals to help to cover their costs and ease other barriers that exist in developing countries. Both jurisdictions benefit from such an arrangement by remaining up-to-date on the progress of the request for assistance. Developed jurisdictions also could consider providing communications technology and equipment to developing jurisdictions to enhance communication, especially on high-profile and complex investigations to recover stolen assets.

Jurisdictions should also use liaison magistrates and customs and police attachés to promote cooperation between central authorities and direct contacts between competent prosecutors, judges, FIU liaison officers, and law enforcement officers. Such contacts are consistent with UNCAC, which requires states to cooperate, through, among other things, consideration of the posting of liaison officers to enhance coordination between authorities.[26]

MLA practitioners in all jurisdictions should take advantage of any opportunities to broaden the scope of their personal contacts, including, for example, the UNCAC asset recovery working group. Asset recovery networks and groups, such as CARIN, ARINSA and IBERRED,[27] help establish networks of contacts that can act as advisory groups to other appropriate authorities and promote trust across jurisdictions. Face-to-face contact and the spontaneous sharing of information and intelligence were both identified as effective ways to develop trust among practitioners.[28] Spontaneous sharing of information occurs when a jurisdiction uncovers information in a domestic investigation that suggests that assets may have been illegally obtained from another jurisdiction, and passes that information on to the victim jurisdiction without any formal request. Because such spontaneous sharing is an effective way to develop trust between two jurisdictions with little or no experience working together, jurisdictions should enact specific provisions, such as memoranda of understanding, allowing such sharing, and should further consider making such sharing mandatory.

---

26. UNCAC, Article 48(1)(e).
27. CARIN (Camden Assets Recovery Inter-Agency Network) is an informal group and network of contacts of mostly European members whose aim is to increase the effectiveness of its members' efforts in depriving criminals of their illicit gains. Launched in 2009, ARINSA (Asset Recovery Inter-Agency Network for Southern Africa) is a network similar to CARIN. It acts as an informal gateway for communication and coordination between authorities in asset recovery. IBERRED (Red Iberoamericana de Cooperacion Juridica Internacional) is an asset recovery network working primarily in Latin America, Spain, Andorra, and Portugal.
28. The third session of Conference of State Parties to UNCAC recommended in November 2009 that states take a proactive approach to international cooperation in asset recovery by, among other things, initiating requests for assistance and making spontaneous disclosures to other states of information on proceeds of offenses: Resolution 3/3 found at www.unodc.org/unodc/en /treaties/CAC/CAC-COSP.html.

Jurisdictions should promote direct contact between practitioners at the institution-to-institution level and establish registries of practitioners that are periodically updated. Jurisdictions should develop policies that allow practitioners from other jurisdictions access to such registries in an effort to expedite cooperation and build contacts and trust between institutions.

Policy Recommendations

a) A requested jurisdiction should not refuse a request for MLA for due process reasons unless it has precise and strong evidence that the originating jurisdiction has not guaranteed due process to the defendants.

b) Developed countries should consider absorbing the costs of communication with developing-country jurisdictions on requests for assistance with recovery of stolen assets; developed countries could also provide developing jurisdictions with communications technology and equipment.

Operational Recommendations

a) Requested jurisdictions should implement policies and procedures that guarantee transparency when dealing with originating authorities and should require that the reasons for rejecting an MLA request be divulged to the originating jurisdiction; they should also give the originating jurisdiction an opportunity to demonstrate that the defendant received due process.

b) To help build trust between jurisdictions, developed countries should establish policies and procedures that facilitate the establishment of personal contacts between originating and requested authorities. In particular, they should establish liaison magistrates, FIU liaison officers, and customs or police attachés[a] to promote enhanced cooperation between central authorities and direct contacts between competent prosecutors, judges, or law enforcement officers.

c) Jurisdictions should provide adequate resources to enable their officials to attend relevant international meetings and forums and to network with their counterparts bilaterally.

d) Jurisdictions should participate in and exploit asset recovery networks and groups such as CARIN, ARINSA, and IBERRED to develop relationships with practitioners in other jurisdictions.

e) Jurisdictions should establish policies and procedures that allow practitioners to develop effective contacts and avenues for communication at an institution-to-institution level, including maintaining contact details in corporate systems. Such systems should be updated on a regular basis.

a. For example, the United States has attachés from the FBI, Drug Enforcement Administration, U.S. Immigration and Customs Enforcement, Internal Revenue Service, and U.S. Secret Service in many embassies overseas. France, Germany, Japan and the United Kingdom also have police, customs, and liaison magistrates in foreign countries.

Barrier 2: Lack of a Comprehensive Asset Recovery Policy

The term "political will" is one of the most elusive and ambiguous terms discussed in international forums. In the context of this report, the concept refers to the demonstrated and credible intent of political actors, civil servants, and organs of the state to combat corruption and recover and repatriate stolen assets. Although difficult to define with precision, this intent is arguably the most relevant precondition for successful and effective international cooperation in asset recovery cases. A country with an effective strategy for combating corruption and recovering stolen assets will provide sufficient resources to the relevant agencies and create incentives for practitioners to prioritize such cases. In such an environment, practitioners will find legal yet creative and unconventional ways to overcome any obstacles present in the system to exact some measure of justice.

Practitioners recognized the absence of a clear policy as a barrier existing in many developed and developing, requested, and originating jurisdictions. Many jurisdictions lack the commitment to initiate and push cases forward or to respond appropriately to initial requests for assistance and requests for additional information. Many jurisdictions, including financial centers, do not sufficiently emphasize asset recovery cases, preferring instead to prosecute a petty domestic drug dealer for money laundering rather than addressing another jurisdiction's request for assistance on a high-profile corruption case. Practitioners recognized that a country's economic interests may also dilute political will to combat corruption. Authorities in a requested jurisdiction may hesitate to vigorously pursue a corruption investigation and asset recovery effort involving a large and influential company located there because of the economic benefits the jurisdiction receives from the company. All these factors reflect a mix of political sensitivities around asset recovery; a lack of priority (and therefore benign neglect); and a failure to align tools, expertise, and resources to sustain a viable asset recovery program.

Where such challenges exist, significant international asset recovery cases are often given lower priority than routine domestic matters. Also, there are indications that practitioners in the developed world—traditionally, jurisdictions whose assistance is requested—view asset recovery cases with a modicum of misgiving. Many judges and prosecutors in some developed jurisdictions continue to consider asset recovery a novelty to be treated with caution. This cautious approach often contributes to time-consuming and ineffective management of processes for repatriating stolen assets, which frequently includes international cooperation.

Some legal traditions view asset recovery strictly as a penalty within the context of a sentence for a predicate crime (the underlying crime that generates the proceeds of crime); this approach raises concerns about the proportionality of asset recovery as a penalty. Many judges are not even aware that criminal assets can be recovered, and both judges and prosecutors do not clearly understand the philosophy behind asset recovery. Given this mindset, such cases become a low priority. Under these circumstances, it is unlikely that these jurisdictions have the requisite commitment to address MLA requests seeking to freeze, seize, or confiscate stolen assets, particularly when resources are not allocated to properly train and enlighten practitioners about asset recovery processes. Such an environment increases the difficulty of stolen asset recovery.

The lack of a comprehensive policy may be reflected differently in originating and requested jurisdictions, or in financial centers and the developing world. Practitioners in the field described the following perceived problems in traditionally requested jurisdictions and financial centers.

- Requested jurisdictions often maintain an unresponsive and inefficient MLA regime and systems that are known to be arduous, discouraging states from submitting requests for assistance.
- Financial center jurisdictions provide insufficient or no response to asset recovery requests. If there is a first response, it may arrive many months after submission of the request, thus compromising any investigative efforts to speedily track assets.
- Some financial centers appear to lack a real commitment to provide truly helpful assistance, as demonstrated by apathy, inefficiency, and a lack of trained practitioners.
- Financial centers often assume a passive stance in responding to MLA asset recovery requests, even though they have significantly more resources and expertise than developing jurisdictions and a greater capacity to trace, freeze, restrain, and confiscate assets.
- Financial centers often seem quick to find reasons, regardless of how trivial, to refuse MLA requests involving asset recovery cases.
- Financial centers often interpret negatively the discretion given to the competent authorities to deny requests.[29]
- Financial centers often prioritize domestic cases over MLA cases, which means the MLA request suffers significantly when the requested jurisdiction has limited resources.

Practitioners also described perceived problems that are particularly prevalent in developing countries and originating jurisdictions.

- Traditional originating jurisdictions, often from the developing world, do not have enough sufficiently skilled practitioners with international experience and an adequate understanding of international conventions and standards to submit legally sufficient requests for mutual legal assistance.
- Traditional originating jurisdictions lack sufficient capacity to conduct complex investigations, which often leads to unsubstantiated requests for cooperation.

---

29. UNCAC, Article 46 (21) states that MLA "may" be refused but does not state that MLA "must" be refused if the request falls under the four categories listed in this section.

- Some jurisdictions may face difficulties because investigating authorities lack independence.
- Traditional originating jurisdictions at times will manifest a lack of commitment to respond positively to offers of cooperation by a traditional financial center.
- Some requests for mutual legal assistance from developing jurisdictions are submitted simply as a "smoke screen," contrived for domestic and international political reasons in a case that would never be seriously prosecuted.
- Developing jurisdictions do not always respond positively when developed countries inform them of the discovery of assets believed to be illegally obtained. This lack of action and intent leads the developed countries to conclude that these jurisdictions lack the political will to pursue these cases. One practitioner succinctly stated that the developing world needs to "raise its game."

Practitioners recognized that the same issues that prevent many asset recovery cases in the developing world from moving forward—a lack of competent practitioners, a lack of resources, a lack of expertise, and more important, a lack of true commitment—are also common in the developed world. Especially problematic in the developed world is the commitment to asset recovery when the case touches on national economic interests.

Traditional financial centers can attempt to address shortcomings in resources and capacity by initiating their own investigations using a variety of legitimate sources, such as FIUs, complaints, and media reports; and by forming and properly resourcing special investigative-prosecutorial units that focus on stolen asset recovery investigations. In addition, jurisdictions that are experienced in asset recovery can proactively take steps to nurture the capacity of originating jurisdictions to perform the necessary financial investigations to support an MLA request. Such steps might include establishing bilateral technical assistance programs, providing hands-on technical assistance on a case-by-case basis, and supporting international organizations that have the capacity to provide assistance. Assistance designed to develop such capacity in other jurisdictions, particularly in the developing world, can also be integrated with other types of assistance provided through multilateral organizations.

Clear objectives, dedicated action, new legislation to overcome barriers to asset recovery, sufficient resources, training for practitioners, and use of the legal tools available in a comprehensive, creative, consistent, and committed manner are all important elements of an asset recovery strategy in any country. The particular actions that can be taken by all jurisdictions, such as the creation of specialized investigative units, are developed in more detail as part of the recommendations to address specific barriers to asset recovery.

Ideally, any asset recovery strategy will be part of an integrated policy plan adopted by high-level officeholders to reduce corruption, deter crime, and achieve broader goals beyond the recovery of assets. The more that financial tools become a regularly utilized aspect of criminal investigations and prosecutions, the greater the success in achieving improvements in asset recovery. Jurisdictions will achieve more with less if they are successful at motivating the private sector and international partners to work toward the same goals. Accountability, established through public statements of commitment and the setting of clear benchmarks, is another important factor in ensuring successful implementation. Departments and agencies, whether specialized units or otherwise, require clear and specific objectives and roles within the broader strategy and must be held accountable. The strategy should also entail the establishment of reporting mechanisms, so that progress can be tracked and results monitored. Clear accountability for results will help create incentives for specialized teams to be proactive in pursuing the proceeds of corruption.

Collage of Good Practices: Strategic Plans

Some jurisdictions have been proactive in developing effective and efficient strategies to combat corruption by identifying, recovering, and repatriating stolen assets. These strategic plans attempt to develop public policy priorities and implement policies and procedures to ensure that asset confiscation is an integral part of corruption investigations and prosecutions. Following are some of the key elements contained in these strategic plans.[a]

- "Buy-in" from high-level officeholders in the state—the president, ministers, parliamentarians—who publicly promote and adopt the national strategy.
- Public statements by high-ranking officials supporting and demonstrating commitment to the national strategy and recognizing their accountability.
- Active civil society engagement that holds public officials accountable for the proper and effective implementation of the national strategy.
- Establishment of strategic planning working groups to develop an effective policy that incorporates the skills of all relevant agencies into an action plan. These groups include representatives from all relevant agencies and components participating in asset confiscation.
- Conduct of needs assessments and advocacy promoting proper allocation of resources.
- New initiatives that make the use of financial tools an integral aspect of all investigatory and prosecutorial work specifically targeting criminal asset recovery.
- Creation of specialized investigative units that focus on stolen asset recovery cases.
- New legislative and operational initiatives that promote the proactive use of powers to freeze assets.
- Articulation of clear objectives for relevant departments and agencies that include effective coordinating structures and accountability.

(continued next page)

- Development of a culture of engagement with the private sector as well as international partners.
- Promotion of "fresh action" at the international level that stimulates new ideas, enhances cooperation, and provides direct assistance and mentors to lower-capacity jurisdictions.

a. Several of these jurisdictions have posted their strategic plans on a Web site. See, for example, http://www.justice.gov/criminal/afmls/pubs/pdf/strategicplan.pdf; or http://www.ustreas.gov/offices/enforcement/teoaf/publications/strategic-plan-2007-2012.pdf.

Good Practices

Example 1

The United Kingdom and the United States have secured funding to support specialized units within their relevant law enforcement agencies to investigate, identify, trace, and retrieve assets resulting from corrupt offenses typically conducted by politically exposed persons (PEPs) in other jurisdictions. These specialized units target PEPs who allegedly either hold assets obtained through corruption or have moved such assets through their country. These specialized units work closely with other countries, often providing on-site technical and capacity support while conducting asset-tracing investigations. This type of coordinated, collaborative effort has been effective even when jurisdictions that lack the political will to move cases forward are involved. In such cases, these specialized units have been able to solicit support by pursuing investigations in their own jurisdiction while obtaining sufficient information and leads from the originating jurisdiction.[a]

Example 2

Swiss officials found themselves somewhat handcuffed when they did not receive the desired cooperation from jurisdictions that were victims of corruption and that lost substantial proceeds as a result of grand corruption. Swiss law did not allow the Swiss authorities to pursue these ill-gotten gains without substantial input from victim states. The need for a change in its laws became evident in connection with bank accounts held by the former president of a foreign jurisdiction, and the family of a former dictator in yet another jurisdiction. In essence, under existing Swiss law, without cooperation by the originating jurisdictions, the Swiss authorities had difficulty proving a nexus between the assets and a criminal offense(s). In response, the Swiss government drafted a new law that allows its federal administrative court to confiscate frozen assets that have been illicitly acquired if the account holder's home country fails to institute proceedings. These assets would then be used to finance programs to benefit the population in the affected jurisdiction(s).

Under this new law, the onus will lie with the depositor to prove the legal origin of the funds, rather than with the plaintiff to prove that they were illegally obtained.

(continued next page)

This law was drafted to supplement existing legislation and focuses on the phe-nomenon of dealing with failed states that cannot contribute actively to mutual legal assistance, which is still the basis of any restitution of stolen funds.[b]

a. http://www.ice.gov/doclib/pi/cornerstone/pdf/cs1008.pdf; http://www.justice.gov/ag/speeches/2010/ag-speech-100725. html; http://www.met.police.uk/scd/specialist_units/economic_specialist_crime.htm.
b. http://www.eda.admin.ch/eda/en/home/topics/finec/intcr/poexp.html.

Example of a Lack of Political Will and Strategy

In one case involving a former ruler suspected of corruption, the jurisdiction where the assets were deposited tried for several years to help the former ruler's jurisdiction regain the assets but to no avail. The episode began when the former ruler's government asked for mutual legal assistance in the case. The requested jurisdiction ordered a partial freezing of the assets as a provisional measure only because the incoming request was insufficient to order a complete freezing of the assets. The freeze continued for more than six years within the framework of international legal assistance. During this period, the requested authorities engaged with the originating jurisdiction on many levels trying to obtain clarifica-tion of the original request, without success.

To prevent return of the assets to the heirs of the suspected corrupt leader, the requested jurisdiction made a decision on the basis of its constitution to freeze the assets for an initial period of three years. The requested jurisdiction decided to prolong the freeze for two additional years, despite the lack of progress made in the matter.

Five months before its freeze was scheduled to expire, the requested jurisdiction warned the originating country that the freeze would be lifted unless the originat-ing country entered discussions to try to find a solution. Although the originating jurisdiction indicated that it was going to try to renew criminal proceedings against the former ruler's heirs and associates, it eventually abandoned that effort and instead decided to negotiate with the former ruler's heirs.

To prevent access by the ruler's heirs to the suspected illegal proceeds in its domain, the requested jurisdiction offered to pay for the services of a lawyer specialized in recovering assets. Following the originating jurisdiction's last-minute consent, the requested jurisdiction extended its freeze for a second time, while the originating country's lawyer prepared a restraint order for the assets.

After the lawyer filed a criminal complaint in the requested jurisdiction, the requested jurisdiction extended the freeze a third time while the competent authority reviewed the complaint. The restraint application was rejected. The requested authorities advised the lawyer to appeal the decision, but contrary to

(continued next page)

Example of a Lack of Political Will and Strategy *(continued)*

all expectations, the originating jurisdiction instructed its lawyer not to appeal that decision, dispelling all hopes of restoring the frozen funds to its own people. Despite its 12-year-long effort to repatriate the corrupt proceeds, the requested jurisdiction had no other option but to unfreeze the assets, allowing the heirs of a suspected corrupt leader access to ill-gotten gains.

Policy Recommendations

a) Jurisdictions should develop and implement a transparent and comprehensive policy for recovery of stolen assets. Such a policy should help communicate the significance of asset recovery as an integral part of broader anti-corruption efforts, assign the relevant authorities with the appropriate resources and with sufficient expertise to trace, seize and confiscate stolen assets and effectively support the relevant authorities in granting the widest range of international assistance.

b) Jurisdictions should create specialized confiscation agencies or units within existing agencies with a clearly defined mandate to facilitate asset recovery (see Barrier 3).

c) Jurisdictions should ensure that their officials, including judges and prosecutors, are well trained on asset recovery matters (see Barrier 3).

d) Where a non-conviction based asset confiscation regime does not exist, jurisdictions that have not already done so should pass and implement legislation that allows them to respond positively to requests to confiscate suspected stolen assets in the absence of a conviction (see Barrier 15).

e) Jurisdictions should explicitly and narrowly define grounds for refusal of a request for mutual legal assistance (see Barrier 22).

Operational Recommendations

a) Jurisdictions should initiate their own stolen asset investigations using a variety of legitimate sources (FIUs, complaints, and media reports); establish bilateral technical assistance programs; provide hands-on technical assistance on a case-by-case basis; initiate and properly resource special investigative-prosecutorial units that focus on stolen asset recovery investigations; and support international organizations that have the capacity to provide assistance (as prescribed in Article 60(2)(3) of UNCAC).

b) When facing a dual criminality requirement, jurisdictions should interpret the originating jurisdiction's definitions of offenses in a broadminded manner, allowing for the widest range of consideration, and, if necessary, use a conduct-based approach to determine if the conduct is a crime in both jurisdictions (see Barrier 22).

Barrier 3: Deficient Resources

The study team's work with practitioners confirmed that originating and requested juris-dictions often do not commit sufficient resources to providing assistance in asset recovery cases. Developed- and developing-country practitioners affirmed that competent authori-ties in both areas of the world are inadequately staffed, insufficiently trained, and inexperi-enced in dealing with MLA requests pertaining to the asset recovery processes. In addition, when more than one agency is involved, the specific roles and functions of agencies and departments involved are often poorly defined. A European study focusing on 21 EU states described the working methods of some competent authorities as inert, nontransparent, or unclear, and found that one of the most important obstacles to cooperation was the lack of qualified investigators. According to this study, the lack of qualified personnel to conduct financial investigations stemmed from a lack of financial resources, the failure of political or law enforcement leadership to prioritize financial investigations, and general personnel issues such as difficulty recruiting qualified and experienced investigators. This study also found evidence of insufficient prosecutorial resources for asset recovery work, a lack of relevant knowledge, and inadequate training of prosecutors and judges.[30]

Jurisdictions should avoid these problems by dedicating the necessary resources to train and staff central authorities, financial investigators, prosecutors, judges, and other competent authorities involved in asset recovery issues.[31] Specialized agencies or units within existing agencies should be given the resources to satisfy their mandate to facil-itate asset recovery, keeping in mind that central authorities themselves are often not directly involved in financial investigations or in asset recovery initiatives but are pri-marily administrative authorities.

Efforts to recover stolen assets are often expensive and may fail to yield results. In many jurisdictions, particularly those that are developing countries, dedicated resources for asset recovery are scarce. Some requested jurisdictions with greater resources have assisted such jurisdictions with legal costs and civil fees, enabling asset recovery to proceed. Other coun-tries have special funds in place to provide mutual legal assistance to jurisdictions with resource issues. Developed countries with greater resources should consider implement-ing such a fund or providing financial assistance on a case-by-case basis to help developing countries mitigate their resource problems. In addition, assets repatriated from successful recoveries could be designated or used by the originating country to expand the expertise of its recovery units. Jurisdictions that provide other assistance through multilateral orga-nizations can also include assistance for asset recovery through those efforts.

In some requested jurisdictions, particularly small jurisdictions with more limited budgets, resource issues are also a significant problem. Requested jurisdictions may be willing to help with drafting requests for mutual legal assistance and other processes,

---

30. Matthias Borgers and Hans Moors, "Targeting the Proceeds of Crime: Bottlenecks in International Coop-eration," *European Journal of Crime, Criminal Law and Criminal Justice* 15, no. 2 (2007), pp. 10, 42, 43.
31. In November 2009 the Conference of State Parties to UNCAC called on States parties to ensure that competent authorities have adequate resources to execute requests. See www.unodc.org/unodc/en /treaties/ CAC/CAC-COSP.html.

provided that some mechanism is in place to share these costs with the originating jurisdiction. Some requested jurisdictions face the additional burden of exposure to a costs order (an order to pay the legal costs of the other side) in non-conviction based (NCB) or asset recovery proceedings, both during the course of proceedings and if restrained assets are ordered released. If claimants to the restrained property have other assets at their disposal, the potential for costs orders against the state can act as a deterrent to providing MLA. Some jurisdictions require an indemnity agreement from the originating state to cover any costs the requested jurisdiction may be required to pay claimants. Many originating states may be unable to provide such an indemnity, however, so alternative means of overcoming this barrier should be explored.

Originating and requested jurisdictions should be aware of the potential issues stemming from scarce resources and be prepared to have frank discussions about cost sharing and, where appropriate, sharing in the recovered assets. To avoid the potential for adverse costs orders, jurisdictions should pass legislation stating that the government will not be liable for legal costs of other parties where it has simply attempted to meet its international obligations to provide MLA. Jurisdictions can also allocate the costs in advance through a mutual legal assistance treaty. In many existing treaties, originating jurisdictions are required to cover any extraordinary costs, which can include costs orders. Many mutual legal assistance treaties require prior consultation between parties when it becomes apparent that expenses of an extraordinary nature are required. Currently, however, there is no objective measure establishing what ordinary costs are. Where possible, jurisdictions should define in advance those costs that will be considered ordinary.

Policy Recommendations

a) Jurisdictions should make it a policy priority to ensure that there are an adequate number of properly trained financial investigators, prosecutors, and judges to address asset recovery cases involving both domestic laws and international conventions and standards.
b) Jurisdictions should pass legislation to ensure that the state cannot be penalized with an adverse costs order in cases where it is addressing its international obligations to provide mutual legal assistance.

Operational Recommendations

a) Jurisdictions should ensure that competent authorities are sufficiently staffed, adequately trained, and experienced in asset recovery matters involving both domestic laws and international conventions and standards.
b) Originating and requested jurisdictions should be prepared to have frank discussions to try to resolve resource issues, including communication about cost sharing and, where appropriate, sharing of recovered assets.

Barrier 4: Lack of Adherence to and Enforcement of AML/CFT Measures

Stolen assets and proceeds of corruption are often moved from victim states to other jurisdictions. In many cases, "gatekeepers"—specialized professionals including legal and financial experts—work on behalf of kleptocrats to move these assets into financial centers where they can be "laundered" and used to buy legal assets. With more effective measures to regulate these gateways into financial centers and stronger enforcement of already existing anti-money laundering controls, some of the barriers discussed in this study would be immaterial. Under an effective anti-money laundering/combating the financing of terrorism (AML/CFT) regime, authorities and financial institutions would intercept assets stolen by corrupt officials, criminals, or terrorists, or prevent such assets from being deposited in their financial institutions. Chapter II, Article 14, of UNCAC focuses on actions to prevent money laundering and Article 52 prescribes stringent measures to prevent and detect the transfer of proceeds of crime. The failure of governments to effectively implement Article 14 and 52 of UNCAC is a barrier to stolen asset recovery. Several Financial Action Task Force (FATF) recommendations also focus on preventive measures and provide clear guidance to jurisdictions on the essential criteria required to mount an effective anti-money laundering regime.[32] Weaknesses in the implementation of the FATF recommendations, especially recommendations 5, 9, 12, 33, and 34, have helped corrupt officials gain access to the financial system. In addition, the FATF analyzes money laundering trends and has provided substantial information about increasing use by kleptocrats and other criminals of specialized professionals— lawyers, accountants, notaries, and other service providers—to facilitate their illegal operations.[33]

The ease with which stolen assets are moved into and through financial centers suggests not only that financial institutions may not adequately implement preventive measures but also that financial institution supervisory agencies may also be deficient in ensuring that banks and other institutions follow anti-money laundering regulations. A recent policy paper by the World Bank and the UN Office on Drugs and Crime (UNODC), prepared under the auspices of the StAR Initiative, found a low level of international compliance with FATF recommendation 6 on monitoring accounts held by politically exposed persons (PEPs)—individuals who are, or have been, entrusted with prominent public functions, together with their family members, and close associates.[34] More than

---

32. FATF is an intergovernmental body whose purpose is the development and promotion of national and international policies to combat money laundering and terrorist financing. Recommendations 5–9, 12, 20, 33, 34, and others involve or are related to preventive measures; International Monetary Fund, *FATF 40+9 Recommendations* (Washington, DC: IMF Legal Department, 2009).

33. FATF, *Report on Money Laundering Typologies 2003–2004*, p. 24–26. http://www.fatfgafi.org/dataoecd/19/11/ 33624379.PDF.

34. Theodore S. Greenberg, Larissa Gray, Delphine Schantz, Michael Latham, and Carolin Garder, *Politically Exposed Persons: A Policy Paper on Strengthening Preventive Measures for the Banking Sector* (Washington, DC: World Bank, 2010), p. 13. The FATF recommendation states that financial institutions should, in addition to performing normal due diligence measures, have appropriate risk management systems to determine whether the customer is a PEP; obtain senior management approval for establishing business relationships with such customers; take reasonable measures to establish the source of

three-fifths of the 124 jurisdictions evaluated were rated noncompliant on this recommendation. The policy paper also found an overall failure among national authorities and banks to effectively implement international PEP standards.[35] Similar conclusions were also reached at recent hearings conducted by the U.S. Senate Permanent Subcommittee on Investigations.[36] In most cases, domestic financial regulations are not adequate to monitor PEPs or prevent money laundering of the proceeds of corruption.

Among the many shortfalls, financial institutions and other reporting entities are not filing suspicious activity and transactions reports with the competent authorities about PEP transactions, and supervisors are not effectively addressing this lack of reporting. Financial institutions are required to take reasonable measures to establish the sources of wealth and of funds deposited by customers and beneficial owners identified as PEPs. However, the apparent volume of illegal proceeds that PEPs move through financial centers, and the apparent ease with which they do it, suggests serious deficiencies in the tracking programs that financial institutions use to comply with this requirement.

Global Witness, an international nongovernmental organization that targets the exploitation of natural resources, has also found what it calls serious gaps in FATF's recommendations themselves, especially in connection with ensuring sufficient transparency over beneficial ownership of assets.[37] Some civil society groups advocate that competent authorities maintain company registries that identify beneficial owners. A forthcoming StAR study into the misuse of corporate vehicles argues that, to be effective, such registries would have to verify the information submitted, which could be quite a tall order. Nonetheless, the study finds that registries can usefully compliment anti-money laundering objectives by implementing minimum standards for the information maintained in the registry and by providing financial institutions and law enforcement authorities with access to adequate, accurate, and timely information on relevant persons connected to corporate vehicles—corporations, trusts, partnerships with limited liability characteristics, foundations, and the like.

---

wealth and source of funds; and conduct enhanced ongoing monitoring of the business relationship. See International Monetary Fund, *FATF 40+9 Recommendations* (Washington, DC: IMF Legal Department, 2009), p. 35.

35. Ibid.

36. During the hearing, Senator Carl Levin remarked that "politically powerful individuals—known internationally as 'politically exposed persons' or PEPs—are taking advantage of the U.S. financial system. In each case, weaknesses in our financial regulations have allowed these PEPs to move millions of dollars into or through U.S. bank accounts, often by using shell company accounts, attorney-client accounts, escrow accounts, or other accounts, or by sending wire transfers that shoot through the system before our banks react." Opening Statement of Sen. Carl Levin quoted in *Keeping Foreign Corruption Out of the United States: Four Case Histories* (Washington, DC: United States Senate Permanent Subcommittee on Investigations, 2010), p. 1.

37. Global Witness, *Undue Diligence: How Banks Do Business with Corrupt Regimes*, November 3, 2009, p. 106, available at www.globalwitness.org.

The FATF Working Group on Terrorist Financing and Money Laundering is currently looking into the challenges financial institutions face regarding PEPs. This work should address the lack of clarity in the definition of PEPs, which has lead to confusion and has subsequently frustrated implementation efforts. UNCAC, for example, requires institutions to apply enhanced due diligence no matter where they reside, whereas FATF recommendations apply only to a financial institution's foreign customers. FATF's adoption of the UNCAC definition of a PEP could provide some clarification and assist efforts toward better implementation of preventive measures. There has also been discussion on the merits of using a risk-based approach to monitoring PEPs as opposed to monitoring PEPs for a prescribed time period. Because some PEPs remain powerfully influential long after they are no longer in office, a risk-based approach would seem to be the more effective monitoring tool.

To overcome this obstacle, financial centers should ensure that an effective preventive regime, including customer due diligence, is in place, properly supervised, and adhered to in their jurisdiction. The StAR policy paper on PEPs put forward several recommendations to improve preventive efforts and due diligence, some of which are listed in the recommendations box below. Moreover, the forthcoming StAR paper on *Misuse of Corporate Vehicles* will make some additional policy recommendations.

In addition, financial centers should take steps to ensure the availability of financial records relating to PEPs. Prosecution of PEPs may be delayed for many years by corruption at the highest levels of the government. As a result, banking records that are destroyed in accordance with usual document retention guidelines can doom the prosecution of PEPs for money laundering and other corruption offenses. To ensure that the necessary banking documents will be available for prosecution of PEPs, jurisdictions should require financial institutions to maintain records relating to PEPs for a longer period of time. This time period may vary according to the level of prominence of the PEP. For example, records relating to a PEP who is a head of state should be kept for a longer period of time because prosecution will likely be impossible as long as the PEP is in power.

Requests through MLA to preserve specific records may be useful. Even before a basis for seizing the records has been determined, a request to preserve such records may be honored. The practice of requesting preservation may avoid a situation where records are inadvertently destroyed between the start of an investigation and the time at which a basis for seizure of the records is determined. These preservation requests can be made through an informal MLA request.[38]

---

38. In general, voluntary "preservation requests" can be useful in both domestic and international litigation. Financial institutions are often cooperative and honor the requests. A request for confidentiality can be included in the request. Along with the preservation request, a request for confidentiality, meaning a request that the bank not inform the customer that his records are being preserved, is also a good idea and likely will be honored as well by the financial institution.

Policy Recommendations

a) FATF should align its definition of a PEP with UNCAC's. This definition should be adopted by all national standard setters and other key stakeholders.[a]
b) Jurisdictions should require financial institutions to review their PEP customers at least yearly, using a risk-based approach, and to document the results of the review.
c) Because PEPs often retain their prominence and influence for several years even after a corruption prosecution begins, jurisdictions should require financial institutions to keep banking records related to PEPs for a longer period than normal, perhaps eight to ten years.

a. Theodore S. Greenberg, Larissa Gray, Delphine Schantz, Michael Latham, and Carolin Garder, *Politically Exposed Persons: A Policy Paper on Strengthening Preventive Measures for the Banking Sector.* (Washington, DC: World Bank, 2010), p. 26.

Operational Recommendations

a) Jurisdictions should ensure implementation of the provisions of Article 14 and Article 52 of UNCAC, the FATF recommendations, and the recommendations set out in the StAR report *Politically Exposed Persons: A Policy Paper on Strengthening Preventative Measures for the Banking Sector.*
b) When a suspicious transaction report (STR) is linked to a foreign PEP, the competent authorities should, after proper analysis supports such dissemination, share this information with the competent authorities in the PEP's home jurisdiction and any other germane jurisdiction.
c) Jurisdictions should report any criminal acts and suspicious information discovered during the yearly review of a foreign PEP to the local FIU using the STR process, or to another competent authority through the appropriate process.
d) Jurisdictions should consider implementing risk management systems to identify PEPs. Such systems should include:
   - Generic indicators and information sources, such as risks associated with certain jurisdictions, products, the seniority of the officeholder, or the type of business.
   - Procurement of relevant information from the customer as part of the normal account application process and ongoing customer due diligence (CDD) and know your client (KYC) processes.
   - A requirement for a written declaration of beneficial ownership under penalty of a criminal offense.
   - Business knowledge and information sharing between financial institutions.
   - Asset and income declaration filing lists.

(continued next page)

- Media and journals containing information that may help banks identify PEPs and keep their customer profile updated.
- Domestic sources of information pertaining to the customer's originating jurisdiction.
- Internet searches, including both large and small search engines.
- Use of commercial PEP database providers.

e) Jurisdictions should ensure that the competent regulators or supervisors properly enforce implementation of the disclosure, reporting, and risk management systems relating to PEPs.

Barrier 5: Too Many Cooks in the Kitchen—Lack of Effective Coordination

MLA becomes a necessity when assets have moved from one jurisdiction to another. If mutual assistance is not achieved in timely fashion, opportunities for seizure are lost and momentum for asset recovery flags. Channels for transmission of MLA requests and follow-up communication are crucial factors in the timeliness of processing requests. The rapid transmission of requests and direct communication with competent officials to provide clarification are highly desirable in an effective MLA process, especially for high-priority cases.

A significant impediment to timely response to MLA requests is the channeling of requests through numerous government agencies or departments, slowing the process unnecessarily. In the case of requests using letters rogatory, the communication must go through diplomatic channels, which can delay action on the request. In some jurisdictions, even if letters rogatory are not the means of request, all communication regarding MLA requests must be channeled into and out of the country though the foreign ministry. In other instances, the central authority acts as a "postbox," forwarding the request, sometimes through three or four offices, to the operational practitioners. Expert practitioners recognized the need for a central control but cautioned that such control processes should not impair efficiency or timely responses to or implementation of requests for assistance.

Practitioners also described challenges in transmitting requests related to politically sensitive PEP cases through the requesting country's foreign ministry, fearing such channeling could jeopardize the integrity of the request. One practitioner recounted that a foreign ministry had held back a request until after the country's elections. In another situation, a request was leaked to the press in the middle of an investigation by the originating jurisdiction because the information was favorable to some members of the government. At the same time, other practitioners sending requests through the foreign ministries sometimes had advantages—the ministry may locate the best contact point, and it cannot hold back a request without a legal basis. On balance, jurisdictions should develop arrangements that will avoid political interference with incoming and outgoing MLA requests by minimizing the number of agencies that need to become involved in the MLA procedure.

Some jurisdictions expressed concerns over the development of direct communication, contending that informality can lower the standards that jurisdictions must meet to ensure that the MLA mechanisms deliver the required results in a lawful and legally admissible manner. On the whole, however, direct communication and informal assistance in the MLA process are valuable tools for dealing with noncoercive measures and can also help to clarify issues and avoid misunderstandings.

Good Practice

Permitting practitioner-to-practitioner communications
The European Union permits direct transmission (judicial authority to judicial authority) for a wide range of informal assistance matters, including investigative actions and freezing and confiscation orders. It also permits direct contact between practitioners dealing with informal assistance requests.[a] Article 48 of UNCAC and some bilateral MLA treaties offer similar avenues of direct cooperation and transmission of requests.

a. Council Framework Decision 2003/577/JHA, July 22, 2003, and Council Framework Decision 2006/783/JHA, October 6, 2006.

One of the impediments identified in the study—lack of coordination between relevant players—applies equally at the international and domestic levels. Several practitioners said that the lack of international coordination could hurt cases, particularly where criminal assets are located in multiple jurisdictions. For example, a jurisdiction that enters into a plea agreement to a lesser offense can create problems for investigations in other jurisdictions if the lesser offense is a misdemeanor, not a felony, or if it precludes the other jurisdiction from obtaining the evidence needed for their investigation. Criminals certainly recognize that globalization allows them to more easily move across borders and to disperse illicit funds and other assets across several different jurisdictions. They also clearly understand that at least some of those stolen assets might be "protected" by the lack of international cooperation and coordination in identifying, tracing, recovering, and returning those assets.[39]

Many practitioners recommended the creation of a joint international task force arrangement to gain a better understanding of the challenges associated with a

---

39. UNCAC mandates and the FATF recommends effective international cooperation, and both have provisions requiring parties to cooperate in criminal matters. UNCAC provides for international cooperation, including cooperation in law enforcement matters (Article 40), mutual legal assistance (Article 46), joint investigations (Article 49), and asset recovery (Chapter V). FATF Recommendations 36 (mutual legal assistance), 37 (dual criminality), 38 (freezing, seizing, and confiscating proceeds of crime), and 40 (other forms of cooperation) set out the FATF standards on international cooperation.

particular request for MLA. Discussions covered the possibility of setting common objectives, joint investigations, and recovery actions. The task force arrangement could be set up any number of ways, for example, an ongoing task force targeted on a particular case to coordinate efforts and benefit from the expertise and experience of both jurisdictions, or a more general task force on MLA issues. Certainly bringing key operatives from originating and requested jurisdictions together in a task force atmosphere would clarify many issues, help each jurisdiction better understand the challenges the other faces, and provide opportunities to share and agree upon strategic and tactical approaches to the case. The task force approach would also provide a means for requesting that certain cases be given a higher priority. (If a task force is already in place, the originating jurisdiction could bring to the task force a request that a case should be given greater priority by the requested jurisdiction.) Some practitioners also suggested that joint task forces could provide an opportunity to explore new and innovative approaches to asset recovery.

Lack of coordination between domestic anticorruption agencies can also impede mutual assistance and asset recovery. The international joint task force approach could be extended to task force arrangements or multiagency working groups at the domestic level. Joint working arrangements facilitate national coordination and cooperation, avoid duplication of effort, and provide an environment for discussing and agreeing on strategies for responding to MLA requests. They can also add value to domestic investigations that may be initiated as a consequence of requests for assistance. A domestic task force can be established as a standing interagency group dealing with MLA requests, or on a case-by-case basis as significant international requests for assistance warrant. Whether the task force is permanent or ad hoc, a lead agency that is responsible for monitoring the progress and reporting on the status of requests is essential. The terms of reference of any multiagency group should also spell out the role and responsibilities of task force members and outline arrangements for task force meetings and reporting.

The Importance of Communication

During the course of this StAR study, some potential originating jurisdictions expressed the opinion that a specific jurisdiction with relevant information or assets would not want to cooperate with originating jurisdictions. The view was based on third-hand accounts and rumors; the jurisdiction in question had never been approached. Similarly, an originating jurisdiction may erroneously interpret a request for further information as indicating that the requested jurisdiction does not want to provide assistance. Some jurisdictions expect, unrealistically, that all requested jurisdictions have the same procedures and access to information and the same level of resources dedicated to recovery actions. If the requested jurisdiction does not respond as expected, the originating jurisdiction may complain of a lack of cooperation, even though the delay or inability to grant the request is a result of differences in procedures and resources.

(continued next page)

Barrier 6: Quick Trigger on Formal MLA Submission

In the context of this study, the term "formal MLA" is used to describe a written request
for mutual legal assistance, a formal process that requires certain prescribed procedures, requirements, and conditions. These requirements, which are described in
greater detail throughout this paper, pose many obstacles to obtaining a positive
response in a timely manner to a formal request for assistance. Depending on the nature
of the request, legal requirements may apply, including requirements for the existence
of criminal charges (Barrier 10), dual criminality (Barrier 22), or mandatory grounds

for refusal (Barrier 22). In addition, the process can be lengthy, with delays caused by any number of factors, such as the exercise of due process rights by the target of the investigation (often for legitimate reasons, but sometimes as an abuse of the process) or by a lack of resources in the responding jurisdiction (see Barrier 3). These requirements may be legitimate and necessary in many cases, but a formal MLA request may not always be required.

Typically, formal MLA is required where the desired assistance involves the use of coercive power by the requested jurisdiction, such as the power to compel production of bank account transaction details or search and seizure orders. At the beginning stages of an investigation and during the collection of information and intelligence, the coercive power of the requested jurisdiction may not be engaged, and a formal MLA request may not be required. At this stage the desired assistance may simply be what is often referred to as informal assistance—assistance through channels other than a formal written MLA request, which is also recognized by many treaties and legislation.[40] Examples of informal assistance include direct communications between the FIUs, police, prosecutors, or investigating magistrates of the two jurisdictions, discussing intelligence or other assistance, with an anticipated formal MLA request to follow.[41]

Such informal assistance is tremendously important to the entire process of asset recovery. With fewer restrictions, practitioners can gather information more quickly than they can under a formal MLA request process, build the necessary substantive foundation for an eventual formal request, and develop a strategy that best accords with the advantages and limitations of both jurisdictions' systems. The importance of these informal channels of assistance and cooperation among counterpart agencies outside the realm of MLA has been emphasized in UNCAC and by FATF.[42]

---

40. Although less formal in the sense that fewer procedural requirements are associated with it, informal assistance should not be taken to include any illegal means or "backroom dealing."

41. The Egmont Group of Financial Intelligence Units, in its Statement of Purpose and Principles of Exchange of Information, encourages members to share financial information related to suspect money laundering and proceeds of crime. The Egmont Group in November 2004 issued a paper on Best Practices for the Exchange of Information Between Financial Intelligence Units; see http://www.egmontgroup.org/library/egmont-documents.

42. UNCAC, Article 48 requires cooperation between States parties to enhance the effectiveness of law enforcement action. See also UNCAC, Article 50, which discusses use of special investigative techniques, and Articles 46(4) and 56 regarding spontaneous transmission of information in MLA and asset recovery cases. States parties to UNCAC discussed direct communication in Resolution 3/3, recommending that states spontaneously disclose information on proceeds of offenses to other States parties, and urging promotion of informal channels of communication by designating officials or institutions as focal points to assist their counterparts in effectively meeting requirements for formal mutual legal assistance. The Open-ended Intergovernmental Working Group on Asset Recovery established by the Conference of State Parties to UNCAC has also recommended the promotion of networks for informal and formal communication (see COSP/WG.2/2009/3).

UNTOC similarly enables States parties to provide "the widest measure of mutual legal assistance in investigations, prosecutions and judicial proceedings in relation to the offences covered by the Convention." States parties are also obliged to "reciprocally extend to one another similar assistance" where the requesting

A number of practitioners who spoke with the study team suggested that less formal contacts always be the starting point in any request for assistance. Concern has been raised that the use of informal procedures may not be appropriate in cases where a jurisdiction provides information to an originating jurisdiction that may be used as evidence. To overcome that concern, the jurisdiction providing the information informally can require that more formal procedures be followed before the originating jurisdiction can use the information as evidence. Requested jurisdictions that will not allow information they provide informally to be used as evidence should make that clear when the information is provided.

In addition to aiding with the collection of information, informal assistance creates a dialogue, acts as a useful prelude to a subsequent formal request, and can help the jurisdictions better understand each other's requirements. Such knowledge can help ensure that the formal MLA request is framed correctly. If it is not, it could be refused because of a deficiency, or returned for additional information, which would slow the process. In some cases informal assistance may result in the requested state helping to draft the letter of request. More than one jurisdiction encourages originating states to submit draft letters of request in more difficult and complicated cases, although originating countries often do not make use of this service.[43]

Considering the challenges involved in obtaining assistance through formal MLA, originating jurisdictions should first ask what forms of informal assistance are available and, wherever possible, move forward with informal assistance before proceeding with a formal MLA request. Authorities in requested jurisdictions should be permitted to provide some information and informal assistance to their foreign counterparts without requiring a formal MLA request. In virtually all jurisdictions, assistance concerning procedures and processes for MLA are available in advance of filing a formal MLA request. Frequently more extensive assistance and cooperation, sometimes involving various creative techniques, are possible even though they appear uncertain. For example, if substantive assistance on a specific case is not available before a formal request is filed, discussions of detailed hypothetical situations may be useful. Moreover, suggestions that the requested jurisdiction preserve specific evidence, if it exists, may be availing, on the theory that even if the requested jurisdiction cannot respond directly to the originating jurisdiction at that time, the requested jurisdiction is aware of any action that could be taken that requires minimal effort on its part. In addition, originating

---

State has "reasonable grounds to suspect" that one or some of these crimes are transnational in nature and that they involve an organized criminal group.

See also Recommendation 40 of the FATF 40: "Countries should ensure that their competent authorities provide the widest possible range of international co-operation to their counterparts. There should be clear and effective gateways to facilitate prompt and constructive exchange directly between counterparts, either spontaneously or upon request, of information relating to both money laundering and the underlying predicate offences."

43. *Combating Money Laundering and Recovering Looted Gains: Raising the UK's Game* (London: Transparency International UK, 2009), p. 44.

jurisdictions should be encouraged to exhaust these informal channels before drafting an MLA request.

Jurisdictions should also ensure that domestic laws authorize direct contact between domestic authorities—including law enforcement agencies, financial intelligence units, and prosecutorial agencies—and their foreign counterparts, as is required by UNCAC. To facilitate such cooperation, some jurisdictions permit authorities to exchange information with other jurisdictions but do not require the exchange to be on a counterpart-to-counterpart basis. For example, one jurisdiction allows law enforcement agencies of the European Union to submit information requests concerning significant money laundering or terrorist finance investigations to domestic financial institutions through their FIU. This practice enables agencies to discover whether a financial institution has established an account or conducted a transaction with a person reasonably suspected, based on credible evidence, of engaging in terrorist activity or significant money laundering. Armed with this limited but important information, the law enforcement agency can follow up using other tools to advance the investigation. Additional information can be requested through MLA requests. If, on the other hand, the institution has no such account or a transaction, that too is valuable information, since it prevents law enforcement agencies from spending additional resources unnecessarily.

The information that can be exchanged should, at a minimum, include all noncoercive investigatory measures in that jurisdiction. In addition, to avoid the dissipation of assets, a temporary freeze of 72 hours or less should be available through informal assistance, even if the freeze is regarded as coercive. A recent study by Transparency International also proposes that states be willing to provide the following types of informal assistance without a written formal request:

- provide public records, such as land registry documents, company documents, information about directors and shareholders, and filed company accounts (see Barrier 27);
- contact potential witnesses to determine if the witness is willing to cooperate voluntarily and take witness statements from voluntary witnesses, provided that contact with witnesses is permitted under such circumstances;
- provide basic subscriber details from communication and service providers that do not require a court order.[44]

---

44. *Combating Money Laundering and Recovering Looted Gains: Raising the UK's Game* (London: Transparency International UK, 2009), p. 45.

Good Practices

Some jurisdictions encourage a practice of identifying the assistance needed by the originating jurisdiction early on in the investigation and recognize the value of informal assistance. These jurisdictions encourage informal assistance because a request that can be executed informally (but that will provide admissible evidence) tends to be acted upon much faster and will not clog an already overloaded MLA transmission network.

Many jurisdictions provide informal assistance through police-to-police and regulator-to-regulator requests to identify and trace persons, bank accounts and balances, real property, businesses, directors, shareholders, and registered addresses of companies. A formal MLA request for this information would impede its timely provision. Originating jurisdictions can ask the requested jurisdiction whether it provides informal assistance, and if so, what sort and through what channels.

Some jurisdictions encourage early requests through the Egmont Secure Web for identification of specific bank accounts and information available on public databases, rather than submit an MLA request to restrain "any and all accounts and assets of. . . ." These jurisdictions also encourage direct contacts with their law enforcement attachés to determine whether other information may be available in an informal context.

Policy Recommendations

a) Jurisdictions should develop and implement policies and procedures that ensure that informal assistance channels are available to foreign practitioners for noncoercive measures and temporary freezes of 72 hours or less, without disproportionate or unduly restrictive conditions.
b) Jurisdictions should establish policies and procedures that create communication channels outside the formal process at all stages: before, during, and after the final preparation and communication of a formal MLA request.

Operational Recommendations

a) Originating jurisdictions should exhaust informal assistance channels before making a formal MLA request.
b) Requested jurisdictions should inform originating jurisdictions, at an early stage, of types of information that can be provided without the need for a formal MLA request. Guidance should be provided through relevant government Web sites (see Barrier 23).

(continued next page)

c) Jurisdictions should not require a formal request before making public records available, such as land registry documents, registered company documents, and information about directors and shareholders. Jurisdictions should also provide copies of annual reports and associated documents without a formal request.

d) If requested, jurisdictions should be willing to contact potential witnesses without a formal request to determine if the witness is willing to cooperate with the originating authorities voluntarily. States should take witness statements from voluntary witnesses without a formal request, provided that contact with the witness is permitted under such circumstances.

Legal Barriers and Requirements
that Delay Assistance

Barrier 7: Differences in Legal Traditions

Differences in legal traditions between jurisdictions introduce challenges and frustrations throughout the asset recovery process. Practitioners said these differences were a common reason that many requests are sent back for more information. These differences also can lead to frustration for practitioners unfamiliar with the procedures and capabilities of a particular jurisdiction, whether it is a civil law, common law, or hybrid jurisdiction. For example, the time needed to respond to particular types of requests varies from one jurisdiction to another. Practitioners may become frustrated if they do not appreciate that some investigative techniques can be applied quickly in some jurisdictions but not in others.

The following differences between civil law and common law jurisdictions may introduce barriers to the asset recovery process.

- *Terminology:* Differences in terminology extend to the names of offenses (which can affect determinations of dual criminality) and confiscation terms that have different meanings in different jurisdictions. In a civil law jurisdiction, the measure used to obtain bank documents may be called a "search and seizure order"; in a common law jurisdiction, it may be known as a "production order" or "subpoena." Some practitioners in civil law jurisdictions said the common law term "civil recovery" is misleading because they automatically associate it with civil procedure, even though the case may have criminal aspects. Similarly, "civil forfeiture" or "civil confiscation," terms used in some common law jurisdictions to describe *in rem* confiscation (confiscation directed at property) without a conviction, can be problematic in civil law jurisdictions where they are equated to a private legal action and thus is not within scope for MLA assistance. Practitioners should try to be aware of these differences and to avoid the use of problematic terminology in their requests. For example, participants preferred the substitution of the terms "non-conviction based forfeiture" or "non-conviction based confiscation" when referring to "civil confiscation" or "civil forfeiture."
- *Tools available for restraint or confiscation:* Although jurisdictions with the same legal tradition may use different legal tools, the difference is even more pronounced between different legal traditions. Practitioners in civil law jurisdictions can often make use of extended confiscation (confiscation of property from criminal activities not directly related to the offense) and confiscation following

conviction for illicit enrichment. Unlike most civil law jurisdictions, common law jurisdictions can confiscate assets using a lower standard of proof, plea agreements, and legislative presumptions. The orders that can be obtained through civil (private law) actions in common law jurisdictions also vary significantly, as does the standard of proof (balance of probabilities or preponderance of the evidence in common law versus proof beyond a reasonable doubt or intimate conviction—proof that intimately convinces a judge—in civil law).

- *Evidentiary requirements:* The evidentiary requirements of the systems also differ, as well as the standards of proof required. For example, searches in common law jurisdictions must be authorized by a judge and require proof of probable cause to believe that an offense has been committed and that evidence is in the place to be searched, whereas many civil law jurisdictions permit the investigating magistrate or prosecutor to conduct all acts necessary to establish the truth.[45] Jurisdictions also vary on what type of evidence needs to be submitted. If practitioners do not understand the different procedures within the two systems, they may improperly collect evidence that turns out to be inadmissible.
- *Requirements for admissibility:* Common law jurisdictions generally require affidavits and certification of documents for the evidence to be admissible in a court, whereas many civil jurisdictions do not have such requirements.
- *Procedures to obtain assistance:* Investigating magistrates and prosecutors in civil law jurisdiction usually have the authority to freeze assets and therefore can take swift action; in common law jurisdictions, they must often apply to a court before they can take action.

Overcoming the obstacles created by these differences in legal tradition requires diligence by both originating and requested jurisdictions, as well as willingness on the part of the requested jurisdiction to be transparent about its process for fulfilling requests. See Barrier 23 for particular recommendations on how to increase transparency and facilitate the exchange of information between originating and requesting jurisdictions.

Although legal differences can make mutual legal assistance more difficult to obtain and to provide, requested jurisdictions can help to overcome these challenges by exploring all procedural laws that may permit them to execute an MLA request. Several multilateral conventions allow for flexibility in complying with procedural forms. The UNCAC builds on previous similar provisions and stipulates that a request shall be

---

45. An example of probable cause: Police receive an anonymous report that persons are selling drugs out of a residence at a certain location in a high drug-trafficking neighborhood and that a supplier wearing a baseball cap and sunglasses visits the house every morning between 7 and 8 a.m. Police conduct surveillance and observe that on three successive mornings, a man fitting that description arrives carrying a large package between 7 and 8 a.m.; and that over the course of the day, every day, at least 20 people arrive at the house, knock, enter, and emerge about five minutes later carrying a small bag. There is no indication that any kind of legitimate business is being conducted from the house. The totality of the circumstances here would amount to probable cause, that is, enough evidence to obtain a warrant to search the house.

executed in accordance with the domestic law of the requested jurisdiction.[46] However, the same provision also states that, where possible, the request shall be executed in accordance with the procedures specified in the request. In the same context, the UNODC Model Treaty on Mutual Assistance in Criminal Matters also enables the request to be executed in the manner specified by the originating jurisdiction to the extent consistent with the law and practice of the requested jurisdiction.[47]

Operational Recommendations

a) To facilitate understandings between jurisdictions with different legal traditions, jurisdictions should provide easy access to information about asset recovery within their legal system, including relevant statutory provisions and information about proof requirements, capacities, types of investigative techniques that are available, and types that are disallowed. Formats should include:

   i) A Web site that provides this information and practical asset recovery case examples that offer guidance on available investigative techniques and how they are used in the jurisdiction.

   ii) Workshops involving international and domestic practitioners to provide information on how to submit MLA requests, capacities, types of investigative techniques that are available, and types that are disallowed.

b) Jurisdictions should use clear, concise, and universal terms when drafting MLA requests, such as those in Article 2 of UNCAC and in UNTOC, and explain concisely the meaning of each term used.

c) Jurisdictions should implement policies and procedures that proactively notify originating jurisdictions about problems with terminology or other substantive issues.

d) Requested jurisdictions should consider developing and implementing policies and procedures that ensure they can use any and all possible procedures that will permit them to positively execute an MLA request, including their own procedures and the procedures specified in the request.

Barrier 8: Inability to Provide MLA

Jurisdictions generally require one of four legal bases to provide formal MLA in criminal and asset recovery cases: international conventions containing provisions on MLA in criminal matters, such as UNCAC and UNTOC; domestic legislation allowing for international cooperation in criminal cases; bilateral mutual legal assistance agreements; or a promise of reciprocity through diplomatic channels (known in some jurisdictions as letters rogatory). Without one of these bases, jurisdictions are unable to provide MLA.

---

46. UNCAC, Article 46(17). See also the United Nations Convention against Illicit Traffic in Narcotic Drugs and Psychotropic Substances, Article 7(12), and UNTOC, Article 18(17).
47. See http://www.unodc.org/pdf/model_treaty_mutual_assistance_criminal_matters.pdf.

International Conventions

Practitioners cited failure to implement and use the provisions of treaties such as UNCAC and UNTOC as a barrier to asset recovery. Chapters IV and V of UNCAC and Article 18 of UNTOC, for example, require member states to cooperate in the fight against crime and to assist one another in the recovery of the proceeds and instrumentalities of criminal conduct. Both conventions set out specific types of assistance that states should provide to each other, as well as procedural and evidentiary requirements for such cooperation.

Depending on constitutional requirements, countries generally pursue one of two avenues to implement their obligations under international law.[48] Some states must transpose the provisions of international treaties into domestic law, frequently through legislation, before they have legal force. In the absence of corresponding domestic legal provisions, MLA, as set out in international treaties such as UNCAC and UNTOC, may not be granted. The extent of and conditions for such assistance are thus exclusively determined by domestic law.

By contrast, in other jurisdictions the mere act of ratification of a self-executing international convention such as UNCAC and UNTOC makes the treaty provisions part of domestic law and thus directly applicable by national judges and authorities. In these jurisdictions, MLA may be granted directly based on the convention provisions. Corresponding domestic legislation is not required.

One barrier revealed by the study is the lack of complete and accurate transposition of the convention provisions into domestic law, where necessary to give effect to the conventions. In such jurisdictions, domestic laws on MLA frequently fail to allow for all types of assistance as set out in conventions such as UNCAC and UNTOC, provide for overly broad grounds for refusal, or apply overly stringent evidentiary requirements. A few such jurisdictions do not have a domestic MLA framework in place at all. Jurisdictions that require international conventions to be transposed into domestic law should thus ensure that comprehensive legislation on MLA is in place and fully in line with the provisions of UNCAC, UNTOC, and other international conventions.

Surprisingly, practitioners indicated that even in jurisdictions where transposition of international self-executing treaties is not required, these conventions are rarely used as vehicles for cooperation in asset recovery cases. The failure to use UNCAC and UNTOC effectively stems, in part, from the general formulation of some of the provisions and a lack of familiarity by practitioners with the conventions.[49] A large number of jurisdictions that are not required to transpose self-executing treaties have also established MLA

---

48. Alfred Verdross and Bruno Simmar, *Universelles Voelkerrecht: Theorie und Praxis* (Berlin: Duncker & Humblot, 1984), p. 54 ff., p. 539 ff.; Hans Kelsen, *Principles of International Law* (Clark, NJ: Lawbook Exchange, 2003), p. 195 ff.

49. The UNCAC Conference of States Parties and its working groups have passed resolutions urging States parties and signatories to disseminate knowledge on the substantive aspects of UNCAC and to provide technical assistance to requesting countries.

laws to facilitate and regulate cooperation with states that are not parties to UNCAC; to allow for MLA in cases that fall outside the scope of conventions; and to set out more specific rules, procedures, and requirements than those stipulated in international treaties. In dealings with other UNCAC parties, jurisdictions might also apply domestic laws that they consider more favorable to granting MLA requests.

To ensure that the potential of international conventions is fully explored and used, jurisdictions that have the ability to directly apply treaties such as UNCAC and UNTOC domestically should ensure that practitioners know they can use these multilateral conventions as a legal basis to grant and request MLA, and that they are familiar with and know how to correctly apply the treaty provisions, including those dealing with asset recovery. To facilitate this effort and to provide practitioners with sufficient training in this area, resource constraints as outlined in Barrier 3 should be addressed.[50]

Domestic Legislation

While domestic MLA laws play a significant role in implementing countries' obligations under international law, practitioners also noted the importance of domestic legislation for cases where MLA is requested in the absence of or outside the scope of conventions such as UNCAC and UNTOC. All jurisdictions, including those that would not be legally required to transpose international treaties, should thus put in place domestic MLA legislation fully in line with the MLA provisions in Chapters IV and V of UNCAC and Article 18 of UNTOC. Jurisdictions that have not yet done so should accede or ratify and fully implement UNCAC, UNTOC, and other regional or international instruments that facilitate the provision of MLA as soon as possible.

Bilateral MLA Treaties

Besides domestic laws and international conventions, bilateral mutual legal assistance treaties (MLATs) may serve as an additional legal basis for international cooperation in criminal cases. In contrast to multilateral conventions, bilateral treaties are typically not limited in scope to a range of offenses but apply to any criminal activity that falls within their scope of application. They create clear and binding obligations between two jurisdictions to cooperate and set out efficient and comprehensive procedures to be applied. MLATs typically create a closer relationship between the signatory states than multilateral conventions and are customized to fit that relationship. In addition, they are typically quicker and easier to negotiate and amend than multilateral conventions.

MLATs can nonetheless be time-consuming and expensive, and can involve the challenging process of negotiation. In many instances, particularly in cases involving jurisdictions with limited resources, jurisdictions can avoid the need for a bilateral treaty by allowing for certain types of assistance in the absence of an MLAT, including

---

50. In addition, a soon-to-be published StAR knowledge product, *UNCAC Knowledge Management Consortium and Legal Library*, will be a useful resource.

provisional measures based either on domestic law[51] or the provisions of international treaties such as UNCAC.[52] Practitioners noted that the detailed procedural and evidentiary provisions of conventions such as UNCAC have recently eliminated the need for MLATs in many cases. Jurisdictions should conduct periodic reviews to determine if entering into MLATs would result in more productive international cooperation and address any concerns not already dealt with by international conventions.

However, practitioners also stated that bilateral treaties are still important in cases where existing multilateral treaties are not applicable. For example, where the originating or requested jurisdiction has not ratified a relevant convention, the nature of the request is outside the scope of a relevant convention, or a request was made by an authority that is not considered a competent authority under a relevant convention, an MLAT would provide for streamlined and effective procedures to provide a wide range of assistance. In such cases, the absence of such a treaty could mean that certain forms of assistance could not be provided or that requests would have to be processed through formal and sometimes cumbersome MLA channels or letters rogatory.[53]

Originating jurisdictions, particularly those in the developing world, should be selective in entering into MLAT relationships, choosing jurisdictions with which cooperation based on domestic law or international conventions would otherwise be limited or overly burdensome, or with which cooperation is or will be significant (typically along economic or geographic ties). Existing MLATs should be reviewed and, if required, updated periodically to ensure their continued relevancy.

Requested countries should also recognize that negotiating an MLAT may not be feasible in some circumstances. In those cases requested countries should therefore consider the application of already existing instruments, such as the Council of Europe Convention on Mutual Assistance in Criminal Matters and the Convention on Laundering, Search, Seizure and Confiscation of the Proceeds of Crime and on Financing Terrorism, the Inter-American Convention Against Corruption, and the ASEAN Treaty on Mutual Legal Assistance.[54]

---

51. Model legislation on MLA was elaborated by UNODC in 2007. See http://www.unodc.org/pdf/legal_advisory /Model%20Law%20on%20MLA%202007.pdf.

52. In the absence of an applicable mutual legal assistance treaty, Article 46 of UNCAC provides a mechanism for transmitting and executing requests for the types of assistance mentioned above. If a treaty is in force between the States parties concerned, the rules of the treaty will apply instead, unless the parties agree to apply Article 46(9) to (29). In any case, States parties are also encouraged to apply those paragraphs if they facilitate cooperation. In some jurisdictions, legislation may be required to give full effect to the provisions.

53. In an effort to provide guidance on the conclusion or updating of MLA treaties, UNODC has prepared a Model Treaty on Mutual Assistance in Criminal Matters (General Assembly Resolutions 45/117, annex and 53/112, annex I), which represents a distillation of the international experience gained with the implementation of such mutual legal assistance treaties, in particular between state parties representing different legal systems. The model treaty is available at http://www.unodc.org/pdf/model_treaty_mutual_assistance_criminal_matters.pdf.

54. Both conventions are also open for countries that are not members of the Council of Europe. See, for example, Article 28 of the Convention on Mutual Assistance in Criminal Matters.

Reciprocity through Diplomatic Channels (Letters Rogatory)

As a last resort, MLA may be obtained through letters rogatory on the basis of reciprocity through diplomatic channels. This approach has many disadvantages, however. Communications occur through diplomatic channels, slowing the response as well as the assistance. Moreover, letters rogatory are limited to court-to-court assistance and thus may not be available in the investigative or early stages of the prosecution if criminal charges have not been laid.

Policy Recommendations

a) Jurisdictions that have not yet done so should accede to or ratify and implement UNCAC, UNTOC, and other regional or international instruments that facilitate the provision of MLA.

b) Jurisdictions that need to transpose international conventions into domestic law should ensure that comprehensive and overarching domestic legislation on MLA is in place and fully compliant with Chapters IV and V of UNCAC and Article 18 of UNTOC.

c) Jurisdictions that have the ability to directly apply self-executing international treaties should ensure that practitioners are aware that international conventions such as UNCAC and UNTOC can be used as a legal basis for MLA and are familiar with the convention provisions. Consideration should be given to adopting domestic MLA laws to allow for assistance in the absence of or in cases outside the scope of international conventions.

d) Jurisdictions should consider entering into bilateral MLATs or memoranda of understanding with jurisdictions that provide only limited forms of MLA based on their domestic laws or based on conventions such as UNCAC, UNTOC, or jurisdictions with which cooperation would be overly burdensome without a bilateral agreement. Priority should be given to jurisdictions that have strategic importance including from an asset recovery standpoint.

e) Existing MLATs should be reviewed and, if required, updated periodically to ensure their continued relevance.

Barrier 9: Failure to Observe UNCAC and UNTOC

A number of jurisdictions that participated in the study have either failed to criminalize all UNCAC and UNTOC offenses or do not extend their legislative confiscation framework to all of these offenses. As a consequence, these jurisdictions are often limited in their ability to secure or confiscate property if a foreign request relates to an uncovered UNCAC or UNTOC offense. To eliminate these barriers to asset recovery, jurisdictions should ensure that the scope of their domestic restraint and confiscation framework encompasses all offenses under UNCAC and UNTOC.

Some jurisdictions do not apply the restraint and confiscation framework provided in UNCAC to all types of property included in the convention. Jurisdictions should be able to assist one another in the restraint, confiscation, and return of proceeds of crime, property, equipment, or other instrumentalities used or destined for use in the commission of an UNCAC offense. The term "proceeds of crime" includes transformed or converted and commingled property as well as income or other benefits derived from proceeds of crime. "Property" is defined broadly to include "assets of every kind, whether corporeal or incorporeal, moveable or immoveable, tangible or intangible, and legal documents or instruments evidencing title to or interest in such assets." Jurisdictions that do not apply their domestic restraint and confiscation provisions to all such types of property are necessarily limited in their ability to provide mutual legal assistance in asset recovery cases.

Policy Recommendations

a) Jurisdictions should review domestic criminal laws and the scope of the restraint and confiscation framework to ensure that they are wide enough to encompass all UNCAC and UNTOC offenses.
b) Jurisdictions should apply domestic restraint and confiscation provisions of UNCAC to all of the types of property as provided in UNCAC.

Barrier 10: No Quick Freeze or Restraint Mechanisms

Because assets can be moved within minutes and at the click of a button, investigators need to act in a time-sensitive manner. Any delay in executing a freezing request after the suspect has been arrested or tipped off can be fatal to the recovery of assets. Unfortunately, current MLA processes are not sufficiently agile to address this reality, particularly for tracing, freezing, or seizing of assets. Although many jurisdictions permit MLA during the investigation stages or once there is reason to believe that a proceeding is about to be instituted against the alleged offender, a few jurisdictions require that criminal charges be initiated before restraint or seizing assistance can be provided. Practitioners stated that this approach impairs efforts to preserve assets by providing notice to the asset holder before the necessary provisional measures have taken place. By the time a response is received to a request to restrain assets, they will have been moved.

To avoid this barrier, jurisdictions should not condition the provision of MLA on the imposition of criminal charges.[55] In such cases, the originating jurisdiction may be

---

55. UNCAC takes into account the need to allow for MLA before criminal proceedings are initiated by enabling States parties to expand their cooperation to cover not only criminal matters but also civil and administrative matters relating to corruption. These include, for example, cases brought by administrative authorities for acts punishable under the national law of both the requesting and requested countries, where the decision may lead to criminal corruption proceedings. For comparative purposes, the Second Additional Protocol to the European Convention on Mutual Assistance in Criminal Matters (2001) extends its scope to cover administrative proceedings that may give rise to proceedings before a court having jurisdiction in particular in criminal matters (Article 1, paragraph 3, of the convention). A similar provision is contained in the 2000 European Union Convention on Mutual Assistance in Criminal Matters (Article 3, paragraph 1).

required to show reason to believe that criminal charges and proceedings will be instituted. However, a request for a temporary freeze is to be distinguished from a request to forfeit assets, which is permanent and requires notice to the asset holder in most jurisdictions.

Given the nature of asset recovery cases, jurisdictions also need to adopt mechanisms that allow for a quick freezing of assets. That can be accomplished by permitting a financial intelligence unit or other competent authority to impose a temporary administrative freeze of up to 72 hours, by allowing the investigating magistrate or prosecutor to impose a freeze (if there is reason to believe that a confiscation order might ultimately be issued or that assets are likely to be dissipated), or by allowing automatic freezes upon the instigation of charges or an arrest. For example, one country has a 30-day freeze that can be issued as soon as charges are laid or an arrest is made. This temporary action prevents dissipation of assets while the authorities attempt to obtain a longer freezing order. Jurisdictions should also permit assets to be frozen on an urgent basis without original documents. Even if a signed MLA request will eventually be required, freezing should be permitted in emergencies on the basis of information provided by fax or, where there is a high level of trust, on the basis of direct communication, through e-mail or a phone call. In such instances, the initial restraints can be made under domestic law. Some jurisdictions will need assurances that a freezing order has been issued in the originating jurisdiction and that the order will be submitted with a formal request. This avenue may be foreclosed if in the past the originating jurisdiction did not follow through on such assurances. Because trust is so important in emergency requests, originating jurisdictions should not abuse these processes and should limit their requests to those that are truly urgent (see Barrier 1).

Freezing or seizure of assets infringes on the property rights of the asset holder, but such action is warranted when balanced against the rights of victims to recover stolen funds and the need to secure funds before the asset holder is tipped off.[56] In addition, safeguards can be introduced to ensure that the asset holder has the opportunity to contest the freezing order. One safeguard can be a requirement that a formal MLA request for a freeze be filed within a certain period of time.

Policy Recommendations

a) Jurisdictions should permit the provision of MLA upon commencement of an investigation into potential criminal activity, even if criminal charges have not yet been instigated.
b) Jurisdictions should introduce mechanisms that allow for prompt tracing and temporary freezing of assets before a formal MLA request is filed. A formal MLA request would be required to retain the freeze.

---

56. Indeed, courts in some jurisdictions require the prosecutor to make such a showing to obtain an initial restraint before the initiation of formal charges.

Barrier 11: Unbalanced Notice Requirements that Allow Dissipation of Assets

Some jurisdictions require notification to the asset holder when an MLA request is received, giving the asset holder the right to contest the provision of MLA before any information on the asset holder is sent to the originating jurisdiction. Practitioners stated that notification requirements, particularly of requests for bank or other financial records, alert the asset holder to the investigation, providing an opportunity to hide or dissipate funds, whether the funds are the subject of the investigation or may be traced to the subject account. Practitioners also said that notification can lead to lengthy delays while the asset holder uses all available avenues to block the provision of the requested evidence, including the exhaustion of all appeals, which can take months or years.

Notice or disclosure is an important due process requirement to protect the asset holder, particularly once property is restrained or seized. Notification is always required in confiscation proceedings because the asset holder may be forced to relinquish his holdings permanently. During the investigation phase, however, disclosure must always be balanced against the need to preserve evidence and combat corruption. Investigative and preservation measures are inherently temporary, contain sufficient safeguards to protect the rights of the asset holder, and do not permanently prejudice the rights of the asset holder (see Barrier 13).

Given the risk that the assets will be dissipated or moved if notice of a request for information about those assets is provided, jurisdictions should not provide disclosure to the asset holder until the assets are frozen or restrained. Similarly, to avoid alerting the defendant to the existence of the investigation, jurisdictions should not require notification to customers whenever a bank communicates information requested by foreign jurisdictions in the course of an investigation; rather, they should permit disclosure to be delayed until more coercive measures, such as permanent restraining of assets, are taken.

For those jurisdictions that must provide disclosure to execute an MLA request for financial information, communication and coordination of investigations by originating and requested jurisdictions are critical. When an MLA request is received, or when the information requested is ready for transmission to the originating jurisdiction, the requested jurisdiction should inform the originating jurisdiction that the asset holder will be notified when the information is transmitted. This communication will permit the originating jurisdiction to consider whether to execute the request at that moment or to request monitoring the account and consider freezes on a transaction-by-transaction basis. In other cases, originating jurisdictions will need to be made aware that even though disclosure is not required for an ex parte application to freeze assets, the accused may obtain access to documents and information that formed the basis of the *ex parte* order if it is subsequently challenged.

Some jurisdictions that require disclosure allow an undisclosed temporary freeze to be put in place during an investigation. In one such country, the courts generally permit as much as a six-month temporary freeze without notification to the asset holder. Temporary freezes are not without their own problems, however. The longer an account is temporarily frozen, the more likely the target of the investigation will attempt to make a transaction and discover the investigation. The target could then move money from other accounts that have not yet been identified and frozen. For that reason, if inquiries into a bank account or property reveal that the target of the investigation has interests in other accounts or properties within the requested jurisdiction, MLA should permit the same inquiries to be made in relation to these other accounts and properties. The use of informal assistance outside of formal MLA, such as the spontaneous sharing of information or the sharing of information and intelligence through FIUs, can also help to identify other accounts to be frozen.

Policy Recommendations

a) Jurisdictions should permit MLA to be provided without notifying the asset holder where investigative and preservation measures are involved, provided that sufficient protections of the due process rights of the asset holder exist at those stages of the proceeding that involve coercive or intrusive measures.

b) Jurisdictions should not require mandatory notification of customers when a financial institution communicates information requested by foreign jurisdictions during an investigation. At a minimum, jurisdictions should have the capacity to delay notification until the appropriate stage of the investigation (usually, the point when the lead investigatory body is best prepared to mitigate the risks of disclosure).

Operational Recommendations

a) Jurisdictions that require disclosure should communicate with originating jurisdictions before assistance is provided to determine whether the jurisdiction would prefer to receive the information or would rather take other measures to avoid disclosure to the asset holder. If such a requirement exists, jurisdictions should prominently display this information on their Web site and advise practitioners in other international forums.

b) Jurisdictions that require disclosure when executing formal MLA requests should allow temporary freezes to be put in place during investigations without disclosure to the asset holder.

Barrier 12: Banking Secrecy Laws

Banks and other financial institutions in most jurisdictions are prohibited from divulging personal and account information about their customers except in certain situations mandated by law or regulation. Some jurisdictions deal with banking secrecy by giving prosecutors the ability to obtain information about the existence of an account but requiring that the prosecutor seek a judicial order to obtain additional information about the contents and transactions of the account. In some jurisdictions, a bank cannot divulge any information to a prosecutor about a bank account without judicial approval. It may even be a serious offense to provide information about a bank customer to any third party, including domestic or foreign governments, unless very specific criteria are met. Participants in the study identified these restrictions as an obstacle to successful investigative, restraint, and confiscation efforts. They noted that investigators have few alternatives to obtaining information about specific accounts holding stolen assets where strict banking secrecy laws are in place. Without that information, restraint and confiscation are impossible.

Banking secrecy should not protect against investigations into conduct that both the originating and the requested jurisdiction have criminalized. In such cases, a jurisdiction should provide requested information on bank account activities through the application of multilateral conventions, bilateral treaties, or domestic legislation on MLA.[57]

Banking secrecy laws can prevent law enforcement agencies from sharing banking information and documents with their foreign counterparts, even where these agencies wish to assist the foreign jurisdiction. In some cases, requested jurisdictions will not provide documents covered by banking secrecy laws when specific activities (including tax evasion) are considered criminal in originating jurisdictions but not in requested jurisdictions. To overcome this obstacle, the information is sometimes provided without a formal MLA request. For example, FIUs can obtain information on an FIU-to-FIU basis, and membership in Egmont Group of Financial Intelligence Units helps facilitate this cooperation and expedites the exchange by offering members access to the Egmont secure Web site. Information provided in this manner, however, is often not admissible as evidence in court. In one such jurisdiction, no informal information obtained by an FIU can be admitted as evidence because the source of the information will be disclosed to the defendant. This restriction can mean that the authorities know where the proceeds of corruption are located but are unable to prove it in court and therefore are unable to restrain, seize, or confiscate the assets.

Requested jurisdictions may consider that a request is not supported by enough information or evidence to justify search for and communication of documents or

---

57. In particular, article 46(8) of UNCAC provides that States parties shall not decline to render MLA on the ground of bank secrecy. Article 40 of UNCAC provides that each State party shall ensure that, for domestic criminal investigations, appropriate mechanisms are available within its domestic legal system to overcome obstacles that may arise out of the application of bank secrecy laws; Article 31 stipulates that States parties shall not decline to freeze, seize, or confiscate property on the ground of bank secrecy.

information covered by banking secrecy laws. Some jurisdictions may be willing to look for evidence and to identify individuals, bank accounts, or financial transactions on behalf of another jurisdiction, even if that jurisdiction provided only incomplete or uncorroborated evidence. Others will refuse to look for banking information if the originating state does not provide strong evidence or justification of the link between the requested information and the commission of the offense. Often, corrupt officials and other targets of investigations do not leave a simple paper trail to follow. Where gathering the information or evidence needed to obtain MLA assistance is too onerous, an originating jurisdiction may stop the investigation at an early stage.

Some jurisdictions may also limit their assistance to only those elements that were specifically listed in the MLA request even though other germane information clearly exists. Such restrictions can be a real problem where funds have been transferred to bank accounts that are not mentioned in the initial request. In this situation, the requested jurisdiction may divulge only information concerning the bank account that was initially identified. The originating jurisdiction will then need to formulate a new request, which may be ineffective if evidence disappears or if funds move again. Jurisdictions should avoid such limitations and instead allow for "consequential inquiries." If inquiries into a bank account or property reveal that the offender has interests in other accounts or properties within the requested jurisdiction, the same inquiries should be made in relation to the further accounts and properties without the need for a further request.

Legal Privilege

A barrier similar to bank secrecy laws may arise where claims of lawyer-client privilege prevent investigators from looking at transactions involving lawyers. Legal privilege is an important right and should be recognized in all jurisdictions. The privilege should not apply, however, in cases where the lawyer is providing financial services, rather than legal advice, or is acting as a financial intermediary.

Policy Recommendations

a) Jurisdictions should not use banking secrecy as a basis for refusing to cooperate fully in international cases (informal and formal) involving all UNCAC and UNTOC offenses.
b) Jurisdictions should enact legislation that limits, as well as precisely defines, "protected information." This information should be very narrow in scope. In cases where investigators or prosecutors in originating jurisdictions have a legitimate and articulable interest in examining such records, the banking secrecy laws should be broad enough to accommodate such requests.
c) Jurisdictions should not allow banking secrecy to prevent them from extending assistance and providing documents or other information in cases where suspicious transactions involving identified accounts implicate other accounts that were not identified in the request.

Barrier 13: Arduous Procedural and Evidentiary Laws

The variety of legal standards that apply to restraint and confiscation procedures can cause confusion and delay MLA. To confiscate proceeds of corruption offenses, requested authorities seeking court orders for evidence or asset restraint must meet the evidential threshold established by their domestic legislation. The amount of evidence required varies from one jurisdiction to another and also depends on whether international MLA or domestic assistance is being requested.[58] The more intrusive the measure, the more evidence will be required (or the higher the threshold).

Requiring a sufficient evidentiary basis is an important component in all cases; however, overly strict requirements can create a serious impediment to asset recovery. For example, a jurisdiction seeking to trace assets should be required to show only that it has reasonable cause to believe that the assets are held in the requested jurisdiction. The requirements in the early phases of an investigation, when investigators are gathering evidence, tracing assets, and determining whether and which assets need to be frozen or seized, should always be less onerous than the requirements for actual confiscation. In cases of assistance under UNCAC involving noncoercive measures, dual criminality is not a prerequisite.[59]

Investigative and Provisional Measures

For investigative and provisional measures, requested jurisdictions may require standards that are more demanding than those in the originating state. Providing sufficient admissible evidence to meet the evidential threshold in the requested jurisdiction is one of the more difficult aspects of submitting an MLA request, particularly when the exchange is between civil and common law jurisdictions. In common law jurisdictions, search warrants, arrest warrants, and the initial restraint and seizure of assets are usually decided on probable cause or reasonable grounds to believe. For example, a judge will authorize a search if there is probable cause to believe that an offense has been committed, that evidence is in the place to be searched, and that there is no less intrusive measure to obtain the same result. Similarly, a court order is generally necessary to obtain production of bank account information. Some common law jurisdictions may refuse to enforce foreign restraining orders or to enter freezing orders if the originating jurisdiction has not provided a final order of confiscation.

By contrast, legislation in civil law jurisdictions frequently permits the investigating magistrate or prosecutor to conduct all acts necessary to elicit the required

---

58. For example, in one country the evidential threshold is lower for MLA requests than for domestic cases. In MLA requests, the offenses have to be described in a plausible way, but no evidence has to be provided; in domestic cases, the offense must be proved in court.
59. UNCAC, Article 46(9)(b).

proof. As a result, property searches, production of bank account information, or a freeze on assets may not require a court order. In some jurisdictions, however, only assets that can be linked to an offense, rather than all assets subject to confiscation, can be seized or frozen during the investigations. In others, substitute or equivalent-value assets can be frozen, seized, or confiscated if the actual proceeds or instrumentalities of crime cannot be located. In the early stage of an investigation, the requirement that the assets must be linked to an offense may prevent quick action, result in notice to the accused, and ultimately allow the accused to move or dissipate assets that were not yet identified as proceeds or instrumentalities of crime.

Before they agree to restrain assets, some requested jurisdictions require originating jurisdictions to establish that proceedings will be instituted in the originating jurisdiction in the near future. The standard of proof is generally met upon submission of a written statement to that effect. However, if the originating jurisdiction does not file charges within a certain time frame, the requested jurisdiction will lift the restraint order. In complex cases or cases requiring evidence gathering in several foreign jurisdictions before the originating jurisdiction can file charges, the time period could expire before all the necessary investigations are completed. Lifting a restraint order in such cases may give the affected person an opportunity to dispose of or move the assets. Jurisdictions should thus ensure that evidentiary requirements applied to foreign jurisdictions seeking the issuance of domestic restraint orders are not too stringent. Jurisdictions should also permit extension of the time period for initial restraint orders where necessary.

In addition, some jurisdictions, particularly common law jurisdictions, may refuse to provide MLA for requests that are beyond the scope of investigated offenses, do not contain sufficient substantive facts, are not sufficiently precise, or do not establish the required link between the assets and the offense or between the asset and the offender. Practitioners in requested jurisdictions explained that stringent evaluation of requests, even for a measure such as restraint (which may be regarded as a coercive measure) is an important safeguard for the offender and ensures proportionate action by the requested state.

Such requirements can, however, be very difficult to meet when not enough evidence is available to identify the assets with particularity. One practitioner read a letter that refused an MLA request because the jurisdiction was able to process only those requests involving "identifiable assets." The request was rejected because the originating jurisdiction was not precise enough in identifying the assets thought to be held by the target in the requested jurisdiction. In practice, obtaining bank account documents from requested jurisdictions will prove very challenging in the absence of a central register of bank accounts, or if the names of account holders listed in such registries are not alphabetized (see Barrier 27).

Criminal Confiscation

To confiscate assets in a criminal case, common law jurisdictions generally require that a conviction be proven beyond a reasonable doubt. To establish the link between assets and an offense after conviction, some common law jurisdictions apply the balance-of-probabilities or preponderance-of-evidence standard, while others apply the beyond-a-reasonable-doubt standard. The balance-of-probabilities standard (a proposition is more likely to be true than not true) applies in civil confiscation cases. In civil law jurisdictions, criminal convictions and some confiscation regimes require proof that intimately convinces a judge (intimate conviction).

Proving an offense under criminal standards of proof may be difficult in corruption cases. In particular, bribery offenses pose specific challenges. In some jurisdictions, prosecutors must prove that the payment of a bribe was made in application of a corruption pact between the briber and a public official; such evidence is often very difficult to obtain. The standard of proof for parties to UNCAC is less stringent: Article 28 obliges States parties to ensure that "knowledge, intent or purpose required as an element of an offense established in accordance with this Convention may be inferred from objective factual circumstances." Even so, the need for a conviction before confiscation can be a significant barrier, particularly where the accused has died or is a fugitive.

In addition, establishing beyond a reasonable doubt that assets are linked to a specific criminal offense (common law jurisdictions) is no easy matter, nor is furnishing proof that will intimately convince the judge (civil law jurisdictions). Practitioners indicated that the difficulty of meeting these requirements has led to the failure of asset recovery cases.

To facilitate asset recovery in confiscation cases, particularly those involving UNCAC and UNTOC offenses, jurisdictions should take two steps. First, they should ensure that the standard of proof for showing that assets are linked to criminal activity is not too stringent. Second, once the state establishes that the assets are linked to criminal activity in general rather than a specific criminal offense, there should be a rebuttable presumption that the assets are the proceeds of crime.

Several jurisdictions with both conviction and non-conviction based systems have lowered the standard of proof for confiscation to a balance of probabilities and require only "reasonable grounds to believe" or even "reasonable ground to suspect" for the freezing of assets.[60] This standard can greatly facilitate the efforts of originating jurisdictions to investigate and secure assets located abroad. Regardless of the standard of proof applied, domestic MLA laws should define it with great specificity to avoid any uncertainty.

In a growing number of jurisdictions, civil courts can confiscate assets if prosecutors establish by a preponderance of evidence that the assets are instrumentalities or proceeds of a crime. Such confiscation procedures require the existence of a criminal offense, but not the conviction of any person for illegal acts. This approach is particularly useful in cases in which a criminal conviction is not possible, including cases where the property is held by a fugitive or by a criminal who has died.

Practitioners noted that the application of rebuttable presumptions can be very helpful. Where it is permitted, the originating jurisdiction is required to establish only that targeted assets cannot stem from a person's legitimate income, at which point the asset holder has to demonstrate based on the applicable standard of proof (generally by a preponderance of evidence or balance of probabilities) that the assets stem from a legitimate source. If the defendant is not successful in establishing that claim, the government is considered to have met its standard of proof.

Both UNCAC and UNTOC call for States parties to consider requiring offenders to demonstrate the lawful origin of the assets subject to forfeiture.[61] In addition, UNCAC encourages States parties to criminalize illicit enrichment, defined as a "significant increase in the assets of a public official that he or she cannot reasonably explain in relation to his or her lawful income."[62] In illicit enrichment cases, a prosecutor need only show that the legitimate income of a public official cannot explain an increase in assets or expenditures. The public official's legal defense must explain how the property in question accrued from legal sources.[63]

---

60. For more information on the various standards of proof in criminal and civil confiscation procedures, see Theodore S. Greenberg, Linda M. Samuel, Wingate Grant, and Larissa Gray, *Stolen Asset Recovery: A Good Practices Guide for Non-conviction-based Asset Forfeiture* (Washington, DC: World Bank, 2009), www.worldbank.org/star.
61. UNCAC, Article 31(8); UNTOC, Article 12(7). Because countries may have constitutional or other constraints preventing them from imposing such a requirement, States parties to UNCAC are required to consider implementing this measure to the extent that it is consistent with the fundamental principles of domestic law.
62. UNCAC, Article 20.
63. Criminalization of illicit enrichment is also a requirement under the Inter-American Convention against Corruption, and many countries have enacted supporting legislation.

To ensure that these presumptions do not violate constitutional guarantees of presumption of innocence, the burden must remain on the prosecution to establish the constituent elements of the offense and the basis for the presumption, and the claimant must be permitted to offer a reasonable or credible explanation to rebut the presumption.[64] Jurisdictions that have adopted this approach have generally embedded it within specific confiscation procedures that take place after conviction.

Good Practices

In some jurisdictions, legislation permits confiscation of the property of a criminal organization. Swiss authorities made creative use of this legislation in 2005 to declare that a former head of state, his family, and associates constituted a criminal organization. As a result, a court could order the confiscation and return of $458 million of related assets without a formal proof that they were the proceeds of a specific offense. It was sufficient to establish that they were at the disposal of the criminal organization. Under the legislation, any property belonging to a person associated with a criminal organization is "presumed to be at the disposal of the organization until the contrary is proved."[a]

In some countries, a presumption based on "criminal lifestyle" is applied. A defendant convicted of money laundering offenses is considered to have a criminal lifestyle, and all proceeds of crime can be confiscated. To calculate the benefit from the criminal conduct, the court is required to take into account all properties transferred to the defendant or all of the defendant's expenditures during a period of time before proceedings began. Similarly, gifts to third parties, including any sales that are significantly underpriced as of the date of transfer, may be considered tainted. All those properties may be confiscated as proceeds of crime unless the assumption that they are proceeds of crime is proved incorrect. Balance of probabilities is the standard of proof in relation to benefit from general criminal conduct and the recoverable amount.[b]

France has legislation that establishes an offense where a person cannot show sufficient income to correspond to his lifestyle or the origin of property and where he drew a benefit from a regular relationship with a person(s) involved in a felony or misdemeanor punishable by at least five years. This offense, which is punishable by three to seven years imprisonment, allows the state to confiscate the convicted person's entire assets. Moreover, if an offense punishable by at least five years' imprisonment resulted in direct or indirect profit to the defendant, all properties of the defendant may be confiscated unless proven to be of legitimate origin.[c]

a. Criminal Code (Switzerland), Article 72.
b. In South Africa, the presumption extends for a period of seven years before proceedings are initiated: Prevention of Organised Crime Act Second Amendment 1999, Section 22. In the United Kingdom, the period is six years for defendants determined to have a criminal lifestyle: Proceeds of Crime Act (United Kingdom), Section 10(8). See also Criminal Code (France), Article 131-21.
c. Criminal Code (France), Article 321-6.

---

64. For more information, see Greenberg, Samuel, Grant, and Gray, *Stolen Asset Recovery: A Good Practices Guide for Non-Conviction Based Asset* Forfeiture, pp. 58–63.

Policy Recommendations

a) Jurisdictions should consider introducing legislation establishing a rebuttable presumption to help meet the standard of proof for criminal confiscation following conviction, particularly for UNCAC and UNTOC offenses.

b) Jurisdictions should ensure that evidentiary requirements are less onerous in cases involving issuance of temporary restraint orders than in cases involving more permanent measures and those at later stages of the confiscation process.

c) Within the limits of constitutional or fundamental guarantees of due process, jurisdictions should pass new legislation or adopt new practices to help meet evidentiary requirements to facilitate MLA for investigative measures, including the establishment of central registries of bank accounts (see Barrier 27).

d) In both conviction-based and NCB forfeiture cases, jurisdictions should ensure that the standard of proof to show that assets are linked to criminal activity is not too stringent and is clearly set out in relevant domestic laws. Jurisdictions should further ensure that prosecutors need establish a link only between assets and criminal activity in general rather than between assets and a specific criminal offense.

Operational Recommendations

a) Jurisdictions should strictly define expectations for content of MLA requests and provide examples of requests, on a Web site, that do not provide sufficient factual and logical justification to reasonably permit further investigation.

b) Requests for assistance containing incomplete information, but a clear nexus between the offender and the assets, should be accepted if the requested jurisdiction appears likely to be able to locate assets based upon the submitted information or information maintained by the requested jurisdiction.

c) Jurisdictions should prioritize requests and limit the volume of the request by focusing on specific and essential items to increase the possibility that their MLA request will be successful.

Barrier 14: No Provisions for Equivalent-Value Restraint and Confiscation

The concept of equivalent-value restraint and confiscation holds that legitimate assets equivalent in value to proceeds or instrumentalities of crime may be restrained or confiscated in cases where the actual proceeds or instrumentalities are no longer available or cannot be located (also referred to as "substitute assets"). Jurisdictions that do not provide for equivalent-value restraint and confiscation create a significant barrier to recovery of stolen assets.[65] The number of jurisdictions that are applying this principle

---

65. Article 31(5) and (6) of UNCAC provides that where proceeds of crime are intermingled with other assets, all the intermingled assets are liable to confiscation up to the assessed value of the intermingled proceeds of crime.

is increasing. Some of them apply it by issuing value-based seizing and confiscation orders instead of property-based orders.

Practitioners emphasized that these equivalent-value measures can be very helpful in asset recovery cases because proceeds and instrumentalities of crime are frequently commingled with legitimate assets. Establishing a link between specific property and the criminal offense has proven to be one of the most challenging aspects in asset recovery (see Barrier 13).

> ### Policy Recommendations
>
> Jurisdictions should introduce legislation to allow for substitute or equivalent-value asset restraint and confiscation. At a minimum, provisions allowing such measures for commingled property should be put in place, in conformity with UNCAC.

Barrier 15: Lack of a Non-Conviction Based Confiscation Mechanism

Practitioners told the study team that the requirement for conviction before stolen assets can be confiscated can impede asset recovery efforts, particularly in corruption cases. While confiscation without a conviction (non-conviction based, or NCB, confiscation) should never be a substitute for criminal prosecution, in many instances, NCB confiscation may be the only way to recover the proceeds of corruption and to exact some measure of justice. Jurisdictions that do not have the ability to confiscate without a conviction are challenged because they lack one of the important tools available to recover stolen assets. NCB confiscation is valuable because the influence of corrupt officials and other practical realities may prevent criminal investigations entirely or delay them until after the official has died or absconded to a jurisdiction that will shelter the official from prosecution. Alternatively, the corrupt official may have immunity from prosecution in certain jurisdictions. Because an NCB confiscation regime is not dependent on a criminal conviction, it can proceed regardless of death, flight, or any immunity the corrupt official might enjoy (see Barrier 17). An increasing number of jurisdictions have adopted legislation permitting confiscation without a conviction,[66] and the practice is encouraged in multilateral treaties and by international standard setters.[67]

NCB confiscation most often takes place in one of two ways. The first is confiscation within the context of criminal proceedings but without the need for a conviction or

---

66. For a list of jurisdictions and relevant legislation, see Greenberg, Samuel, Grant and Gray, *Stolen Asset Recovery: A Good Practices Guide for NCB Asset Forfeiture*. Note that several countries (notably in the Caribbean) added NCB forfeiture measures following publication of this book.

67. UNCAC, Article 54(1)(c) requires countries to consider such confiscation without a conviction in cases of death, flight, or absence or in other appropriate cases. Recommendation 3 of the FATF 40+9 recommendations requires countries to consider allowing confiscation without a conviction. FATF has also introduced best practices on NCB confiscation, including recognition of foreign NCB confiscation orders: FATF, *Best Practices Paper on Confiscation (R. 3 and 38)*, adopted by the FATF plenary in February 2010.

finding of guilt. In these situations, NCB confiscation laws are incorporated into existing criminal codes, as well as anti-money laundering acts or drug laws, and are regarded as "criminal" proceedings to which the criminal procedural laws apply. The second means is confiscation outside criminal proceedings, such as in a civil or administrative proceeding. This is a separate proceeding that can occur independently of or in conjunction with any related criminal proceedings. In a number of jurisdictions, this means of confiscation is called "civil confiscation" or "civil forfeiture."

Even where NCB confiscation is accepted, international cooperation in these cases can be challenging because the systems vary significantly, both in the identification of the court (civil or criminal) and in the procedural and substantive elements, such as the standard of proof (balance of probabilities, beyond reasonable doubt, or intimate conviction). The NCB order is *in rem* in some jurisdictions (an action asserting a proprietary claim over the assets), but *in personam* in others (a claim against a person for a crime or breach of a legal duty). For *in rem* proceedings, the presence of property in the country is sufficient to establish jurisdiction to proceed with NCB confiscation. Some jurisdictions will pursue NCB confiscation only after criminal proceedings are abandoned or unsuccessful, while others pursue it in parallel to the related criminal proceeding.

Countries without NCB confiscation provisions should introduce domestic legislation permitting the use of this tool. Such laws will not only broaden the measures available to combat corruption and the laundering of proceeds domestically but can also assist originating jurisdictions that may choose to delegate the case to the requested jurisdiction. Practitioners highlighted the usefulness of NCB confiscation because it can be quicker and more efficient and may be the only recourse when the offender is dead, has fled the jurisdiction, or is immune from prosecution.

Although it is best not to limit the scope of NCB confiscation, it should apply, at a minimum, to circumstances where the perpetrator is dead, a fugitive, absent, or unknown, as well as in "other appropriate cases" (to allow for jurisdictions that may go beyond the minimum requirements). Jurisdictions themselves should then determine *how* NCB confiscation is implemented, whether in the context of criminal laws and proceedings or through a separate system or law outside criminal proceedings. The advantage to a separate proceeding is that it is fully independent of any criminal case and may be initiated in a separate court, thereby possibly avoiding any undue influence that may be brought to bear in the criminal case.

While NCB confiscation is a valuable tool in many cases, if criminal prosecution is possible, NCB confiscation may not be the best way to proceed with a case. International cooperation may be difficult if the requested jurisdiction does not permit NCB confiscation.[68] In addition, confiscating assets after a criminal conviction may be advantageous

---

68. Some practitioners said that NCB confiscation can be a concern in jurisdictions that require losing parties to pay court costs to the successful party, resulting in a substantial cost risk to the jurisdiction that does not exist where assets are confiscated after a criminal conviction. Some jurisdictions require undertakings or an agreement to pay costs and damages. Greenberg, Samuel, Grant, and Gray, *Stolen Asset Recovery: A Good Practices Guide to NCB Asset Forfeiture*, p. 79, box 23.

where that jurisdiction permits recovery of all of an offender's assets, whether tainted or legitimate, under special provisions related to criminal lifestyle.

In addition, jurisdictions must have the capacity to enforce a confiscation order of another jurisdiction. Domestic laws need to be flexible to account for the differences in legal systems. Several jurisdictions allow for direct enforcement of such orders only if dual criminality is met, or only if the order has been issued by a jurisdiction that has been designated by the requested jurisdiction as one whose orders will be enforced. These kinds of limitations should not be overly onerous or too strictly applied (see Barrier 22).

NCB legislation should also include applicable procedures for enforcement and a listing of defenses that will be recognized, including whether the property owner can challenge the underlying decision. (For additional information and guidance on the key concepts to be included in NCB legislation, see *Stolen Asset Recovery: A Good Practices Guide for Non-Conviction Based Asset Forfeiture* published in 2009 by the StAR Initiative).

Good Practices

Providing for more than one method of asset recovery provides prosecutors with the tools they need, depending on the circumstances of the case. A number of jurisdictions have two main schemes of asset recovery: criminal confiscation, which requires a conviction, and NCB confiscation, which does not. Under value-based confiscation, a link between the criminality and the assets realized does not have to be established to satisfy a final order; rather there must be evidence that the assets are linked to a person who has been accused or convicted of a crime. Under NCB confiscation, a link must be established between criminal activity in general and the assets that are being pursued, but a criminal conviction is not necessary.

Another jurisdiction permits direct enforcement of external confiscation orders based on the purpose of the order rather than on whether the order originates from a civil or criminal court. To permit both criminal and NCB enforcement, this jurisdiction defines an external order as "an order made by a court for the purpose of recovering the proceeds of crime or the value representing the proceeds of crime."

Some jurisdictions enforce foreign NCB orders even if their domestic scheme permits only conviction-based forfeiture.[a] In some Latin American countries, this practice is called "homologation," and the NCB restraining order is filed with a civil court for enforcement. Other jurisdictions in the Caribbean region will enforce an NCB restraining order as long as a criminal case is pending or is issued in connection with a criminal investigation.

a. Hong Kong SAR, China: Jersey-Civil Asset Recovery (International Cooperation) Law 2007; and France. French Courts recognized and executed a foreign NCB confiscation order from Italy pursuant to the 1990 Convention Council of Europe Convention on Laundering, Search, Seizure and Confiscation of the Proceeds of Crime despite the fact that France did not have a system of NCB confiscation: Cour de cassation 13 November 2003, No. 3 03-80371, case Crisafulli. The courts considered two factors. First, the evidence establishing that the property was the product of a criminal offense was sufficiently similar to that required for a criminal decision, thus likened to a criminal case. Second, the consequences on the property of the person were similar to a criminal penalty.

a) Jurisdictions should enact domestic legislation permitting confiscation with-
    out a conviction. At a minimum, non-conviction based confiscation should be
    permitted when the perpetrator is dead, a fugitive, absent, immune from
    prosecution, or in other appropriate cases.
b) Jurisdictions should, at a minimum, allow for enforcement of foreign NCB
    orders.

Barrier 16: Inability to Enter into Plea Agreements

In many common law jurisdictions, plea agreements allow prosecuting authorities to
let the defendant plead to a lesser charge, or decrease the number of counts charged, in
exchange for substantial cooperation.[69] Part of that cooperation generally includes the
defendant's willingness to disclose where and how illicit assets are concealed, thus eliminating the need for complex and lengthy investigations, resulting in a more effective
and swift asset recovery and conserving valuable resources of law enforcement and the
judicial system. Some practitioners perceived the lack of a plea bargain mechanism for
motivating the defendant to cooperate as a barrier to asset recovery. Another perceived
barrier was the inability of some jurisdictions without plea bargain mechanisms to
honor such agreements reached in another jurisdiction concerning the confiscation or
release of assets.

Many jurisdictions reject the concept of plea agreements out of concern that the
truth-finding process will be distorted, leading to an incorrect legal outcome. Nevertheless, jurisdictions that do not officially allow for plea agreements should consider introducing other mechanisms that allow law enforcement authorities to secure
the defendant's substantial cooperation, particularly with regard to the identification
of and voluntary forfeiture of illicit assets, as well as provisions that honor such
agreements reached in foreign jurisdictions. Even practitioners in jurisdictions that
officially reject the plea bargain concept acknowledge that plea agreements can be
effective investigatory tools. Moreover, some practitioners without a tradition of plea
agreements admitted that such arrangements occur in practice without any formal
basis.

Generally, a court must review and accept plea agreements and will make its own
judgment on sentencing or penalty (such as fines). Typically the court considers the
recommendations presented by the prosecution describing the merits of the plea
agreement. In international asset recovery cases, any contemplated plea agreement
should be discussed among all jurisdictions having any litigation, including confiscation

---

69. At least one civil law jurisdiction has also introduced plea agreements for criminal organizations. For
information, see the Good Practices box in this section.

measures, related to the matter. If a penalty is to be imposed, discussions should occur regarding the allocation of that penalty, which may include a confiscation provision. Such agreements should take into account the differing governing constitutional and statutory provisions in multiple jurisdictions. For example, in one case where a penalty allocation under a plea agreement was unconstitutional in one of the jurisdictions involved, the court emphasized the importance of ensuring that both jurisdictions had the constitutional and legal power to enter into such an agreement, including the agreement to allocate the penalty or confiscation, but then ruled in favor of the prosecutor's penalty recommendation in the interest of justice.[70]

In addition, plea agreements can have adverse effects on ongoing, related investigations in other jurisdictions. For example, a plea agreement that states that the file will be closed and not available to practitioners in other jurisdictions could stymie those other investigations, create ill will between the jurisdictions, and arguably prevent justice from being served. For that reason, jurisdictions that are considering a plea agreement should coordinate with other foreign jurisdictions investigating the defendant to ensure that they have the evidence necessary to carry on with their own investigation and prosecution.

Good Practices

One of the important strategic steps taken by the government of Peru in the early phases of the investigation into Vladmiro Montesinos, chief of Peru's intelligence service under President Alberto Fujimori, was the adoption of Law 27.738. Montesinos was convicted of embezzlement, illegal assumption of his post as intelligence chief, abuse of power, influence peddling, illegal arms trafficking, and bribing TV stations. Montesinos was also investigated for money laundering, drug smuggling, corruption, and other criminal activity. The law, which established a plea agreement mechanism for investigations into organized crime, was unique because the concept of "guilty pleas" and plea agreements do not exist in Peru or many other civil law jurisdictions, as they do in many common law jurisdictions. The law allowed members of a criminal organization subject to prosecution, with the exception of leaders and some public officials, to engage with prosecutors in plea agreements, often providing information in exchange for a reduced sentence. Plea agreements entered into under this law produced evidence that helped secure Montesinos' conviction and avoided years of litigation. Most important, the new law enabled the Peruvian authorities to quickly obtain information on the flow of funds and—through a waiver process—recover assets located in foreign jurisdictions amounting to over $175 million.

---

70. An example occurs when a defendant is extradited from country A to country B and enters a plea agreement in country B regarding assets located in country A. If the defendant acknowledges that the property belongs to him and not to a third party, and agrees to voluntarily relinquish his interest in some of the assets for confiscation, the prosecutor in country B may agree to release some of the assets back to the defendant or his family, particularly if the assets are not directly connected to the crime. However, such an agreement may violate constitutional or statutory provisions of country A, which may still be obligated to pursue confiscation.

Barrier 17: Immunity Laws that Prevent Prosecution and MLA

Practitioners point out that international immunities conferred by law upon foreign states and officials often constitute barriers to MLA in corruption cases or to prosecution of foreign officials holding assets in financial centers. Some countries grant functional immunity to foreign officials performing acts of state, protecting them from criminal liability or civil suits arising from acts performed in their official capacity, even after they leave office. Courts have frequently held that legal proceedings against individuals acting in their official capacity, including civil suits, are the equivalent of suing the foreign state itself. Countries also grant personal immunity, usually to a small group of foreign officials (heads of state or government, senior cabinet members, foreign ministers, and diplomatic agents in a host country), from criminal proceedings arising from both official and private activities. This type of immunity, which may extend to civil suits, normally ceases when the official has left his or her post.

Any type of international immunity is a significant barrier to criminal proceedings against officials, particularly for heads of state or government, ministers of foreign affairs, and diplomats in a host state.[71] In addition, foreign officials may claim state immunity for activities relating to state sovereignty (as opposed to commercial activities). This kind of immunity acts as a barrier where, for example, bank accounts are set up in the name of a jurisdiction but are used to finance personal expenses of dishonest officials who attempt to claim immunity on the basis that the activities related to state sovereignty.

While the intention of immunity provisions is to enable a foreign official to act freely, such laws also have had the effect of shielding officials suspected of corruption from criminal prosecution. In the absence of a pending criminal investigation, MLA channels are not available and a request to seize foreign assets may not be made. This situation is highly problematic given that asset recovery cases frequently involve current or

---

71. Some jurisdictions also include defense and finance (or treasury) ministers.

former high-level politicians and government leaders. These officials may use immunities to avoid prosecution until applicable statutes of limitation have expired. In addition, offenders who have participated in corrupt activities, including an official's family members or intermediaries, may benefit from immunity laws by obtaining public positions or diplomatic passports solely to be able to organize or commit crimes with impunity.

International and national courts have defined the scope and the limits of international immunities, however, and in recent years have circumscribed their applications in corruption matters. As a result, authorities now may prosecute foreign officials and provide MLA in a number of circumstances.[72] First, foreign officials other than heads of state, heads of government, ministers of foreign affairs, and diplomats in a host state do not enjoy international immunity for acts committed in their personal capacity. In addition, former heads of state, heads of government, and ministers of foreign affairs may be tried in foreign courts for acts committed before or subsequent to their period of office, as well as for private acts taken while in office. Authorities and courts in requested jurisdictions may find no legal obstacle to providing MLA or to prosecuting foreign officials in such circumstances.

Second, there is no international immunity for officials prosecuted by their own jurisdiction. Incumbent or former heads of state, heads of government, ministries of foreign affairs, and diplomats in a host state may be tried in their home courts in accordance with relevant domestic laws. Officials can also be prosecuted if the state that they represent or have represented decides to waive that immunity. In such situations, the foreign jurisdiction may provide legal assistance to competent authorities in the prosecuting jurisdiction.

Third, international immunity may not apply when funds belonging to a foreign state are held by private companies or are replaced by and managed as commercial or private property. Similarly, proceeds of corruption or embezzled funds held by offshore corporate vehicles representing that they act in the name of a state may be legally seized and frozen despite claims that they were covered by immunity of states. In such circumstances, it is necessary to look behind the name of the state and consider the function and character of the corporate vehicle. Moreover, assets held by family members of a current head of state are not ordinarily protected by any international immunity.

A rigorous application of these principles in compliance with international customary laws and treaties may assist victim jurisdictions in their efforts to overcome or mitigate the difficulties posed by immunity laws, as shown in the good practices example described in this section. In addition, when dealing with an UNCAC or UNTOC offense, jurisdictions should consider whether those immunities should apply or be

---

72. Arrest Warrant of 11 April 2000 *(Democratic Republic of Congo v. Belgium)*, Preliminary Objections and Merits, Judgment, ICJ Rep 2002, 3.

waived for that particular case.[73] Although immunities are important to protect officials from meritless and frivolous lawsuits, this protection must be balanced against the public interest in combating public corruption. In such cases, the overwhelming public interest in stopping public corruption tips the balance from immunity toward permitting prosecution.

Good Practices

In the United States, courts issued temporary restraining orders against corporate vehicles controlled by Ferdinand Marcos, former president of the Philippines. Judges ruled that the doctrine of acts of state did not apply when the (new)Philippine government asked the U.S. government to investigate allegations that Marcos, while president, had abused his position to commit financial crimes. A civil action was filed in the Philippines against Marcos, his wife, Imelda Marcos, and other persons involved in the frozen properties. One year later, the competent court rejected the former president's appeal and ruled that a receiver should be appointed. The mortgaged properties were sold, and the balance after payment of mortgages was turned over to the originating jurisdiction.[a]

In the Philippines, waiver of immunity of former president Marcos facilitated the recovery of stolen public funds by permitting the freezing and then the return of funds he had deposited in banks in Switzerland.

a. *Republic of Philippines v. Marcos*, 806 F. 2d 244 (CA 2d Cir. 1986).

Policy Recommendations

a) Jurisdictions should, where necessary, enact legislation to ensure that the scope of international immunities applicable in their jurisdiction does not extend beyond the limits defined by international law and jurisprudence. The legislation should permit prosecution, confiscation of assets, and mutual legal assistance where:
    i)   the acts involved are committed in a personal capacity;
    ii) the foreign officials are being prosecuted by their own jurisdiction; or
    iii) the foreign officials are the beneficial owners of assets managed as private resources or in the name of family members and associates.
b) Jurisdictions should enact legislation that provides for the suspension of applicable statutes of limitation until foreign officials shielded by immunities leave their positions or lose that immunity.

---

73. At the third session of the Conference of States Parties to UNCAC in November 2009, States parties were encouraged to limit domestic legal immunities, in accordance with their legal systems and constitutional principles.

a) Jurisdictions should not consider immunities to be an obstacle when they are waived by the state of the official.

b) Jurisdictions should carefully examine each case involving corruption offenses to determine whether immunities apply or prosecution is possible. If immunities apply and they cannot be waived, prosecutors should be encouraged to consider other avenues of pursuing justice, including civil suits, NCB confiscation, or charges against other people or entities involved or implicated in the crimes.

Barrier 18: Fleeting Statutes of Limitations

In most jurisdictions, initiating criminal proceedings after the expiration of a legally determined period of time starting from the commission of the offense is prohibited. Such provisions are known as "periods of prescription" or "statutes of limitation." If the period of prescription has expired in either the originating or the requested jurisdiction, legal authorities in requested jurisdictions may refuse to extend MLA, fail to prosecute corruption and money laundering cases, or decline to enforce foreign confiscation orders. Limitations periods may reward offenders who succeed in concealing their conduct or who operate in an environment that prevents prompt initiation of investigations. Official corruption is particularly difficult, and sometimes impossible, to discover, investigate, and prosecute while the violator is in office. Practitioners identified limitations periods that are too short to permit prosecution of money laundering and corruption offenses as an obstacle to asset recovery.

In practice, the time limitation varies according to the jurisdiction and the offense. The disparity of laws in different jurisdictions highlights the complexity of the issue. One country has no time limitations for money laundering offenses. By contrast, in another jurisdiction, the statute of limitation for these offenses is 7 years, but the limitation period may be longer (15 years) when the money laundering activities involve proceeds of specific predicate offenses (including breach of trust, fraud, and theft) or when money laundering offenses were committed by a criminal organization, a gang, or in the exercise of a professional activity. In yet another jurisdiction, prosecuting a money laundering offense is not possible when funds are laundered after the period of prescription of the underlying offense has passed.

If the limitation period for an offense has expired in the requested jurisdiction, that jurisdiction may not consider the offense to be a crime and may refuse to provide assistance on the basis of dual criminality. In such cases, however, the time limitation in the originating jurisdiction should govern because the prosecution of the crime will occur in the originating jurisdiction.

For procedural reasons, the expiration of a limitation period that bars money laundering proceedings or prevents other forms of MLA in the requested country could be viewed as unacceptable in large-scale corruption cases involving regimes or officials who amassed stolen assets to the detriment of the security or the health of their population. Grand corruption cases not only damage public finances in the developing world but, by diverting public resources, also endanger the lives of people threatened by starvation, deprive others of the aid they need to fight poverty, and deny still others access to health services they need to survive. In addition, those spoliations are sometimes committed to strengthen dictatorships and finance political violence or illegal wars. As such, they could be considered violations of basic human rights. Officials who use or betray their mandate to commit these crimes should be held to higher standards of accountability. For these reasons, jurisdictions should consider passing or amending legislation to eliminate the limitation period for large-scale or egregious corruption-related offenses that endanger the lives of entire populations. If eliminating limitation periods appears difficult to realize given the traditional principles that justify them, jurisdictions could at least lengthen the prescription periods for corruption and the laundering of proceeds of corruption.

Authorities should also look closely at the circumstances involved to determine whether the limitation period was suspended or interrupted for a period of time, or whether the offense involved is continuous. In most jurisdictions, the "clock" can be stopped (suspended) or even restarted by certain legal events, including investigations by law enforcement agencies or prosecutors or when the individual has fled the jurisdiction. Where international immunities prevent prosecution, the clock should not begin to run until the immunity is waived or no longer applies and prosecution is possible. Even at that point, the limitation period should not begin to run until the offense is complete or discovered. This principle is already applied in many jurisdictions. For example, in one country, the limitation period in cases of breach of trust or embezzlement of public funds starts to run only when the offense is discovered by law enforcement agencies or prosecutors. In another jurisdiction, the five-year time limitation for money laundering offenses begins on the date when the offense is complete. If an offense is continuous, however, the statute of limitations is extended beyond its stated term. As an example, where an overt act is required for a conspiracy, the statute of limitations on a continuing conspiracy does not begin to run until the last overt act in furtherance of the conspiracy is committed.

Where the limitation period on a criminal offense has expired, authorities should consider whether there are related offenses that can be prosecuted or any civil action that can be taken. Criminal investigations into a crime with an expired limitation period may lead to the discovery of other, fresher offenses. As an example, prosecuting a bribery offense may be impossible if the time limitation has expired. However, if fictitious invoices recorded in accounting books have concealed bribes paid to an intermediary, the starting point of the limitation period may be delayed until the actual discovery of the publication of false accounting statements, indicating fraud or embezzlement.

Policy Recommendations

a) Where possible, jurisdictions should consider repealing statutes of limitation for large-scale and egregious corruption offenses, to be defined within the legislation. For example, the limitation period might be repealed for offenses involving assets in excess of a specific amount.
b) If repeal is not feasible, jurisdictions should lengthen the applicable limitation period for UNCAC offenses.
c) Jurisdictions should introduce or apply laws or jurisprudence delaying the start of the time limitation period until there is no immunity preventing prosecution.
d) Jurisdictions should introduce or apply laws or jurisprudence delaying the start of the time limitation period until discovery of the crime.

Operational Recommendations

a) In cases where statutes of limitation act as a barrier to recovering stolen assets, jurisdictions should encourage prosecutors to identify possible charges (such as embezzlement, money laundering, and possession of stolen assets) or other avenues—including civil actions and NCB confiscation—to which a more favorable statute of limitations regime can be applied.
b) Requested jurisdictions should agree to provide MLA without consideration of their own limitation period because it is the limitation period in the originating jurisdiction that should govern.

Barrier 19: Inability to Recognize and Enforce Foreign Confiscation and Restraint Orders

Under UNCAC, States parties are required to take steps to give effect to foreign freezing or seizing (restraint) and confiscation orders.[74] In practice, foreign orders are generally implemented in the requested jurisdiction based on a decision by a domestic court (an *exequatur* ruling) that the foreign order meets the requirements of domestic law. Because foreign orders are not being reviewed on the merits of the case, thus eliminating the need to initiate domestic proceedings and to repeat evidentiary submission, this process is efficient and speedy. By the same token, requested jurisdictions that do not give effect to foreign orders create barriers to MLA and asset recovery by requiring the originating jurisdiction to prove its case again before assets can be restrained and eventually confiscated.

In some countries, domestic law does not impose criminal liability on legal (as opposed to natural) persons, such as corporations, and thus prevents enforcement of confiscation proceedings and orders. The Financial Action Task Force on Money Laundering

---

74. UNCAC, Article 54(2)(a).

recommends that criminal liability be extended to legal persons.[75] At the least, criminal liability should extend to all legal persons for the purpose of recognizing and enforcing foreign orders. Where that is not possible, civil or administrative liability should apply.

The majority of jurisdictions participating in the study give effect to both foreign confiscation and restraint orders. Some jurisdictions give effect to restraint orders only if a confiscation order has been or is expected to be issued in the originating jurisdiction. One country gives effect to foreign orders only from jurisdictions with which it has a bilateral MLAT, which necessarily limits the number of jurisdictions that may request such a measure.

To allow for asset recovery cases to be conducted in an efficient and timely manner, all jurisdictions should have mechanisms in place to give effect to foreign freezing, seizure, and confiscation orders, as required by UNCAC.[76] Direct enforcement should be preferred as a speedier way to initiate confiscation proceedings and should apply to legal as well as natural persons and to all jurisdictions.

> **Policy Recommendation**
>
> Jurisdictions should put mechanisms in place to give effect to foreign freezing, seizure, and confiscation orders, including value judgments in the criminal context. Limitations on the jurisdictions or the types of persons to which such direct enforcement can be applied should be removed. The legislation should also allow for the entry of judgments against substitute assets or value-based criminal orders.

Barrier 20: Inability to Return Assets to Originating Jurisdictions

Pursuant to Article 57 of UNCAC, States parties should have in place such legislative and other measures as may be necessary to enable its competent authorities to return all confiscated property (minus expenses incurred) to the jurisdiction from which it was stolen.[77] In comparison, Article 14(3)(b) of UNTOC requires jurisdictions to merely consider entering into an agreement to share recovered assets with originating jurisdictions.

---

75. FATF 40+9 recommendations, recommendation 2 (2.3).

76. The third session of the Conference of the States Parties to UNCAC urged in November 2009 that States parties expand cooperation in the enforcement of foreign judgments: Resolution 3/3, www.unodc.org/ unodc/en /treaties/CAC/CAC-COSP.html.

77. UNCAC, Article 57(2) requires that States parties adopt such legislative and other measures as may be necessary to enable their competent authorities to return confiscated property, when acting on the request made by another State party. An interpretative note indicates that the legislative and other measures referred to in paragraph 2 would mean the national legislation or regulations that enable the implementation of this article by States parties: A/58/422/Add.1, para. 68.

While the UNCAC provisions clearly go beyond the requirements of UNTOC, many jurisdictions allow only for the sharing of confiscated assets, rather than their return, and require an asset-sharing agreement or a government decision to do so, meanwhile retaining certain portions of the amounts confiscated for themselves. Only a very limited number of jurisdictions have the legal authority to return 100 percent of stolen assets in cases relating to UNCAC offenses and directly based on domestic law.

Only sovereign jurisdictions may negotiate bilateral asset-sharing agreements. Given the large number of offshore jurisdictions that qualify as crown dependencies or overseas territories, such as the Channel Islands, this requirement severely limits the number of jurisdictions with which assets may be shared and thus constitutes a significant barrier.

Another pitfall is that case-by-case sharing agreements tend to be negotiated only after assets have been confiscated. At that point, the requested jurisdiction has possession of or owns the confiscated assets, including in those cases where the confiscation took place at the request of another jurisdiction and on the basis of a foreign confiscation order. Originating jurisdictions may find themselves in a weak negotiating position even after having provided all of the evidence necessary to obtain the confiscation order.

Negotiating asset-sharing agreements can be a lengthy process, which may result in considerable delays in the return of assets. In addition, the substantial resources required to negotiate such agreements are often not available to originating jurisdictions. To eliminate this barrier, jurisdictions should enact legislation allowing for the return of confiscated assets in accordance with UNCAC, or directly based on domestic law.

Policy Recommendations

a) For UNCAC offenses, jurisdictions should put in place legislation that allows for the return of all assets confiscated upon foreign request (minus expenses) in accordance with UNCAC Article 57.

b) For all other offenses, including those set out in UNTOC, jurisdictions should put in place legislation that allows for direct sharing of assets based on domestic law in the absence of a bilateral asset-sharing agreement. Bilateral sharing agreements setting out how assets are to be disposed of or shared may still be reached on a case-by-case basis.

Operational Barriers and Communication Issues

Barrier 21: Absent or Ambiguous Focal Points

The lack of information available to an originating jurisdiction on the appropriate focal point, or designated point of contact, in a requested jurisdiction, whether for formal MLA or other assistance, may impede the ability of an originating jurisdiction to initiate an effective request for assistance. Increasingly, mutual legal assistance treaties and multilateral conventions containing MLA provisions require that jurisdictions designate a central authority (generally the Ministry of Justice) to whom requests can be sent, thus providing an alternative to diplomatic channels.[78] Some jurisdictions have two central authorities and numerous contact points for requests for assistance. In others, however, it can be difficult, if not impossible, to identify a focal point, and in still others central authorities are unable to obtain reliable information quickly because data related to assets is so compartmentalized and administered by a diverse number of agencies.

The lack of clarity about relevant focal points at the beginning of the process can affect cooperation between jurisdictions and result in delays in potential informal assistance. Personal contacts can be a valuable means of identifying appropriate focal points in foreign counties. However, if the personal contacts break down because individuals leave their organizations or move to a different role, the focal points can also be lost or difficult to identify for new practitioners.

The designation of a central authority in both the originating and requested states is essential to fostering cooperation. The judicial authorities of the originating jurisdiction can then communicate directly with the central authority in the requested jurisdiction. Today, to an increasing degree, even more direct channels are being used, in that an official in the originating state can send the request directly to the appropriate official in the other state. This trend demonstrates the importance of a competent national central authority as a prerequisite for rendering mutual legal assistance more effectively. Moreover, central authorities should be staffed with practitioners who are

---

78. UNCAC, Article 46(13) requires that States parties designate a central authority. The Conference of State Parties to UNCAC has repeatedly highlighted both the importance of establishing central authorities with focal points and the need for those focal points to cooperate closely to facilitate the swift exchange of information. See Resolutions 1/4, 2/3, and 3/3, www.unodc.org/unodc/en/treaties/CAC/CAC-COSP.html.

legally trained, who have developed institutional expertise, and who are ensured access to up-to-date information.

Based on discussions with practitioners, the most useful measure is for each central authority to develop focal point contact information and make sure that the information is readily available to central authorities and practitioners in other jurisdictions. To be effective, these contacts should be able to provide information on how to make an MLA request. Jurisdictions can and should provide information about focal points in a number of ways, including on their Web sites and through INTERPOL[79] and other international and regional networks. The information should be kept up-to-date for maximum effectiveness. All requests should designate a specific individual as a contact person and include all necessary contact information.

In addition, asset recovery networks facilitate establishment of networks of contact points, act as advisory groups to other appropriate authorities, promote the exchange of information and good practices, and with time can develop into centers of expertise on tackling the challenges of asset recovery.[80] These networks can also advise practitioners on topics relating to recovering stolen assets and encourage more effective cooperation with the private sector on matters relating to the proceeds of crime. To avoid fragmentation, existing networks should be used, where possible. If no existing network is available, jurisdictions should support the creation of new networks.

In addition to information about the central authority, jurisdictions should disseminate information about informal focal points, which may be outside the central authority. These focal points might include the financial intelligence unit, investigative agencies, regulators and supervisors, and other competent authorities involved with recovering stolen assets. The Third Session of the Conference of State Parties of the UN Convention against Corruption encouraged States parties to promote informal channels of communication, particularly before making formal requests for mutual legal assistance, by, among other things, designating as focal points those officials or institutions with technical expertise in international cooperation in asset recovery. As focal points their role is to assist their counterparts in effectively meeting requirements for formal mutual legal assistance.

---

79. INTERPOL, in partnership with the StAR Initiative, has launched a focal point database to strengthen the coordination of law enforcement bodies that are investigating and prosecuting individuals and organizations involved in the illegal looting of public resources. The database provides a 24-hour, 7-day a week StAR Focal Point Contact List of officials who can respond to emergency requests for assistance from foreign countries (http://www.worldbank.org/publicsector/star_site/law_enforcement.html).

80. Examples of existing asset recovery networks are Camden Asset Recovery Inter-Agency Network (CARIN), Asset Recovery Inter-Agency Network for Southern Africa (ARINSA), and Red Iberoamericana de Cooperacion Juridica Internacional (IBERRED).

Operational Recommendations

a) Jurisdictions should identify a primary and secondary focal point within their central authority, as initial contact point for inquiries on making requests for assistance. Jurisdictions should also identify other competent authorities as focal points for managing informal inquiries. Focal point information should be kept current and include the name and address of the central or competent agency, the position or title of the focal point, contact details (e-mail, telephone, facsimile) and the languages spoken.

b) Jurisdictions should implement policies and procedures to ensure that focal points within central authorities have the capacity and knowledge to provide information on how to make a request for international assistance.

c) Jurisdictions should use a variety of avenues to provide information on focal points within their system and to ensure that focal point details remain current; options include use of domestic government Web sites, INTERPOL, and international or regional networks such as CARIN, ARINSA, and IBERRED.

d) Jurisdictions should strengthen existing asset recovery networks or include asset recovery within an existing regional network. Where no such networks exist, jurisdictions should support their creation, requesting assistance from international organizations when necessary.

Barrier 22: Onerous Legal Requirements to MLA and Overly Broad MLA Refusal

As a prerequisite to providing formal MLA, most jurisdictions require dual criminality and reciprocity. These requirements may be difficult to meet, stalling MLA and thus introducing obstacles to asset recovery. Dual criminality requires that the offense be criminalized in both the originating and requested jurisdictions. Practitioners identified this requirement as a barrier to the provision of MLA. Illicit enrichment, corruption of foreign public officials, and violations of foreign exchange control laws are examples of activities that are not criminalized in all jurisdictions. Moreover, because jurisdictions use different terminology to describe the offenses and required elements for proof, the assessment of dual criminality can prove problematic when it is based solely on the category and title of the offense without consideration of the criminalized conduct itself. The central authority in a requested jurisdiction might refuse the request because the originating jurisdiction cannot provide a reciprocity assurance to the requested jurisdiction.[81]

Some jurisdictions have removed the dual criminality and reciprocity requirements to facilitate the MLA process. Other jurisdictions consider waiving requirements in

---

81. For jurisdictions that have ratified UNCAC, reciprocity is not a valid reason for refusal of MLA; see UNCAC, Article 46(21).

certain cases or assume that reciprocity is met unless and until experience suggests otherwise. Where appropriate, this practice should be considered. In addition, some requested jurisdictions may not provide assistance if the originating jurisdiction considers corruption to be a capital offense.[82] A jurisdiction that is concerned about the possibility of capital punishment should seek assurances that, if it provides assistance, the originating jurisdiction will not apply capital punishment in the case or will impose a sentence that does not exceed the maximum permitted under the requested jurisdiction's laws. Because these initiatives assist in overcoming some of the barriers to MLA requests, jurisdictions should take such steps where appropriate.

UNCAC mandates and the Financial Action Task Force on Money Laundering recommends that where dual criminality cannot be waived, jurisdictions should use the conduct-based approach to determine if dual criminality can be met, focusing on whether the conduct is a criminal offense under the laws of both jurisdictions, not on whether the names of the offenses are the same.[83] The criminal conduct should be considered within the factual context of the offense to help in determining whether it is a criminal offense in both jurisdictions. This approach avoids a formalistic application of dual criminality in a way that could foreclose MLA unnecessarily. For example, suppose the originating jurisdiction is proceeding on charges for bribery of a government official, an offense that is not criminal in the requested jurisdiction. Under the conduct-based approach, the dual criminality requirement would be met if the requested jurisdiction criminalizes bribery of a national official.

Some requested jurisdictions have incorporated the statute of limitations into the dual criminality requirement and will refuse to provide assistance to an originating jurisdiction if the limitations period has expired in the requested jurisdiction. However, the expiration of a limitation period in the requested jurisdiction should never be used as a reason to deny assistance under dual criminality. The originating jurisdiction is only asking the requested jurisdiction to provide information or to freeze accounts, it is not seeking to prosecute the defendant in the requested jurisdiction. Because the actual prosecution will occur in the originating jurisdiction, that limitation period should govern, not that of the requested jurisdiction.

In addition, some jurisdictions restrict the jurisdictions to which they can provide assistance. Practitioners noted that assistance may be provided only to jurisdictions that are named or "designated" in domestic legislation or by certain domestic agencies such as foreign affairs ministries. Other jurisdictions will only help "sovereign countries," meaning that assistance cannot be extended to any crown dependencies.[84] Jurisdictions should avoid limiting the applicability of MLA to specific jurisdictions or using terminology that limits the jurisdictions that can apply for MLA. In addition, jurisdictions

---

82. See UNCAC, Article 46(21)(c).

83. UNCAC, Article 43(2) requires that countries apply this conduct-based approach. See also FATF 40+9, recommendation 37.

84. The crown dependencies include the Channel Island bailiwicks of Jersey and Guernsey in the English Channel, and the Isle of Man in the Irish Sea. They are independently administered jurisdictions that do not form part of the United Kingdom or the European Union.

should adopt domestic MLA legislation that introduces MLA procedures in the absence of bilateral or multilateral treaty between the two jurisdictions.

Most MLA agreements and domestic MLA laws, as well as UNCAC, permit or require the requested state to refuse assistance in certain circumstances. These circumstances commonly include requests that could prejudice the essential interests of the requested state; that involve property of a *de minimis* value (as defined by the jurisdiction); that touch on current proceedings or investigations in the requested state; or that permit punishment that the requested jurisdiction believes is too severe (such as the death penalty); and in cases where the offender is immune from prosecution or the due process rights of the offender were violated. These grounds can be an obstacle if they are not properly defined or are too expansive. For example, "essential interests" may be interpreted broadly to include sovereignty, public order, security, or excessive burden on resources. If a requested jurisdiction refuses extradition in a case involving a political offense, the requested jurisdiction should still attempt to address other aspects of an MLA request, where domestic law permits.[85]

To avoid an overly broad application of the grounds for refusing an MLA request, jurisdictions should ensure that their grounds for refusal are not mandatory and that they are able to exercise discretion in applying them in a particular case. Some jurisdictions have already adopted this approach. In addition, the grounds for refusal should be limited to those that are absolutely necessary and fundamental to the requested state, should be reasonable in light of what is being requested, and should not go beyond those grounds set out in UNCAC.[86] In other words, the requirements should be less onerous and more flexibly interpreted for MLA than for extradition, when liberty is at stake. Within MLA itself, there can be a gradation between investigatory measures, restraint and seizure, and confiscation, with fewer requirements and more flexibility in the earlier stages of the case. Finally, jurisdictions should clearly define the grounds for refusal and indicate how they are to be assessed.

When determining whether to refuse MLA on the basis of due process, jurisdictions should look at the particular facts of the case, not solely at what the legal system does or does not require. For example, due process may have been provided on the facts of the case, although laws may not require it. The legal system may not require that a defendant be served or notified of a proceeding, but if the jurisdiction has nonetheless served the defendant and provided a chance to respond, due process has been respected. Similarly, trials *in absentia* should not be a basis for refusal to provide MLA, so long as due process was provided to the defendant in the originating jurisdiction.

---

85. UNCAC, Article 44(4) on extradition states that where domestic law so permits, States parties extraditing under UNCAC should not consider any UNCAC offense to be a political offense. Article 46(17) on mutual legal assistance states that requests "shall be executed in accordance with the domestic law of the requested State Party." Article 46(21)(d) says a request may be refused "if it would be contrary to the legal system of the requested State Party relating to mutual legal assistance."
86. UNCAC, Article 46(9)(b) and (21).

The economic interests of a jurisdiction should never be a permissible reason for denying an MLA request. Practitioners stated that even though economic interests are not an enumerated ground for refusal, jurisdictions may be reluctant to provide assistance to another jurisdiction whose MLA request relates to a company of national importance. One practitioner advised that in one EU country, a guide to corporate prosecutions states that prosecution may not be carried out where the conviction would have adverse consequences under European law. This language suggests that a company could not be prosecuted for fraud on the ground that, if convicted, it would be prohibited under European law from bidding on public procurement projects, which could in turn adversely affect the economy, employment, and tax base of the country. Such practices and policies should be prohibited.

Some jurisdictions prohibit MLA if the request relates to an offense that involves, even partially, a fiscal offense such as tax evasion or tax fraud. In some cases, even if a tax offense is not the subject of the request, the asset holder will argue against the granting of the request on the basis that the subject offense amounts to a tax offense. Both Article 46(22) of UNCAC and FATF Recommendation 40 prohibit MLA refusals on the sole ground that the offense is considered to involve fiscal matters. Jurisdictions should ensure that requests cannot be refused on these grounds.

Policy Recommendations

a) Where reciprocity is required, jurisdictions should assume that reciprocity is met unless experience tells otherwise.
b) Jurisdictions should not refuse to provide assistance on the basis of dual criminality because a limitation period has expired in the requested jurisdiction.
c) Where dual criminality is required, jurisdictions should use a conduct-based approach in determining whether the requirement can be met.
d) When concerned about capital punishment, requested jurisdictions should seek assurances that if assistance is provided, the originating jurisdiction will not apply capital punishment.
e) Jurisdictions should avoid limiting the jurisdictions that can apply for MLA.
f) Jurisdictions should limit the grounds for refusal of MLA with regard to the provisions of UNCAC and UNTOC and, where required, define any grounds for refusal as clearly as possible, having regard to the nature of the request.
g) Jurisdictions should not set up mandatory grounds for refusal of MLA but rather clarify criteria for consideration and leave room for the exercise of discretion depending on the circumstances.
h) Jurisdictions should ensure that MLA requests cannot be refused on the ground that the offense involves fiscal matters.
i) Jurisdictions should ensure that MLA requests cannot be refused on grounds related solely to economic interests.

Barrier 23: Lack of Information on MLA Requirements

Practitioners identified failure to provide access to or properly explain the applicable laws, procedures, evidentiary requirements, and other MLA requirements as impediments to international cooperation in the recovery of assets. Effective cooperation requires accessibility to information and understanding of the systems and their limitations operating in participating countries.

Some jurisdictions make relevant laws and regulations on MLA available on the Web site of the central authority or on another government Web site. In some instances, laws are accessible through third-party Web sites, such as the International Money Laundering Information Network (IMoLIN)[87] database and the soon-to-be-developed UNCAC Legal Library, which are administered by the UNODC. Providing access to templates and relevant forms is also an important factor in assisting jurisdictions to prepare and transmit requests in the appropriate way. The level of online information and guidance provided by the 16 financial centers reviewed in this study is inconsistent. Internet research revealed that seven of the centers provided access to laws on international cooperation; five centers made laws, regulations and guidance available; and only two also provide samples or templates for making requests for assistance.

A representative of one of the 16 financial centers stated that while the government posted relevant laws and treaties on government Web sites, guidance on how to make an MLA request is not available on the Internet out of concern that criminals will find the information and use it to their advantage. That concern, however, is outweighed by the many advantages gained from disseminating detailed guidance on preparing and submitting MLA requests. In sum, ready availability of such information facilitates MLA requests by foreign jurisdictions and aids the fight against criminals. This study did not uncover any specific examples where open access to guidance notes proved beneficial to criminals and thwarted asset recovery action. Practitioners said that such information can be "sanitized" so that it can be made public, yet still assist practitioners in understanding the MLA process in that jurisdiction. Alternatively, information can be password protected so that access is restricted to practitioners in other jurisdictions. Jurisdictions that provide online access to laws and regulations but no further guidance should also provide contact details for a focal point so that originating jurisdictions can quickly identify and contact the appropriate authority for more detailed guidance (see Barrier 21). In addition, StAR has published the *Asset Recovery Handbook*, which includes a template for MLA requests, while the UNODC is working to update its MLA Request Writer Tool.

---

87. See www.imolin.org/.

Some jurisdictions have prepared "how to" guides to asset recovery in their jurisdiction that describe the necessary content of an MLA request, sample forms, points of contact, and the process for making a request. One such guide contains practitioners as named points of contact for each stage of the process who can provide real, practical assistance.[a]

a. The United Kingdom and Hong Kong SAR, China, have guides available upon request; Singapore provides guidance on a Web site: http://www.agc.gov.sg/criminal/mutual_legal_asst.htm.

Operational Recommendations

a) Jurisdictions and organizations should use government Web sites, MLA focal points, and third-party databases to make available MLA laws, regulations, and tools, along with explanatory guidelines and sample requests for assistance, preferably in at least one of the internationally accepted languages. Examples of outlets are UNODC IMoLIN, UNCAC Legal Library, the StAR initiative, and the ICAR (International Centre for Asset Recovery) Web site.

b) Central authorities designated as focal points for MLA requests should, in partnership with relevant domestic agencies:
   i) provide ready access to laws and regulations on MLA on the Internet;
   ii) issue and regularly update guidelines for foreign jurisdictions on requirements for making MLA or other requests, including a template for a request and sample requests, and update them regularly;
   iii) issue written policies and procedures on MLA to assist relevant staff to initiate and transmit MLA requests and to facilitate the timely processing of requests from foreign jurisdictions; and
   iv) provide relevant staff with formal and on-the-job training on MLA laws, regulations, and policies and on procedures for making MLA requests and processing incoming MLA requests.

Barrier 24: Lack of Problem-Solving Ingenuity

A number of practitioners noted that requested jurisdictions do not respond to or provide assistance on deficient or poorly drafted requests. Requested jurisdictions identify these drafting problems and deficiencies to include inappropriate requests, requests with irrelevant information, unclear requests, unfocused requests, and poor translation. Many originating jurisdictions, however, believe that developed countries have well-developed and -resourced central authorities that could assist less knowledgeable or less resourced jurisdictions to overcome these deficiencies.

Some jurisdictions have taken steps to provide assistance to other jurisdictions seeking MLA, including online guidance on preparing requests, making available sample requests or templates, providing access to liaison officers (if the requested jurisdiction has a presence in the originating jurisdiction), and reviewing draft requests for assistance before formal submission. When faced with a poorly drafted request, requested jurisdictions should communicate the deficiencies to the originating jurisdiction, a process that should improve the quality of future requests and ensure that the request will be executed as desired. Originating jurisdictions should try to ensure that their requests are clear and focused and do not use legal terms without explanation.

Mentoring of asset recovery specialists is another effective way to assist originating jurisdictions. This approach provides the opportunity for knowledge and skill transfers over an extended period of time and has the added advantage of sustainable capacity building at the institutional level. The UNODC, the World Bank, and several developed countries have mentor programs operating in several developing countries to provide advice and coaching on dealing with corruption and money laundering matters, including proceeds of crime and other aspects of international cooperation. Because these programs have provided tangible benefits to participating jurisdictions, international organizations and developed countries should consider opportunities to broaden the scope of their mentor programs. Developed countries can integrate assistance with mentoring and capacity-building programs as part of their assistance packages through multilateral organizations.

Some practitioners suggested that competent and accepted international bodies like the World Bank or UNODC, perhaps working through the StAR Initiative, provide direct assistance to developing countries by facilitating the MLA process. To avoid becoming involved in the chain of evidence and creating substantial disclosure issues for prosecutors, international organizations should limit their assistance to helping resolve capacity issues and clarify the content of formal MLA requests. These organizations typically do not investigate the substance of any request. Practitioners said that this limited involvement would improve the quality of requests, provide valuable training to developing-country practitioners, and facilitate the entire process. In addition, UNODC is currently engaged in upgrading its existing tool, MLA Request Writer Tool, to include asset recovery.

Several jurisdictions also give bilateral assistance to selected originating jurisdictions. One country, for example, paid the fees for private legal services provided to a developing country seeking recovery of stolen assets. Another jurisdiction provides bilateral assistance through its network of law enforcement attachés, many of whom are located in developing countries.

The requirement that originating jurisdictions translate requests into the language of the requested jurisdiction or an internationally accepted language was a subject of discussion among practitioners. Requested jurisdictions highlighted poor translation as a barrier to understanding the specifics of a request. This problem, of course, is exacerbated when the request is poorly drafted in the native language of the originating jurisdiction before any translation is undertaken,[88] or when the request uses excessive legal jargon. One way to solve this problem is for the requested jurisdiction to review a translated version of the initial draft. This translation should be of a professional standard so that the requested jurisdiction is able to provide clarification and feedback regarding changes that may need to be made in the draft document.

The cost of translation can be a major obstacle for developing countries. To produce a quality translation, the originating jurisdiction needs to engage the services of accredited professional translators from within the central authority, another government agency, or externally. Professional translation is particularly important because terms in one language may not have an equivalent term in another language. As a result, the term may be misunderstood, ignored, or translated into a substitute term, altering the meaning of the original text. To minimize poor-quality translation, requested jurisdictions could assist the process by funding professional translations of draft and final requests for some developing countries.

Finally, as noted in Barrier 23, jurisdictions should publish guidelines and provide sample formats for making MLA requests. Such tools and information will assist originating jurisdictions to focus their requests and ensure that they are in an appropriate form.

Good Practices

Estonia has established a national translation center with experts who are available to undertake legal translations on behalf of the central authority. This arrangement has added benefit as the legal translators become even more productive through repeated dealings with MLA matters.[a]

The United Kingdom has had positive results in aligning capacity building with casework. By providing technical assistance directly to originating jurisdictions, experts in London's Metropolitan Police Service help build the capacity of those who will actually execute the request.[b]

a. www.just.ee.
b. The experts are funded by the UK Department for International Development.

---

88. Article 46(14) of UNCAC states that MLA requests shall be formulated in a language acceptable to the requested country and that the Secretary-General shall be notified of the language acceptable at the time of depositing instruments of ratification. This information is available from http:///www.unodc.org/unodc/en/treaties/CAC/signatories-declarations-reservations.html.

a) Requested jurisdictions should, under agreement, provide assistance and training through the placement of liaison magistrates, prosecutors, attachés, or legal mentors in originating jurisdictions, particularly those with a significant number of requests or high-value matters. Developed jurisdictions should consider providing financial support, either directly or through assistance packages via multilateral organizations, to developing countries for placement of a liaison officer or attaché in the requested jurisdiction.

b) Jurisdictions should develop policies and procedures that provide and publicize resources available to originating jurisdictions to assist them in making a request for assistance. Resources could include online information, names of liaison officers, and details of contact persons who can review draft requests.

a) Originating jurisdictions should increase the quality of translation by using professional translation services and avoid the excessive use of legal jargon in requests.

b) Where a request is required to be submitted in a foreign language, developed countries should consider assisting developing countries by providing or arranging for translation services.

c) Providers of technical assistance should consider developing programs that allow, at the request of developing countries, the placement of mentors in originating jurisdictions to build capacity and transfer knowledge on MLA and other elements of international cooperation, potentially aligning such efforts with casework.

Barrier 25: Indistinct Channels and No Feedback

Another difficulty some practitioners encounter is finding out the status of a request or who to contact, in a timely manner, to provide additional information on a request, if need be. Both originating and requested jurisdictions said this problem was a barrier to asset recovery efforts. Ready availability of names, e-mail addresses, and telephone numbers of practitioners in both originating and requested jurisdictions is essential for timely communication between relevant personnel, and this information must be kept current. In addition, a requested jurisdiction that denies an MLA request should promptly advise the originating jurisdiction of the denial so that the jurisdiction can attempt asset recovery using other means. To help originating jurisdictions avoid future problems with their MLA requests, the grounds for refusal and the underlying facts supporting that refusal should be provided in writing. Explaining the grounds for refusing requests will also encourage requested jurisdictions to deny requests only for legitimate reasons solidly based in fact (see Barrier 22).

Switzerland has established a Web site for MLA requests. A practitioner seeking information about the status of a request enters a docket number and instantly obtains information about the status of the request, regardless of the time of day.

a) Jurisdictions making an MLA request should include contact details of the practitioner who is responsible for the request, including information about the languages spoken by that individual.
b) Jurisdictions should implement policies and procedures for responding to MLA requests. An important element is an acknowledgment receipt that includes names and contact details that the originating jurisdiction may use to follow up on the status of the request. This acknowledgment should be submitted within two weeks after receipt of the request.
c) Requested jurisdictions should promptly advise originating jurisdictions in writing when an MLA request is denied, including the grounds for refusal and the underlying facts supporting the refusal.

Barrier 26: Unreasonable Delays in MLA Responses

Practitioners identified delays in processing and responding to MLA requests as a significant barrier to stolen asset recovery. If the delay is too lengthy and the assets have not been frozen or restrained, they may be dissipated or moved. If delays are extremely lengthy, the existing evidence will grow stale and witnesses may die or go missing. Significant delay may frustrate practitioners, discourage future MLA requests, and undermine the political will to proceed with the cases.

In many cases, delays in processing requests may be related to due process rights. Most jurisdictions recognize the right of the accused to appeal by making application to court. Due process rights are important protections for those accused of crimes, and should be respected and maintained.

The accused, however, sometimes abuse the system and due process rights. Frequently, the accused, as well as their family members and associates, may intentionally initiate baseless litigation strategies designed only to delay the rendering of assistance, knowing that their suits have little chance of ultimate success. To minimize the possibility of undue delay, jurisdictions can enact legislation that limits the types of challenges an asset holder can raise so that litigants do not have an opportunity to make the same argument twice, once in the requested jurisdiction and again in the originating jurisdiction. Jurisdictions should also consider implementing mechanisms to accelerate the process in all stolen asset recovery cases and to enforce penalties, such as costs orders, against parties that submit groundless applications clearly designed to unnecessarily delay procedures.

Due process rights must also be balanced with the needs of investigators to secure evidence without prejudicing the case and the objectives of UNCAC or national laws to combat corruption.[89] For confiscation orders, the balance favors the asset holder because of the finality of the order or penalty. As such, the asset holder should have the opportunity to object or defend at this stage of the proceedings. Investigative and preservation (freezing or restraint) measures, on the other hand, do not imply or establish guilt, nor are they punitive, and various safeguards can be implemented to ensure that they are not abused. For example, some courts require applicants to show potential prejudice before the court will order a freeze without notice; in addition, they may also require notice to the asset holder after the preservation order has been granted. If notice is not supplied within a certain period of time, the freeze order is lifted. Jurisdictions should permit investigative and preservation measures to proceed without notice to the asset holder, provided that sufficient protections of the due process rights of the asset holder exist at other stages of the proceedings.

The exercise of due process rights is not the only cause of delay to requests for MLA. Other common delays are caused solely by the internal processes and procedures of requested jurisdictions. Practitioners said that sometimes months can elapse before requested jurisdictions acknowledge receipt of the request and subsequently attend to it. Practitioners also identified circumstances in which both originating and requested jurisdictions failed to prioritize requests adequately. In some instances, practitioners complained that originating jurisdictions submit requests involving assets of minimal value and expect immediate action. Conversely, originating practitioners complained that the requested jurisdictions do not prioritize their requests, despite pleas about the urgency of a matter. In addition, there was a sense that jurisdictions always prioritize domestic investigations ahead of international requests for assistance.

To eliminate this barrier, originating jurisdictions should prioritize their requests based on the seriousness of the offense, the value of the assets involved, the stage of the investigation, and the impact that the case has on the public interest. Prioritizing requests in this manner will help requested jurisdictions not only respond more quickly but use their limited resources on the most important requests. Originating jurisdictions should also communicate the degree of urgency of the request and the reasons for the urgency, so that requested jurisdictions are better able to prioritize the deployment of their resources. Finally, originating jurisdictions should establish a reasonable monetary value threshold for assets below which they will not seek assistance unless there is high public interest in the recovery of the assets. Submission of too many requests, particularly requests involving only a small amount of assets, can cause fatigue in financial centers beset by many such requests and could erode political will within those jurisdictions for providing MLA in asset recovery cases.

---

89. UNCAC, Article 1.

Policy Recommendations

a) Jurisdictions should permit investigative and preservation measures to proceed without notice to the asset holder, provided that sufficient protections of the due process rights of the asset holder exist at other stages of the proceeding.

b) Jurisdictions should put statutory limitations on the types of challenges an asset holder can raise in cases where the jurisdiction has been asked to provide assistance to another jurisdiction. They also should, in cases where they are the originating jurisdiction, prohibit asset holders from raising any challenges that could be raised in the litigation pending in the requested jurisdiction. In both situations, the jurisdiction would be denying asset holders the opportunity to make the same argument twice.

Operational Recommendations

a) Jurisdictions should enforce penalties (such as costs orders) against parties that submit groundless applications solely to delay procedures unnecessarily.

b) To avoid unnecessary delay in processing requests, jurisdictions should implement procedures for all MLA requests that:
   i) acknowledge receipt of the request within two weeks, providing contact information for the practitioner responsible for managing the request, including an e-mail address, to the originating authority;
   ii) establish clear lines of communication between originating and requested jurisdictions; and
   iii) provide information to originating jurisdictions about process, timeline, expectations, and any other relevant matters related to the process.

c) Requested jurisdictions should prioritize requests when informed of the urgency and create special procedures to expedite requests where originating jurisdictions advise that the assistance is urgently required.

d) Practitioners should communicate with originating jurisdictions to ensure that all aspects of the request are understood, especially if the dollar value is low but the public interest is high.

Barrier 27: Lack of Publicly Available Registries

Article 55 of UNCAC requires originating jurisdictions to provide a description of the property to be restrained or confiscated, including the location and estimated value of the property, as well as a statement of the facts underlying the request. Some jurisdictions, however, require overly specific property designation requirements, which may be difficult for originating jurisdictions to meet. For example, one jurisdiction requires the lot registry number instead of the address of a real estate property, and the account and bank branch numbers instead of the names of the account holder and bank. Given that originating jurisdictions often do not have the means or available resources to research the information required, overly specific information requirements may delay and thus dilute the effectiveness of restraint and confiscation measures. Jurisdictions should therefore take steps to eliminate overly specific property designation requirements where the property description submitted is sufficient to identify the asset in question.

To enable originating jurisdictions to identify and include the necessary information in requests for the seizing or confiscation of assets, jurisdictions should develop and maintain publicly available registries, such as company registries, land registries, registries of nonprofit organizations, and other databases. If possible, such registries should be centralized and maintained in electronic and real-time format, so that they are searchable and updated at all times. The availability of such registries will minimize delay by making it easier for originating jurisdictions to obtain the necessary information to make a successful MLA request without asking the requested jurisdiction to undertake investigatory measures outside the usual course of MLA assistance. These registries should include, but not be limited to, names, personal identifying data, corporate director and officer information, shareholder information, and beneficial owner information.

Operational Recommendations

a) Jurisdictions should develop and maintain publicly available registries, such as company registries, land registries, and registries of nonprofit organizations. If possible, such registries should be centralized and maintained in electronic and real-time format, so that they are searchable and updated at all times.

b) Jurisdictions should eliminate requirements for overly specific descriptions of the property to be restrained or confiscated, such as requirements for the lot registration number rather than the street address; jurisdictions should also ensure that the requirements applied do not inhibit effective implementation of the requested measure.

Barrier 28: Identifying Foreign Bank Accounts

Some jurisdictions require overly specific information to implement requests for seizing or confiscating assets and bank accounts (see Barrier 27). One reason for this requirement is that in the absence of specific information, the authorities trying to identify specific accounts might have to query every bank operating domestically. Needless to say, this process would be very long and tedious, particularly in larger jurisdictions and those with a large financial sector. At a minimum, therefore, most jurisdictions require that any request for restraint or seizure identify the financial institution(s) where the assets are thought to be held.

In many MLA requests, the identification of the particular account holding the assets can be one of the most significant difficulties encountered in the early stages of a case. Several practitioners indicated that central bank account registries would be highly useful tools in asset recovery cases because they allow competent law enforcement authorities to conduct electronic searches using an individual's name or the identification elements of a specific bank account. Because criminals often use other individuals, attorneys, and legal persons to hide assets, such tools would be even more useful if they identify the beneficial owner of the account and any power of attorney related to the account. By helping to identify accounts, central bank account registries thus eliminate the need to impose overly specific property designation requirements on originating jurisdictions and speed the work of law enforcement authorities in asset recovery cases.

Jurisdictions should also be willing to provide information from such registries to foreign jurisdictions conducting investigations without requiring a formal MLA request. This minimizes delay without alerting the asset holder to the investigation, thereby avoiding the risk that the assets will be moved or dissipated before the investigation is complete.

Operational Recommendations

a) Jurisdictions should establish a national bank registry to retain account iden-
    tification information, including beneficial owners and powers of attorney.
b) Requested jurisdictions should enact legislation or develop policies and
    procedures that make available from its national bank registry account
    identification data, beneficial owner information, and powers of attorney
    without the submission of a formal MLA request by the appropriate, compe-
    tent authorities in another jurisdiction.

Barrier 29: Using Restrained Funds to Pay Legal Fees; Depletion of Confiscated Assets by Contingency Fee Payments; Asset Mismanagement

In many jurisdictions, the owner of seized or restrained property is entitled to or can request payment of legal fees associated with the proceeding or a related proceeding from the restrained assets. Practitioners identified this practice as a barrier that can significantly dissipate the seized assets, particularly where the legal fees are exorbitant. There is also the potential of abuse by improper access and spending of the restrained funds. An originating jurisdiction that recovers significantly less than expected in one case may hesitate before attempting asset recovery in the future, particularly where the monetary amounts are less significant. The failure to recover all the assets in question may also deplete political will to combat corruption in the future (see Barrier 2).

To combat abuse, jurisdictions can place limits on the amount of the assets that can be used for legal fees or require the owner to show that no other assets are available to satisfy the fees. One jurisdiction, for example, intends to pass legislation to bar the payment of legal fees out of the seized proceeds of corruption altogether. These measures should balance the rights of the accused to access funds to mount a legal defense against the rights of the victims to recover the stolen assets.

Legal fees incurred by the originating jurisdictions to recover the stolen assets can also significantly deplete the asset once it is confiscated.[90] Asset recovery can be a costly and time-consuming exercise. It frequently requires lawyers, financial investigators, forensic accountants, other experts, translation services, and expensive international travel. Laws in developed countries are more complex and restrictive than those in the developing world and often feature increased procedural and evidentiary requirements. Although these requirements are not easily managed, they often cannot be avoided.

Many developing countries do not have the capacity to meet these requirements and choose to solicit the services of private law firms to manage a stolen asset recovery action on their behalf. Many private law firms have such expertise, including some with experience in high-profile cases. The legal fees in these arrangements can be exorbitant, however, and often significantly diminish the amount of proceeds recovered and repatriated. Moreover, when the recovery is not successful, the victim jurisdiction often is still liable for legal fees incurred. The prospects of these considerable costs might discourage some developing countries from attempting to recoup their stolen assets.

To assist developing countries in recovering stolen assets, jurisdictions should encourage law firms to provide such services pro bono to jurisdictions that lack the capacity or financial resources to engage in time-consuming and expensive litigation. To entice such participation, leaders can establish public awards and make public declarations in support of professionals that regularly provide services pro bono to assist with MLA. In addition, if a developed country receives a request from a developing country seeking assistance to recover stolen assets, the developed country should provide financial assistance to the developing country to pay for legal representation. For example, some practitioners advised that their jurisdictions have a special fund available to assist developing countries with such cases.

Contingency fee arrangements can also assist victim jurisdictions by providing them with access to legal representation that they could not otherwise afford. In addition, these arrangements also prevent the initiation of implausible actions by developing countries, saving their resources for actions with a greater chance of success. While contingency fee arrangements can help to overcome this obstacle, some practitioners did not agree with these arrangements because they were prohibited in their jurisdiction. Others were concerned that that the legal fees from these arrangements may be so great that they inappropriately deplete the confiscated assets. To avoid such abuse, these arrangements should be transparent, equitable, and in the best interest of the victim jurisdiction.

---

90. Article 57(4) of UNCAC states that, where appropriate and unless States parties decide otherwise, the requested State party may deduct reasonable expenses incurred in investigations, prosecutions, or judicial proceedings leading to the return or disposition of confiscated property.

UNCAC requires States parties to consider measures to permit their competent authorities to preserve property for confiscation and to adopt legislative and other measures to regulate the administration of frozen, seized, or confiscated property.[91] The function of an asset manager is to preserve the security and value of the assets pending confiscation and to realize assets after confiscation. The failure to manage restrained assets carefully and adequately is a significant obstacle to the recovery of the full value of stolen assets. If assets are not properly managed when restrained or seized, their value may be significantly depleted by the time confiscation occurs. If an originating jurisdiction expected to recover a much greater amount of assets that it actually does, the loss of value can discourage it from attempting asset recovery in the future and deplete political will to combat corruption. Moreover, originating jurisdictions could perceive improper maintenance of assets by requested jurisdictions as objectionable, perhaps creating an antagonistic relationship.

When the proceeds of corruption are traced to a bank account, management of those assets is relatively simple. In other circumstances, they may be traced into operating businesses, real property, art, or other assets that require special storage or active management. In these cases, asset management requires specialized knowledge and attention. In addition, in the case of rapidly depreciating or perishable property, asset managers need to be able to take steps to dispose of the seized property as necessary to preserve its value.

To ensure the preservation of seized or frozen assets, jurisdictions should implement an asset management scheme that includes the ability for timely disposal or sale of the seized property where appropriate. The scheme may contemplate asset management by a number of different players, such as private receivers, the person who holds the property, a court-appointed manager, or a public service office created for this purpose. Many jurisdictions have created a specialized office to manage seized or restrained property pursuant to various domestic confiscation laws. This office usually provides planning and analysis before the assets are restrained or seized plus management of the assets once they are restrained or seized and then realization of the assets after they are formally confiscated.

The asset manager should be involved before restraint or seizure to analyze the costs of managing the property against the value likely to be realized on confiscation. In addition, the asset manager should be required to keep a detailed description of the property and its condition, including, where appropriate, photographs or video images. In some situations, a valuation of the property may also be important.

FATF has recommended as a best practice that jurisdictions implement an asset management scheme to manage frozen and seized property, ideally including the following characteristics:

- a framework to effectively manage frozen, seized, or confiscated property, including designation of the authority responsible for managing the property;
- sufficient resources to handle all aspects of asset management;

---

91. UNCAC, Articles 54(2)(c) and 31(3).

- the involvement of the authority before action is taken to freeze or seize the asset;
- measures to deal with the property owner and third-party rights;
- appropriate record keeping;
- the requirement that the authority take responsibility for any damages to be paid following legal action by an individual in respect of damage or loss of the property; and
- statutory authority to permit a court to order a sale, particularly where the property is perishable or rapidly depreciating.

For additional information, see the StAR publication *Asset Recovery Handbook: A Guide for Practitioners.*

Operational Recommendations

a) Jurisdictions should develop policies and procedures that ensure that appropriate limits are placed on access to restrained assets, such as limits on exorbitant fees and a requirement that the defendant show that no other sources of funds are available for legal representation. These policies and procedures should balance the rights of the accused to access funds for a defense against the rights of the victim to recover stolen assets.

b) Developed jurisdictions should consider creation of a special fund to provide financial assistance to developing countries seeking to recover stolen assets located within the developed jurisdiction.

c) Jurisdictions should encourage law firms to provide services to assist with asset recovery pro bono for jurisdictions that lack the capacity or financial resources to engage in time-consuming and expensive litigation. Alternatively, developed countries that receive requests from developing countries for the return of stolen assets should consider providing financial assistance to the developing country to pay for legal representation.

d) Jurisdictions should support contingency fee arrangements between private law firms and developing countries seeking the return of their stolen assets in corruption cases and the use of confiscated assets for that purpose, provided that such arrangements are made public, equitable, in line with industry best practices, and in the best interest of the victim country.

e) Jurisdictions, possibly the central and judicial authorities, should take steps to ensure that legal fee arrangements are not abused.

f) Jurisdictions should ensure that effective asset management measures exist to protect against depletion of restrained or seized assets, as required by UNCAC.

g) Jurisdictions should include provisions that permit the disposal of rapidly depreciating or perishable seized property where necessary to preserve the value.

Appendix A. Table of Recommendations

Recommendation	Barrier	Type
A requested jurisdiction should not refuse a request for MLA unless it has precise and strong evidence that the originating jurisdiction has not guaranteed due process to the defendants.	1	Policy
Developed countries should consider absorbing the costs of communication with developing-country jurisdictions on requests for assistance with recovery of stolen assets; developed countries could also provide developing jurisdictions with communications technology and equipment.	1	Policy
Requested jurisdictions should implement policies and procedures that guarantee transparency when dealing with originating authorities and should require that the reasons for rejecting a MLA request be divulged to the originating jurisdiction; they should also give the originating jurisdiction an opportunity to demonstrate that the defendant received due process.	1	Operational
To help build trust between jurisdictions, developed countries should establish policies and procedures that facilitate the establishment of personal contacts between originating and requested authorities. In particular, they should establish liaison magistrates, FIU liaison officers, and customs or police attachés[a] to promote enhanced cooperation between central authorities and direct contacts between competent prosecutors, judges or law enforcement officers.	1	Operational
Jurisdictions should provide adequate resources to enable their officials to attend relevant international meetings and forums and to network with their counterparts bilaterally.	1	Operational
Jurisdictions should participate in and exploit asset recovery networks and groups such as CARIN, ARINSA, and IBERRED to develop relationships with practitioners in other jurisdictions.	1	Operational
Jurisdictions should establish policies and procedures that allow practitioners to develop effective contacts and avenues for communication at an institution-to-institution level, including maintaining contact details in corporate systems. Such systems should be updated on a regular basis.	1	Operational
Jurisdictions should develop and implement a transparent and comprehensive strategy for recovery of stolen assets that explicitly and narrowly defines grounds for refusal of a request for mutual legal assistance.	2	Policy

a. For example, the United States has attachés from the FBI, Drug Enforcement Administration, U.S. Immigration and Customs Enforcement, Internal Revenue Service, and U.S. Secret Service in many embassies overseas. France, Germany, Japan, and the United Kingdom also have police, customs, and liaison magistrates in foreign countries.

Recommendation	Barrier	Type
Jurisdictions should create specialized confiscation agencies or units within existing agencies with a clearly defined mandate to facilitate asset recovery.	2	Policy
Jurisdictions should ensure that their officials, including judges and prosecutors, are well trained on asset recovery matters.	2	Policy
Where a non-conviction based asset confiscation regime does not exist, jurisdictions that have not already done so should pass and implement legislation that allows them to respond positively to requests to confiscate suspected stolen assets in the absence of a conviction.	2	Policy
Jurisdictions should explicitly and narrowly define grounds for refusal of a request for mutual legal assistance.	2	Policy
Jurisdictions should initiate their own stolen asset investigations using a variety of legitimate sources (FIUs, complaints, and media reports); establish bilateral technical assistance programs; provide hands-on technical assistance on a case-by-case basis; initiate and properly resource special investigative-prosecutorial units that focus on stolen asset recovery investigations; and support international organizations that have the capacity to provide assistance (as prescribed in Article 60(2)(3) of UNCAC).	2	Operational
When facing a dual criminality requirement, jurisdictions should interpret the originating jurisdiction's definitions of offenses in a broadminded manner, allowing for the widest range of consideration, and, if necessary, use a conduct-based approach to determine if the conduct is a crime in both jurisdictions.	2	Operational
Jurisdictions should make it a policy priority to ensure that there are an adequate number of properly trained financial investigators, prosecutors, and judges to address asset recovery cases involving both domestic laws and international conventions and standards.	3	Policy
Jurisdictions should pass legislation to ensure that the state cannot be penalized with an adverse costs order in cases where it is addressing its international obligations to provide mutual legal assistance.	3	Policy
Jurisdictions should ensure that competent authorities are sufficiently staffed, adequately trained, and experienced in asset recovery matters involving both domestic laws and international conventions and standards.	3	Operational
Originating and requested jurisdictions should be prepared to have frank discussions to try to resolve resource issues, including communication about cost sharing and, where appropriate, sharing of recovered assets.	3	Operational
FATF should align its definition of a PEP with UNCAC's. This definition should be adopted by all national standard setters and other key stakeholders.	4	Policy
Jurisdictions should require financial institutions to review their PEP customers at least yearly, using a risk-based approach, and to document the results of the review.	4	Policy

Recommendation	Barrier	Type
Because PEPs often retain their prominence and influence for several years even after a corruption prosecution begins, jurisdictions should require financial institutions to keep banking records related to PEPs for a longer period than normal, perhaps eight to ten years.	4	Policy
Jurisdictions should ensure implementation of the provisions of Article 14 and Article 52 of UNCAC, the FATF recommendations, and the recommendations set out in the StAR report *Politically Exposed Persons: A Policy Paper on Strengthening Preventative Measures for the Banking Sector*.	4	Operational
When a suspicious transaction report (STR) is linked to a foreign PEP, the competent authorities should, after proper analysis supports such dissemination, share this information with the competent authorities in the PEP's home jurisdiction and any other germane jurisdiction.	4	Operational
Jurisdictions should report any criminal acts and suspicious information discovered during the yearly review of a foreign PEP to the local FIU using the STR process, or to another competent authority through the appropriate process.	4	Operational
Jurisdictions should consider implementing risk management systems to identify PEPs. Such systems should include: • Generic indicators and information sources, such as risks associated with certain jurisdictions, products, the seniority of the officeholder, or the type of business. • Procurement of relevant information from the customer as part of the normal account application process and ongoing customer due diligence (CDD) and know your client (KYC) processes. • A requirement for a written declaration of beneficial ownership under penalty of a criminal offense. • Business knowledge and information sharing between financial institutions. • Asset and income declaration filing lists. • Media and journals containing information that may help banks identify PEPs and keep their customer profile updated. • Domestic sources of information pertaining to the customer's originating jurisdiction. • Internet searches, including both large and small search engines. • Use of commercial PEP database providers.	4	Operational
Jurisdictions should ensure that the competent regulators or supervisors properly enforce implementation of the disclosure, reporting, and risk management systems relating to PEPs.	4	Operational
To facilitate international cooperation, relevant jurisdictions should enter into joint task force arrangements or participate in regular international meetings in circumstances when two or more jurisdictions are involved in a significant asset recovery case.	5	Operational

Recommendation	Barrier	Type
Jurisdictions should review domestic arrangements for MLA and take steps to enhance domestic cooperation and coordination. One option is to develop multiagency task forces or joint working group arrangements that meet regularly to discuss strategies and actions.	5	Operational
Where a central authority is the first point of contact for an MLA request, jurisdictions should introduce procedures that allow, encourage, and facilitate practitioner-to-practitioner communication once the process is under way; if necessary, the central authority should be copied on communications. However, jurisdictions should enact policies and procedures that avoid involving agencies that are not essential to the MLA process.	5	Operational
Jurisdictions should develop and implement policies and procedures that ensure that informal assistance channels are available to foreign practitioners for noncoercive measures and temporary freezes of 72 hours or less, without disproportionate or unduly restrictive conditions.	6	Policy
Jurisdictions should establish policies and procedures that create communication channels outside the formal process at all stages: before, during, and after the final preparation and communication of a formal MLA request.	6	Policy
Originating jurisdictions should exhaust informal assistance channels before making a formal MLA request.	6	Operational
Requested jurisdictions should inform originating jurisdictions, at an early stage, of types of information that can be provided without the need for a formal MLA request. Guidance should be provided through relevant government Web sites.	6	Operational
Jurisdictions should not require a formal request before making public records available, such as land registry documents, registered company documents, and information about directors and shareholders. Jurisdictions should also provide copies of annual reports and associated documents without a formal request.	6	Operational
If requested, jurisdictions should be willing to contact potential witnesses without a formal request to determine if the witness is willing to cooperate with the originating authorities voluntarily. States should take witness statements from voluntary witnesses without a formal request, provided that contact with the witness is permitted under such circumstances.	6	Operational

Recommendation	Barrier	Type
To facilitate understandings between jurisdictions with different legal traditions, jurisdictions should provide easy access to information about asset recovery within their legal system, including relevant statutory provisions and information about proof requirements, capacities, types of investigative techniques that are available, and types that are disallowed. Formats should include: • A Web site that provides this information and practical asset recovery case examples that offer guidance on available investigative techniques and how they are used in the jurisdiction. • Workshops involving international and domestic practitioners to provide information on how to submit MLA requests, capacities, types of investigative techniques that are available, and types that are disallowed.	7	Operational
Jurisdictions should use clear, concise, and universal terms when drafting MLA requests, such as those in Article 2 of UNCAC and in UNTOC, and explain concisely the meaning of each term used.	7	Operational
Jurisdictions should implement policies and procedures that proactively notify originating jurisdictions about problems with terminology or other substantive issues.	7	Operational
Requested jurisdictions should consider developing and implementing policies and procedures that ensure they can use any and all possible procedures that will permit them to positively execute an MLA request, including their own procedures and the procedures specified in the request.	7	Operational
Jurisdictions that have not yet done so should accede to or ratify and implement UNCAC, UNTOC, and other regional or international instruments that facilitate the provision of MLA.	8	Policy Legal
Jurisdictions that need to transpose international conventions into domestic law should ensure that comprehensive and overarching domestic legislation on MLA is in place and fully compliant with Chapters IV and V of UNCAC and Article 18 of UNTOC.	8	Policy Legal
Jurisdictions that have the ability to directly apply self-executing international treaties should ensure that practitioners are aware that international conventions such as UNCAC and UNTOC can be used as a legal basis for MLA and are familiar with the convention provisions. Consideration should be given to adopting domestic MLA laws to allow for assistance in the absence of or in cases outside the scope of international conventions.	8	Policy Legal

Recommendation	Barrier	Type
Jurisdictions should consider entering into bilateral MLATs or memoranda of understanding with jurisdictions that provide only limited forms of MLA based on their domestic laws or based on conventions such as UNCAC, UNTOC, or jurisdictions with which cooperation would be overly burdensome without a bilateral agreement. Priority should be given to jurisdictions that have strategic importance including from an asset recovery standpoint.	8	Policy Legal
Existing MLATs should be reviewed and, if required, updated periodically to ensure their continued relevance.	8	Policy Legal
Jurisdictions should review domestic criminal laws and the scope of the restraint and confiscation framework to ensure that they are wide enough to encompass all UNCAC and UNTOC offenses.	9	Policy Legal
Jurisdictions should apply domestic restraint and confiscation provisions of UNCAC to all of the types of property as provided in UNCAC.	9	Policy Legal
Jurisdictions should permit the provision of MLA upon commencement of an investigation into potential criminal activity, even if criminal charges have not yet been instigated.	10	Policy Legal
Jurisdictions should introduce mechanisms that allow for prompt tracing and temporary freezing of assets before a formal MLA request is filed. A formal MLA request would be required to retain the freeze.	10	Policy Legal
Jurisdictions should permit MLA to be provided without notifying the asset holder where investigative and preservation measures are involved, provided that sufficient protections of the due process rights of the asset holder exist at those stages of the proceeding that involve coercive or intrusive measures.	11	Policy Legal
Jurisdictions should not require mandatory notification of customers when a financial institution communicates information requested by foreign jurisdictions during an investigation. At a minimum, jurisdictions should have the capacity to delay notification until the appropriate stage of the investigation (usually, the point when the lead investigatory body is best prepared to mitigate the risks of disclosure).	11	Policy Legal
Jurisdictions that require disclosure should communicate with originating jurisdictions before assistance is provided to determine whether the jurisdiction would prefer to receive the information or would rather take other measures to avoid disclosure to the asset holder. If such a requirement exists, jurisdictions should prominently display this information on their Web site and advise practitioners in other international forums.	11	Operational
Jurisdictions that require disclosure when executing formal MLA requests should allow temporary freezes to be put in place during investigations without disclosure to the asset holder.	11	Operational

Recommendation	Barrier	Type
Jurisdictions should not use banking secrecy as a basis for refusing to cooperate fully in international cases (informal and formal) involving all UNCAC and UNTOC offenses.	12	Policy Legal
Jurisdictions should enact legislation that limits, as well as precisely defines, "protected information." This information should be very narrow in scope. In cases where investigators or prosecutors in originating jurisdictions have a legitimate and articulable interest in examining such records, the banking secrecy laws should be broad enough to accommodate such requests.	12	Policy Legal
Jurisdictions should not allow banking secrecy to prevent them from extending assistance and providing documents or other information in cases where suspicious transactions involving identified accounts implicate other accounts that were not identified in the request.	12	Policy Legal
Jurisdictions should consider introducing legislation establishing a rebuttable presumption to help meet the standard of proof for criminal confiscation following conviction, particularly for UNCAC and UNTOC offenses.	13	Policy Legal
Jurisdictions should ensure that evidentiary requirements are less onerous in cases involving issuance of temporary restraint orders than in cases involving more permanent measures and those at later stages of the confiscation process.	13	Policy Legal
Within the limits of constitutional or fundamental guarantees of due process, jurisdictions should pass new legislation or adopt new practices to help meet evidentiary requirements to facilitate MLA for investigative measures, including the establishment of central registries of bank accounts.	13	Policy Legal
In both conviction-based and NCB forfeiture cases, jurisdictions should ensure that the standard of proof to show that assets are linked to criminal activity is not too stringent and is clearly set out in relevant domestic laws. Jurisdictions should further ensure that prosecutors need establish a link only between assets and criminal activity in general rather than between assets and a specific criminal offense.	13	Policy Legal
Jurisdictions should strictly define expectations for content of MLA requests and provide examples of requests, on a Web site, that do not provide sufficient factual and logical justification to reasonably permit further investigation.	13	Operational
Requests for assistance containing incomplete information, but a clear nexus between the offender and the assets, should be accepted if the requested jurisdiction appears likely to be able to locate assets based upon the submitted information or information maintained by the requested jurisdiction.	13	Operational

Recommendation	Barrier	Type
Jurisdictions should prioritize requests and limit the volume of the request by focusing on specific and essential items to increase the possibility that their MLA request will be successful.	13	Operational
Jurisdictions should introduce legislation to allow for substitute or equivalent-value asset restraint and confiscation. At a minimum, provisions allowing such measures for commingled property should be put in place, in conformity with UNCAC.	14	Policy Legal
Jurisdictions should enact domestic legislation permitting confiscation without a conviction. At a minimum, non-conviction based confiscation should be permitted when the perpetrator is dead, a fugitive, absent, immune from prosecution, or in other appropriate cases.	15	Policy Legal
Jurisdictions should, at a minimum, allow for enforcement of foreign NCB orders.	15	Policy Legal
Jurisdictions should consider creating mechanisms that permit proportionate cooperation from defendants in asset recovery cases.	16	Policy Legal
Before entering into a plea agreement or similar arrangement, jurisdictions should attempt to coordinate with other jurisdictions with a vested interest in the investigation to avoid jeopardizing related investigations being conducted in those jurisdictions.	16	Operational
Jurisdictions should, where necessary, enact legislation to ensure that the scope of international immunities applicable in their jurisdiction does not extend beyond the limits defined by international law and jurisprudence. The legislation should permit prosecution, confiscation of assets, and mutual legal assistance where: • the acts involved are committed in a personal capacity; • the foreign officials are being prosecuted by their own jurisdiction; or • the foreign officials are the beneficial owners of assets managed as private resources or in the name of family members and associates.	17	Policy Legal
Jurisdictions should enact legislation that provides for the suspension of applicable statutes of limitation until foreign officials shielded by immunities leave their positions or lose that immunity.	17	Policy Legal
Jurisdictions should not consider immunities to be an obstacle when they are waived by the state of the official.	17	Operational
Jurisdictions should carefully examine each case involving corruption offenses to determine whether immunities apply or prosecution is possible. If immunities apply and they cannot be waived, prosecutors should be encouraged to consider other avenues of pursuing justice, including civil suits, NCB confiscation, or charges against other people or entities involved or implicated in the crimes.	17	Operational

Recommendation	Barrier	Type
Where possible, jurisdictions should consider repealing statutes of limitation for large-scale and egregious corruption offenses, to be defined within the legislation. For example, the limitation period might be repealed for offenses involving assets in excess of a specific amount.	18	Policy Legal
If repeal is not feasible, jurisdictions should lengthen the applicable limitation period for UNCAC offenses.	18	Policy Legal
Jurisdictions should introduce or apply laws or jurisprudence delaying the start of the time limitation period until there is no immunity preventing prosecution.	18	Policy Legal
Jurisdictions should introduce or apply laws or jurisprudence delaying the start of the time limitation period until discovery of the crime.	18	Policy Legal
In cases where statutes of limitation act as a barrier to recovering stolen assets, jurisdictions should encourage prosecutors to identify possible charges (such as embezzlement, money laundering, and possession of stolen assets) or other avenues—including civil actions and NCB confiscation—to which a more favorable statute of limitations regime can be applied.	18	Operational Legal
Requested jurisdictions should agree to provide MLA without consideration of their own limitation period because it is the limitation period in the originating jurisdiction that should govern.	18	Operational Legal
Jurisdictions should put mechanisms in place to give effect to foreign freezing, seizure, and confiscation orders, including value judgments in the criminal context. Limitations on the jurisdictions or the types of persons to which such direct enforcement can be applied should be removed. The legislation should also allow for the entry of judgments against substitute assets or value-based criminal orders.	19	Policy Legal
For UNCAC offenses, jurisdictions should put in place legislation that allows for the return of all assets confiscated upon foreign request (minus expenses) in accordance with UNCAC Article 57.	20	Policy Legal
For all other offenses, including those set out in UNTOC, jurisdictions should put in place legislation that allows for direct sharing of assets based on domestic law in the absence of a bilateral asset-sharing agreement. Bilateral sharing agreements setting out how assets are to be disposed of or shared may still be reached on a case-by-case basis.	20	Policy Legal
Jurisdictions should identify a primary and secondary focal point within their central authority, as initial contact point for inquiries on making requests for assistance. Jurisdictions should also identify other competent authorities as focal points for managing informal inquiries. Focal point information should be kept current and include the name and address of the central or competent agency, the position or title of the focal point, contact details (e-mail, telephone, facsimile), and the languages spoken.	21	Operational

Recommendation	Barrier	Type
Jurisdictions should implement policies and procedures to ensure that focal points within central authorities have the capacity and knowledge to provide information on how to make a request for international assistance.	21	Operational
Jurisdictions should use a variety of avenues to provide information on focal points within their system and to ensure that focal point details remain current; options include use of domestic government Web sites, INTERPOL, and international or regional networks such as CARIN, ARINSA, and IBERRED.	21	Operational
Jurisdictions should strengthen existing asset recovery networks or include asset recovery within an existing regional network. Where no such networks exist, jurisdictions should support their creation, requesting assistance from international organizations when necessary.	21	Operational
Where reciprocity is required, jurisdictions should assume that reciprocity is met unless experience tells otherwise.	22	Policy Legal
Jurisdictions should not refuse to provide assistance on the basis of dual criminality because a limitation period has expired in the requested jurisdiction.	22	Policy Legal
Where dual criminality is required, jurisdictions should use a conduct-based approach in determining whether the requirement can be met.	22	Policy Legal
When concerned about capital punishment, requested jurisdictions should seek assurances that if assistance is provided, the originating jurisdiction will not apply capital punishment.	22	Policy Legal
Jurisdictions should avoid limiting the jurisdictions that can apply for MLA.	22	Policy Legal
Jurisdictions should limit the grounds for refusal of MLA with regard to the provisions of UNCAC and UNTOC and, where required, define any grounds for refusal as clearly as possible, having regard to the nature of the request.	22	Policy Legal
Jurisdictions should not set up mandatory grounds for refusal of MLA but rather clarify criteria for consideration and leave room for the exercise of discretion depending on the circumstances.	22	Policy Legal
Jurisdictions should ensure that MLA requests cannot be refused on the ground that the offense involves fiscal matters.	22	Policy Legal
Jurisdictions should ensure that MLA requests cannot be refused on grounds related solely to economic interests.	22	Policy Legal
Jurisdictions and organizations should use government Web sites, MLA focal points, and third-party databases to make available MLA laws, regulations, and tools, along with explanatory guidelines and sample requests for assistance, preferably in at least one of the internationally accepted languages. Examples of outlets are UNODC IMoLIN, UNCAC Legal Library, the StAR initiative, and the ICAR (International Centre for Asset Recovery) Web site.	23	Operational

Recommendation	Barrier	Type
Central authorities designated as focal points for MLA requests should, in partnership with relevant domestic agencies: • provide ready access to laws and regulations on MLA on the Internet; • issue and regularly update guidelines for foreign jurisdictions on requirements for making MLA or other requests, including a template for a request and sample requests, and update them regularly; • issue written policies and procedures on MLA to assist relevant staff to initiate and transmit MLA requests and to facilitate the timely processing of requests from foreign jurisdictions; and • provide relevant staff with formal and on-the-job training on MLA laws, regulations, and policies and on procedures for making MLA requests and processing incoming MLA requests.	23	Operational
Requested jurisdictions should, under agreement, provide assistance and training through the placement of liaison magistrates, prosecutors, attachés, or legal mentors in originating jurisdictions, particularly those with a significant number of requests or high-value matters. Developed jurisdictions should consider providing financial support, either directly or through assistance packages via multilateral organizations, to developing countries for placement of a liaison officer or attaché in the requested jurisdiction.	24	Policy
Jurisdictions should develop policies and procedures that provide and publicize resources available to originating jurisdictions to assist them in making a request for assistance. Resources could include online information, names of liaison officers, and details of contact persons who can review draft requests.	24	Policy
Originating jurisdictions should increase the quality of translation by using professional translation services and avoid the excessive use of legal jargon in requests.	24	Operational
Where a request is required to be submitted in a foreign language, developed countries should consider assisting developing countries by providing or arranging for translation services.	24	Operational
Providers of technical assistance should consider developing programs that allow, at the request of developing countries, the placement of mentors in originating jurisdictions to build capacity and transfer knowledge on MLA and other elements of international cooperation, potentially aligning such efforts with casework.	24	Operational
Jurisdictions making an MLA request should include contact details of the practitioner who is responsible for the request, including information about the languages spoken by that individual.	25	Operational

Recommendation	Barrier	Type
Jurisdictions should implement policies and procedures for responding to MLA requests. An important element is an acknowledgment receipt that includes names and contact details that the originating jurisdiction may use to follow up on the status of the request. This acknowledgement should be submitted within two weeks after receipt of the request.	25	Operational
Requested jurisdictions should promptly advise originating jurisdictions in writing when an MLA request is denied, including the grounds for refusal and the underlying facts supporting the refusal.	25	Operational
Jurisdictions should permit investigative and preservation measures to proceed without notice to the asset holder, provided that sufficient protections of the due process rights of the asset holder exist at other stages of the proceeding.	26	Policy
Jurisdictions should put statutory limitations on the types of challenges an asset holder can raise in cases where the jurisdiction has been asked to provide assistance to another jurisdiction. They also should, in cases where they are the originating jurisdiction, prohibit asset holders from raising any challenges that could be raised in the litigation pending in the requested jurisdiction. In both situations, the jurisdiction would be denying asset holders the opportunity to make the same argument twice.	26	Policy
Jurisdictions should enforce penalties (such as costs orders) against parties that submit groundless applications solely to delay procedures unnecessarily.	26	Operational
To avoid unnecessary delay in processing requests, jurisdictions should implement procedures for all MLA requests that: • acknowledge receipt of the request within two weeks, providing contact information for the practitioner responsible for managing the request, including an e-mail address, to the originating authority; • establish clear lines of communication between originating and requested jurisdictions; and • provide information to originating jurisdictions about process, timeline, expectations, and any other relevant matters related to the process.	26	Operational
Requested jurisdictions should prioritize requests when informed of the urgency and create special procedures to expedite requests where originating jurisdictions advise that the assistance is urgently required.	26	Operational
Practitioners should communicate with originating jurisdictions to ensure that all aspects of the request are understood, especially if the dollar value is low but the public interest is high.	26	Operational

Recommendation	Barrier	Type
Jurisdictions should develop and maintain publicly available registries, such as company registries, land registries, and registries of nonprofit organizations. If possible, such registries should be centralized and maintained in electronic and real-time format, so that they are searchable and updated at all times.	27	Operational
Jurisdictions should eliminate requirements for overly specific descriptions of the property to be restrained or confiscated, such as requirements for the lot registration number rather than the street address; jurisdictions should also ensure that the requirements applied do not inhibit effective implementation of the requested measure.	27	Operational
Jurisdictions should establish a national bank registry to retain account identification information, including beneficial owners and powers of attorney.	28	Operational
Requested jurisdictions should enact legislation or develop policies and procedures that make available from its national bank registry account identification data, beneficial owner information, and powers of attorney without the submission of a formal MLA request by the appropriate, competent authorities in another jurisdiction.	28	Operational
Jurisdictions should develop policies and procedures that ensure that appropriate limits are placed on access to restrained assets, such as limits on exorbitant fees and a requirement that the defendant show that no other source of funds are available for legal representation. These policies and procedures should balance the rights of the accused to access funds for a defense against the rights of the victim to recover stolen assets.	29	Operational
Developed jurisdictions should consider creation of a special fund to provide financial assistance to developing countries seeking to recover stolen assets located within the developed jurisdiction.	29	Operational
Jurisdictions should encourage law firms to provide services to assist with asset recovery pro bono for jurisdictions that lack the capacity or financial resources to engage in time-consuming and expensive litigation. Alternatively, developed countries that receive requests from developing countries for the return of stolen assets should consider providing financial assistance to the developing country to pay for legal representation.	29	Operational
Jurisdictions should support contingency fee arrangements between private law firms and developing countries seeking the return of their stolen assets in corruption cases and the use of confiscated assets for that purpose, provided that such arrangements are made public, equitable, in line with industry best practices, and in the best interest of the victim country.	29	Operational

Recommendation	Barrier	Type
Jurisdictions, possibly the central and judicial authorities, should take steps to ensure that legal fee arrangements are not abused.	29	Operational
Jurisdictions should ensure that effective asset management measures exist to protect against depletion of restrained or seized assets, as required by UNCAC.	29	Operational
Jurisdictions should include provisions that permit the disposal of rapidly depreciating or perishable seized property where necessary to preserve the value.	29	Operational

Appendix B

Canada

A. MLA Legal Framework and Preconditions to Cooperation (General)

A.1. Relevant Laws, Treaties, and Conventions Dealing with or Including a Component Relevant for MLA and Asset Recovery

- The *Mutual Legal Assistance in Criminal Matters Act* (MLACMA) (http://laws. justice.gc.ca/eng/M-13.6/index.html) allows for the provision of MLA. Canada may not provide MLA directly based on multilateral conventions but only pursuant to the provisions of the MLACM.
- The *Canada Evidence Act* (EA) (http://laws.justice.gc.ca/eng/C-5/index.html) Section 46 allows for the provision of certain forms of MLA, including certain coercive measures, based on letters rogatory if criminal proceedings are pending abroad.
- Canada has entered into bilateral treaties with 33 countries, namely Argentina; Austria; Australia; Bahamas; Belgium; China; Czech Republic; France; Greece; Hong Kong SAR, China; Hungary; India; Israel; Italy; Republic of Korea; Mexico; Netherlands; Norway; Peru; Poland; Romania; Russian Federation; South Africa; Spain; Sweden; Switzerland; Thailand; Trinidad and Tobago; Ukraine; United Kingdom; United States; and Uruguay.
- Canada has ratified the Merida Convention, the Inter-American Convention on Mutual Legal Assistance in Criminal Matters, the Vienna and Palermo Conventions, the Organization of American States Inter-American Convention on Mutual Assistance in Criminal Matters, and the Organisation for Economic Co-operation and Development's Convention on Combating Bribery of Foreign Public Officials in International Business Transactions.

A.2. Legal Preconditions for the Provision of MLA

- Dual criminality is generally not required for requests based on bilateral or multilateral treaties. Administrative agreements with nontreaty states may be concluded only for indictable offenses under Canadian law and thus require dual criminality.
- Foreign restraint and seizing orders may be enforced directly in Canada only if they relate to an indictable offense under Canadian law.

- Reciprocity is required and assumed for countries that have signed a relevant treaty, convention, or administrative agreement with Canada. Administrative agreements may be entered into for specific cases and in the absence of an applicable treaty.

A.3. Grounds for Refusal of MLA

Pursuant to MLACMA Section 9.4, the minister of justice must refuse requests if there are:

- Reasonable grounds to believe that the request has been made for the purpose of punishing a person by reason of his or her race, sex, sexual orientation, religion, nationality, ethnic origin, language, color, age, mental or physical disability, or political opinion.
- Enforcement of the order would prejudice an ongoing proceeding or investigation.
- Enforcement of the order would impose an excessive burden on the resources of federal, provincial, or territorial authorities.
- Enforcement of the order might prejudice Canada's security, national interest, or sovereignty.
- Refusal of the request is in the public interest.

Further grounds for refusal may be contained in applicable bilateral, multilateral, or administrative agreements.

B. MLA General Procedures

B.1. Central Authority Competent to Receive, Process, and Implement MLA Requests in Criminal Matters

- The Ministry of Justice is the central authority to receive any requests for MLA.
- In practice, the ministry performs its function as central authority through the International Assistance Group (IAG), which reviews and coordinates the implementation of MLA requests. The IAG may receive requests either through diplomatic channels or directly from the central authority of the requested entity or state.

B.2. Language Requirements

- Requests have to be submitted in English or French.

C. Asset Recovery Specific

C.1. Stage of Proceedings at Which Assistance may be Requested

- Tracing measures under the MLACM are available once a criminal investigation has been initiated in the requesting country.
- The measures under the EA, including direct enforcement of foreign freezing and seizing orders, are available only after formal charges have been brought before a foreign court or tribunal. It is not required that a conviction has been obtained.

Tracing

C.2. Available Tracing Mechanisms

- Under MLACMA Section 11 and 12, search warrants may be issued by a Canadian court if there are reasonable grounds to believe that an offense has been committed under the law of the requesting country, evidence of the commission of the offense or information on the whereabouts of a suspect will be found in the place to be searched, and it would not be appropriate to issue a production order. The person executing the search warrant may seize any thing he believes will afford evidence of, has been obtained by, is intended to be used, or has been used in the commission of an offense.
- Under MLACMA Section 18, a Canadian judge may issue a production order if there are grounds to believe that an offense has been committed under the law of the requesting country, and evidence of the commission of the offense or information on the whereabouts of the suspect will be found in Canada. Items or documents subject to privilege or nondisclosure under Canadian law cannot be compelled. EA Section 46 also allows for the issuance of production orders and for the compelled testimony of witnesses by Canadian courts if criminal charges have been brought in the requesting country.
- Other measures provided for under the MLACMA and the EA include video or audio-link of a witness in Canada to proceedings in a foreign jurisdiction, an order for the lending of exhibits that have been tendered in Canadian court proceedings, an order for the examination of a place or site in Canada, the transfer of a sentenced prisoner to testify or assist in an investigation, and service of documents and account monitoring orders.

C.3. Access to Information Covered by Banking or Professional Secrecy

- Privileged information can be obtained pursuant to an MLAT search warrant if any information over which privilege is claimed is sealed and filed with the court.

Provisional Measures (Freezing, Seizing, and Restraint Orders)

C.4. Direct Enforcement of Foreign Freezing or Seizing Orders

- MLACMA Section 9.3 allows for the direct enforcement of foreign restraint or seizing orders if a person has been charged with an offense in the requesting jurisdiction and if the offense would be an indictable offense in Canada.
- Upon approval by the minister of justice, the attorney general may file the order with the Superior Court of Criminal Jurisdiction of the relevant province. The order is then entered as an order of that court and may be executed in Canada.

C.5. Issuance of Domestic Provisional Measures upon Request by a Foreign Jurisdiction

- **Legal basis:** There are no provisions that permit domestic provisional measures within the Criminal Code to be used by a foreign state.

- **Procedure:**
- **Evidentiary requirements:**
- **Time limit:**

Confiscation

C.6. Enforcement of Foreign Confiscation Orders

- **Legal basis:** MLACMA Section 9.
- **Procedure:** Subject to approval by the minister of justice, MLACMA Section 9 allows for the direct enforcement of foreign confiscation judgments in Canada. Upon approval by the minister, the attorney general may file the judgment with the Superior Court of Criminal Jurisdiction of the relevant province. The order is then entered as the judgment of that court and may be executed in Canada pursuant to domestic law.
- **Evidentiary requirements:** Foreign confiscation judgments may be enforced in Canada if the affected person has been convicted of an offense in the requesting country, if the offense would be an indictable offense under Canadian law, and if the judgment is final. The judgment may extend to any offense-related property or any proceeds of crime.

C.7. Applicability of Non-Conviction Based Asset Forfeiture Orders

- Some but not all provinces in Canada can enforce civil forfeiture orders.

C.8. Confiscation of Legitimate Assets Equivalent in Value to Illicit Proceeds

- A foreign confiscation order may be enforced under MLACMA section 9 (see C.6.).

D. Types of Informal Assistance

- Informal assistance may be provided by the FINTRAC (FIU and FI Supervisor) (http://www.fintrac.gc.ca/), the Office of the Superintendent of Financial Institutions (http://www.infosource.gc.ca/inst/sif/fed04-eng.asp), provincial securities regulators, and the police.
- MOUs are required only by FINTRAC (both as supervisor and as FIU). All other authorities are empowered to provide decentralized types of assistance also in the absence of MOUs.
- Canada maintains and uses attaché offices.[92]

---

92. Practitioners should contact the nearest Canadian embassy to determine the appropriate attaché office.

Cayman Islands

A. MLA Legal Framework and Preconditions to Cooperation (General)

A.1. Relevant Laws, Treaties, and Conventions Dealing with or Including a Component Relevant for MLA and Asset Recovery

- *Criminal Justice (International Cooperation) Law* (CJICL) allows for MLA in the context of all serious offenses under Cayman Islands law if requested by a country listed in the annex to the CJICL (the list is identical with list of signatories to the Vienna Convention).
- *Proceeds of Criminal Conduct Law* (PCCL) later repealed and replaced by the *Proceeds of Crime Law, 2008,*[93] and *Misuse of Drugs Law* (MDL) govern the registration and/or enforcement of external confiscation orders. Requests for the enforcement of such orders may be requested only by countries listed in the annex to the law (list is identical with list of signatories to the Vienna Convention).
- *Evidence (Proceedings in other Jurisdictions)(Cayman Islands) Order* (EO) enables the Grand Court to provide assistance to foreign courts in obtaining evidence in criminal and civil cases in which charges have been brought against the defendant. Requests are to be made through letters rogatory. The measures may be requested by any country.
- Cayman Islands may not provide MLA directly based on international treaties but only based on the CJICL, the PCCL, the MDL, or the EO.
- The Cayman Islands have entered into a bilateral MLA Treaty with the United States. The United Kingdom's ratification of the Vienna Convention has been extended to the Cayman Islands. The United Kingdom's ratification of the Merida Convention has not yet been extended to the Cayman Islands.

A.2. Legal Preconditions for the Provision of MLA

- Dual criminality is a requirement in all cases, but technical differences in the categorization of offenses do not pose an impediment to MLA.
- Reciprocity is required in all cases.

A.3. Grounds for Refusal of MLA
A request for MLA may be refused if:

- Form requirements as stipulated in the applicable laws are not met.
- The request does not establish reasonable grounds for believing that a criminal offense has been committed.
- The request does not establish reasonable grounds for believing that the information sought relates to the offense and is located in the Cayman Islands.
- The request is likely to prejudice the security, public order, or other essential interests of the Cayman Islands.

---

93. The PCCL still applies to offenses committed before September 2008.

- The authorities in the Cayman Islands would be prohibited by law from carrying out the action requested if the offense had been committed in the Islands.
- It is contrary to the laws of the Cayman Islands to grant MLA in circumstances to which the request relates.
- The request is received from a foreign body other than juridical (courts or tribunals exercising jurisdiction) or law enforcement authorities (attorneys generals, prosecutorial and investigative authorities).

B. MLA General Procedures

B.1. Central Authority Competent to Receive, Process, and Implement MLA Requests in Criminal Matters

- The central authority for all requests made pursuant to the CJICL, the MDL, and the PCCL is the attorney general; counsel in the attorney general's chambers will be instructed to execute the request.
- The central authority for all requests made through letters rogatory based on the EO is the Grand Court of the Cayman Islands. In practice, all letters rogatory are handled by the attorney general, who instructs counsel in his chambers to apply to the Grand Court for granting of the request. If the Grand Court grants the request, the evidence will be transmitted to the requesting court by the clerk of the Grand Court.
- The central authority to receive MLA requests based on the bilateral treaty with the United States is the chief justice.

B.2. Language Requirements

- All requests for MLA must be submitted in English.

C. Asset Recovery Specific

C.1. Stage of Proceedings at Which Assistance may be Requested

- Assistance based on the CJICL may be granted during the investigative stage if there are reasonable grounds for suspecting that a specified person has committed or has benefited from an offense.
- Assistance based on the MDL and the PCCL may be granted only after proceedings have been instituted against the defendant but before they have concluded and an external confiscation order has been made or appears likely to be made, or if the Grand Court is satisfied that proceedings will be instituted against the defendant within 21 days.
- Assistance based on the EO may be granted only after charges have been brought against the defendant.

Tracing

C.2. Available Tracing Mechanisms

Pursuant to CJICL Section 3, the measures available to respond to formal MLA requests include:

- The taking of evidence or statements from persons.
- Production orders for information and items of evidence, including originals or certified copies of relevant bank, financial, corporate, or business records, may be issued if there are reasonable grounds to suspect that a specified person has carried out or has benefited from a serious offense, the material to which the application relates is of substantial value to the request and is not subject to legal privilege, and it is in the public interest that the material be produced or access to the requested information be given.
- Searches and seizures for evidentiary purposes may be ordered by the Grand Court if a production order has not been complied with; or if there are reasonable grounds to suspect that a specified person has carried out or has benefited from a serious offense and it would not be practical to issue a production order in relation to the material, or the investigation could be seriously prejudiced unless immediate access to the material is secured; or if there are reasonable grounds to believe that a specific person has carried out or benefited from a serious offense and that material relating to the specified person or to a serious offense is on the premise and of substantial value to the request. Any material, other than items subject to legal privilege, that is likely to be of substantial value to the investigation for which the warrant was issued may be seized.
- Proceeds, property, instruments, or such other things may be identified and traced for the purposes of evidence.
- Criminally obtained assets may be immobilized.
- Assistance may be given in proceedings related to forfeiture and restitution.
- Pursuant to CJICL Section 10, based on a request by a foreign jurisdiction, the central authority may apply to the court for the taking of testimony.

C.3. Access to Information Covered by Banking or Professional Secrecy

- Access to information covered by confidentiality may be provided through issuance of a production or a search and seizure order. Confidential information may be provided only if it is needed for the investigation or prosecution of a criminal offense abroad and if the governor has specifically authorized the disclosure of the confidential information. For requests through letters rogatory, the Grand Court, rather than the governor, has to authorize and determine the extent to which information may be shared.

Provisional Measures (Freezing, Seizing, and Restraint Orders)

C.4. Direct Enforcement of Foreign Freezing/Seizing Orders

- Foreign freezing or seizing orders may not be directly enforced in the Cayman Islands. Any form of assistance with the restraining or seizing of property has to be provided based on the MDL and PCCL or the CJICL as outlined below.

C.5. Issuance of Domestic Provisional Measures upon Request by a Foreign Jurisdiction

- **Legal basis:** MDL or the PCCL (depending on the crime involved).
- **Procedure:** The Cayman Islands Court may issue a domestic restraint order based on a foreign request.
- **Evidentiary requirements:** A restraint order may be issued if proceedings have been instituted against the defendant in the requesting country, the proceedings have not concluded, and either an external confiscation order has been made or there are reasonable grounds to believe that such an order may be made; or if it appears that proceedings are about to be instituted against the defendant and there are reasonable grounds to believe that such a confiscation order may be made in the course of such proceedings. Restraint orders may be applied to all realizable property held by a specified person, including property transferred to him after the making of the restraint order, or to property specified in the order.
- **Time limit:** If after 21 days of the taking of the restraint measure in the Cayman Islands the proceedings have not been instituted in the requesting country, the provisional measure will be lifted. Proceedings are considered to be instituted in the requesting country when charges have been brought against a defendant or an application for an external confiscation order has been made.

Confiscation

C.6. Enforcement of Foreign Confiscation Orders

- **Legal basis:** PCCL Sections 43–48 or the relevant provisions of the MDL.
- **Procedure:** External confiscation orders may be registered and consequently directly enforced in the Cayman Islands Court by the Grand Court based on a request by the attorney general.
- **Evidentiary requirements:** External confiscation orders may be registered if the amount payable under the order is at least $30,000 or it is in the public interest to register the order; if at the time of registration, the order is in force and not subject to appeal; in cases where the person against whom the order was made did not appear in the proceedings, and the defendant received notice of the proceedings in sufficient time to enable him to defend them; and when enforcing the order in the Cayman Islands is not contrary to the interests of justice.

C.7. Applicability of Non-Conviction Based Asset Forfeiture Orders

- It is unclear whether and under what circumstances foreign civil forfeiture orders may be enforced against funds or assets in the Cayman Islands. In certain cases (*Montesinos-Torres, Re Codelco, Canadian Arab Financial Corporation and others v. Player*), the Court allowed for the enforcement of civil forfeiture orders, whereas *In the Matter of Falcone*, the court did not interpret domestic legislation to allow the enforcement of civil forfeiture judgments.

C.8. Confiscation of Legitimate Assets Equivalent in Value to Illicit Proceeds

As discussed in sections 16, 18, 19, 44(a)–45, 133–135, 70–71, 78–79, and 45(2) of the *Proceeds of Crime Law (2008)*, similar to the United Kingdom, it is common in the Cayman Islands to restrain all assets during criminal investigation, even beyond the amount alleged in the crime, because not only can the Cayman Islands recover from legitimate assets but there are occasions when the defendant may be required to prove that all assets acquired in the previous six years are from legitimate sources; otherwise, the assumption is that they are the proceeds of crime. Even legitimate gifts in certain circumstances can be restrained and confiscated.

The Court ultimately conducts an exercise where it determines the "recoverable amount" (the amount representing the proceeds of crime) and the "available amount" (the asset base, legitimate or illicit, of the person from which the recoverable amount can be taken).

D. Types of Informal Assistance

- Informal assistance may be provided by CAYFIN (FIU) (http://www.fra.gov.ky/), the Cayman Islands Monetary Authority (CIMA) (http://www.cimoney.com.ky/), as well as the police and customs and tax authorities.

France

A. MLA Legal Framework and Preconditions to Cooperation (General)

A.1. Relevant Laws, Treaties, and Conventions Dealing with or Including a Component Relevant for MLA and Asset Recovery

- Pursuant to the Code of Criminal Procedures (CPC) Article 694, France may provide MLA directly based on international conventions and agreements. France has ratified the Merida, Vienna, Palermo, and Terrorism Financing Conventions as well as the European Convention in Mutual Assistance in Criminal Matters and its additional protocol, the Council of Europe Convention on Laundering, Search, Seizure and Confiscation of the Proceeds of Crime and the OECD Convention on Combating Bribery of Foreign Public Officials in International Business Transactions.
- In the absence of an international convention, France may provide MLA based on letters rogatory and pursuant to the provisions of the CPC Title X Articles 694 to 696–47 (http://www.legifrance.gouv.fr/html/codes_traduits/code_penal_textan.htm).
- France has entered into bilateral MLA treaties with Brazil and South Africa.

A.2. Legal Preconditions for the Provision of MLA

- Dual criminality is not required for MLA pursuant to the CPC. Depending on the provisions of applicable treaties and agreements, however, dual criminality may be required.
- Reciprocity is required as a precondition to MLA in the absence of an applicable convention. Requesting countries should offer reciprocity in their MLA request and may refer to past cases where assistance was provided to France.

A.3. Grounds for Refusal of MLA

- Pursuant to CPC Article 694-4, requests that threaten public order or the fundamental interests of France may be partially or totally denied.

B. MLA General Procedures

B.1. Central Authority Competent to Receive, Process, and Implement MLA Requests in Criminal Matters

- All requests for MLA must be sent to the Ministry of Justice through diplomatic channels and are carried out by the district prosecutor or the investigating judge of the territorially competent district court. In urgent cases, requests may be sent directly to the competent authorities. Requests received from member states of the European Union may always be sent directly to the competent judicial authority in France.

- As a general principle, all MLA requests are to be executed by the district prosecutor. However, procedural acts that may not be ordered or executed in the course of a preparatory investigation have to be executed by the investigating judge.

B.2. Language Requirements

- Letters rogatory should be in French.
- Translation into the language of the requested country is required by most of the MLA treaties signed by France.

C. Asset Recovery Specific

C.1. Stage of Proceedings at Which Assistance may be Requested

- MLA may be provided as soon as an investigation for a specific offense has commenced in the requesting country.

Tracing

C.2. Available Tracing Mechanisms

- CPC Articles 78 and 101–121 allow interrogation of witnesses and compelled appearance by witnesses who have not responded to a summons before the courts.
- CPC Article 76 allows court warrants for the search of houses during an investigation and the seizing of items and documents if the judge considers the measure necessary for the foreign investigation.
- CPC Articles 92–99-4 allows the search of premises where items or electronic data useful for the discovery of the truth may be found and the seizing of such evidence. A court order is required for both measures.
- Article 77-1-1 allows production orders with respect to any person, establishment, or organization and for any documents or data relevant to the foreign investigation. The production order may also extend to items covered by professional secrecy and information held by financial institutions.
- CPC Article 100-1–100-7 allows interception of telecommunications if the investigation involves a crime punishable with imprisonment of two years or more and the investigation calls for such a measure. Requests for such a measure have to indicate the link to be intercepted, the offense that justified the measure, and the requested duration of interception.
- For EU member states, there is also the possibility to set up Joint Investigation Teams pursuant to CPC Articles 695-2 and 693-3 and to freeze property or evidence under the European Framework Decision pursuant to CPC Articles 695-9-1–695-9-9. Provisions are also made with respect to assistance requested through Eurojust.

C.3. Access to Information Covered by Banking or Professional Secrecy

- Production orders pursuant to CPC Article 77-1-1 and seizing orders pursuant to CPC Articles 92–94 may also extend to items covered by professional secrecy. Documents covered by banking secrecy can be compelled or seized by judicial authorities.

Provisional Measures (Freezing, Seizing, and Restraint Orders)

C.4. Direct Enforcement of Foreign Freezing and Seizing Orders

- Orders to "prevent the destruction, transformation, displacement, transfer or alienation of material liable to be confiscated" issued by EU member countries may be directly enforced in France pursuant to CPC Article 695-9-1 and through a seizing order pursuant to CPC Articles 92–94-4.

C.5. Issuance of Domestic Provisional Measures upon Request by a Foreign Jurisdiction

- **Legal basis:** In the absence of an MLA treaty providing for such measures, CPC Article 694-10 provides for seizure of any asset of any kind that constitutes direct or indirect proceeds of crime, and of any asset whose value corresponds to the proceeds.
- **Procedure:**
- **Evidentiary requirements:**
- **Time limit:** There is no time limitation for seizing orders under the CPC.

Confiscation

C.6. Enforcement of Foreign Confiscation Orders

- **Legal basis:** CPC Article 659-9-1 for confiscation orders issued by EU courts. Direct enforcement of confiscation orders is possible only for EU member states.
- **Procedure:**
- **Evidentiary requirements:**

C.7. Applicability of Non-Conviction Based Asset Forfeiture Orders

- Although France does not provide for non-conviction based forfeiture, the High Court has enforced foreign non-conviction based orders to the extent that confiscation would have been possible under French law in similar circumstances.

C.8. Confiscation of Legitimate Assets Equivalent in Value to Illicit Proceeds

- Under CPC Article 131-21, value-based confiscation is permitted where the assets cannot be located or are no longer available.

D. Types of Informal Assistance

- Assistance may be provided by TRACFIN (FIU).
- France has liaison magistrates posted in Canada, Czech Republic, Germany, Italy, Morocco, Netherlands, Spain, United Kingdom, and United States.[94]

---

94. Practitioners should contact the nearest French embassy to determine the appropriate attaché office.

Germany

A. MLA Legal Framework and Preconditions to Cooperation (General)

A.1. Relevant Laws, Treaties, and Conventions Dealing with or Including a Component Relevant for MLA and Asset Recovery

- Germany may provide MLA based on the *Law on International Assistance in Criminal Law Matters* (LIACM) (http://www.gesetze-im-internet.de/irg/index.html) as well as on the basis of multilateral and bilateral treaties. Where an international treaty exists, the LIACM is applied only to cases that are not, or are not conclusively, covered by the treaty provisions.
- Germany has ratified the Vienna, Palermo, and Terrorism Financing Conventions and the Council of Europe Convention on Laundering, Search, Seizure and Confiscation of the Proceeds from Crime. Germany has signed but not yet ratified the Merida Convention.

A.2. Legal Preconditions for the Provision of MLA

- Only requests for application of coercive measures, including search and seizing measures, are subject to the requirement of dual criminality. Other forms of assistance may be granted even in the absence of dual criminality.

A.3. Grounds for Refusal of MLA
MLA may be refused if:

- The request is made under circumstances in which German courts or authorities could not render mutual assistance to one another.
- Granting a request would conflict with essential principles of the German legal system.
- The execution of the request would contravene the principles contained in Article 6 of the Treaty on European Union.

B. MLA General Procedures

B.1. Central Authority Competent to Receive, Process, and Implement MLA Requests in Criminal Matters

- The Federal Ministry of Justice through the Federal Office of Justice in Bonn is the central authority to receive and decide on foreign request for MLA.
- In practice, the Federal Office of Justice executes requests through delegation to the local public prosecutor within the regional courts. Requests relating to *laender* (states) may be delegated to the *laender* authorities by way of an agreement.

B.2. Language Requirements

- Requests have to be submitted in German, English, or French.

C. Asset Recovery Specific

C.1. Stage of Proceedings at Which Assistance may be Requested

- MLA may be provided as soon as an investigation for a criminal offense has been initiated in the requesting country.

Tracing

C.2. Available Tracing Mechanisms

- LIACM Section 67 subsection 2 allows search and seizing orders for evidentiary purposes if dual criminality is met. Search and seizing warrants may generally be issued only by the courts. In exceptional circumstances, the prosecutor may order search and seizing measures without court involvement.
- LIACM Section 66 subsection 1 allows surrender of property and documents that may serve as evidence in foreign proceedings; that was obtained for or from the offense forming the basis of the request or as a result of the sale of an object obtained for or from the offense forming the basis of the request; or that was obtained as compensation for the destruction, damage, or withdrawal of such property; or that emanated from or were used or intended for use in the commission or preparation of the offense forming the basis of the request. The measure is subject to dual criminality and may be taken only if the requesting authority submits a seizing order for the property or a declaration showing that the requirements for seizure would be met under the law of the requesting state and if there is no final and enforceable foreign ruling pertaining to the property.

C.3. Access to Information Covered by Banking or Professional Secrecy

- Under German law, "banking secrecy" does not preclude the provision of MLA in criminal matters.

Provisional Measures (Freezing, Seizing, and Restraint Orders)

C.4. Direct Enforcement of Foreign Freezing and Seizing Orders

- Pursuant to LIACM Article 66 subsection 1, foreign seizing orders may be applied directly in Germany if dual criminality is met.

C.5. Issuance of Domestic Provisional Measures upon Request by a Foreign Jurisdiction

- **Legal basis:** AIMC Section 66 subsection 1; LIACM Section 58 in combination with Section 111b to 111d of the Code of Criminal Procedure.
- **Procedure:** Foreign countries may request securing measures in Germany (securing of objects through seizure, and *in rem* attachment of property) to prepare a confiscation in the requesting country.

- **Evidentiary requirements:** Requests may be granted only if dual criminality is met and if the requirements for a seizure would be met under the law of the requesting state.

Confiscation

C.6. Enforcement of Foreign Confiscation Orders

- **Legal basis:** LIACM Section 48.
- **Procedure:** The LIACM allows for the direct enforcement of foreign confiscation orders by virtue of an *exequatur* decision. Once a request has been granted, the foreign order is implemented as a domestic order pursuant to the relevant provisions of the Criminal Procedure Code.
- **Evidentiary requirements:** Foreign confiscation orders may be enforced directly only if a complete, legally binding, and enforceable ruling is submitted with the request; if the sentenced person had an opportunity to be heard and to defend himself; and if the sanctions were imposed by an independent court; if a confiscation order could have been made under the German Criminal Procedure Code if the proceedings had been conducted in Germany; and if the statute of limitations has not lapsed.

C.7. Applicability of Non-Conviction Based Asset Forfeiture Orders

- LIACM Section 48 allows for the execution of both foreign forfeiture and confiscation orders issued by a court (criminal or other court) in the requesting country, provided the order is based on a punishable offense.

C.8. Confiscation of Legitimate Assets Equivalent in Value to Illicit Proceeds

- Pursuant to LIACM section 49, foreign confiscation orders can be enforced if an order of this kind could have been issued in accordance with German law irrespective of the provision in section 73 subsection 1, second sentence of the criminal code. Equivalent-value confiscation is possible under German law.

D. Types of Informal Assistance

- Informal assistance may be provided by the federal criminal police, BaFin, and the financial intelligence unit (http://www.bka.de/). The BKA (Bundeskriminalamt) has attaché offices in some embassies.[95]

---

95. Practitioners should contact the nearest German embassy to determine the appropriate attaché office.

Guernsey

A. MLA Legal Framework and Preconditions to Cooperation (General)

A.1. Relevant Laws, Treaties, and Conventions Dealing with or Including a Component Relevant for MLA and Asset Recovery

- The *Criminal Justice (International Cooperation)(Bailiwick of Guernsey) Law* (CJICL), the *Criminal Justice (Proceeds of Crime)(Bailiwick of Guernsey) Law* (POCL), the *Drug Trafficking (Bailiwick of Guernsey) Law* (DTL), the *Terrorism and Crime (Bailiwick of Guernsey) Law* (TL), and the *Forfeiture of Money in Civil Proceedings (Bailiwick of Guernsey) Law* (FOML) (http://www.guernseylegalre sources.gg/ccm/navigation/orders-in-council/guernsey---bailiwick/c/crime-and-criminal-justice/) allow for a wide range of MLA to any country.
- The *Criminal Justice (Fraud Investigation) (Bailiwick of Guernsey) Law* (FIL) (http://www.guernseylegalresources.gg/ccm/navigation/orders-in-council/ guernsey---bailiwick/c/crime-and-criminal-justice/) serves as a legal basis to grant MLA in cases involving serious or complex fraud.
- The *Companies Securities (Insider Dealing) (Bailiwick of Guernsey) Law* (IDL) (http://www.guernseylegalresources.gg/ccm/navigation/orders-in-council/ guernsey---bailiwick/c/crime-and-criminal-justice/) serves as a legal basis to grant MLA in cases involving insider dealing.
- The *Proceeds of Crime Law (Enforcement of Overseas Confiscation Orders) Ordinance* (PCLOCO), the *Drug Trafficking (Designated Countries and Territories) Ordinance* (DTDCTO), the *Terrorism and Crime (Enforcement of External Orders) Ordinance* (TLEO) (http://www.guernseylegalresources.gg/ccm/naviga tion/ordinances/guernsey---bailiwick/c/crime-and-criminal-justice/), and the *Forfeiture of Money, etc in Civil Proceedings (Designation of Countries) (Bailiwick of Guernsey) Regulations* (FOMR) (http://www.guernseylegalresources.gg/ccm/ navigation/statutory- instruments/2008/2009/guernsey---bailiwick/c/crime-and-criminal-justice/) govern the issuance of seizing orders and the registration and enforcement of external confiscation orders relating to the proceeds of crime and terrorist funding. These enactments apply to the proceeds of all offenses that would be "triable on indictment" under Guernsey law and upon request by "designated countries." All offenses that are not classified as exclusively summary offenses are indictable. There are very few summary offenses, and they are mostly minor public order and traffic offenses.
- Guernsey has entered into Double Taxation Arrangements (DTAs) with the United Kingdom and Jersey, both of which contain provisions for the exchange of information in tax matters. Negotiation of DTAs with 6 other countries is expected to commence shortly. In addition, Guernsey has signed 15 Tax Information Exchange Agreements (TIEAs) to date. TEIA negotiations are currently being conducted with more than 20 countries.

A.2. Legal Preconditions for the Provision of MLA

- Mutual legal assistance under the FOML requires reciprocity.

- Search and seizure orders pursuant to CJICL Section 7 may be issued only for conduct that would be a criminal offense punishable with imprisonment under Guernsey law.
- Any measures taken pursuant to FIL Section 2 or IDL Section 10 require dual criminality.
- Seizing and confiscation measures pursuant to the POCL, the DTL, the TL, the FOML, and the designating ordinances and regulations listed below require that the conduct would constitute an "offense triable on indictment" under Guernsey law.
- Measures pursuant to the POCL, the DTL, the TL, and the FOML (except for civil seizure) are available only to a list of "designated countries" under the PCLOCO, the DTDCTO, the TLEO, and the FOMR.

A.3. Grounds for Refusal of MLA

- Assuming that any dual criminality, designation, or reciprocity requirements are met, there are no legal provisions governing the refusal of MLA.
- In practice, the attorney general will always exercise his powers in a manner that complies with Guernsey's human rights law. Mutual legal assistance will not be provided to a jurisdiction where assistance is requested in connection with an offense that is subject to the death penalty, unless an undertaking is given that such a sentence will not be imposed.
- In practice, assistance may not be provided in cases where it can be demonstrated that the request is politically motivated. The attorney general will, as a matter of course in these cases, consult the U.K. authorities.

B. MLA General Procedures

B.1. Central Authority Competent to Receive, Process, and Implement MLA Requests in Criminal Matters

- The attorney general is the central authority for all MLA requests.
- In practice, requests received by the attorney general are handled by a member of the criminal team in the Chambers of the Law Officers of the Crown, who will arrange the date on which the evidence will be given before the court, inform the requesting state of the date, summon the witnesses, or take any other measure required to implement the request. Eventually, the matter is taken before the attorney general, who approves the proposed course of action, issues the relevant notices for implementation, and refers the case to one of the courts in the Bailiwick.

B.2. Language Requirements

- All requests have to be submitted in English or with English translation.

Asset Recovery Specific

C.1. Stage of Proceedings at Which Assistance may be Requested

- Most measures pursuant to the CJICL, the FIL, the POCL, the DTL, the TL, and the IDL may be taken as soon as an investigation for an offense has been initiated in the requesting country. Assistance may be granted under the FOML as soon as a civil forfeiture investigation has been initiated in the requesting country.
- Search and seizing warrants pursuant to the CJICL may be taken if criminal proceedings have been instituted in the requesting country. Proceedings are considered to be instituted in the requesting country once the defendant has been notified in writing that proceedings relating to a specific offense have begun.

Tracing

C.2. Available Tracing Mechanisms

- Under POCL Section 45, DTL Section 63, and FOML Section 20, an *ex parte* application to the court may be made for an order requiring a named person to deliver up specified material. Under POCL Section 46, DTL Section 64, TL Schedule 5, FIL Section 1, and FOML Section 22, the court may grant a warrant to search specified premises and seize material found there. CJICL Section 7 grants similar powers, which may be exercised if criminal proceedings have been instituted or an arrest been made or if there are reasonable grounds to believe that proceedings will be instituted or an arrest be made in the requesting country; if the conduct in question would constitute an offense punishable with imprisonment had it been committed in Guernsey; and if there are reasonable grounds to suspect that evidence relating to the offense is in Guernsey.
- Under POCL Section 48A, DTL Section 67A, TL Schedule 6, and FOML Section 28, the court may make customer information orders, which require financial services businesses to provide specified information related to the assets and identity of a particular customer if that person is the subject of an investigation into money laundering or terrorist financing, or in related matters such as the whereabouts of the proceeds of criminal conduct or terrorist property.
- The court may also make account monitoring orders under POCL Section 48H, DTL Section 67H, TL Schedule 7, and FOML Section 35. These orders require named financial services businesses to provide information about any dealings relating to the account or group of accounts named in the order, for a period not exceeding 90 days. Again, it is a requirement that there be a relevant investigation into money laundering or related issues.
- Under FIL Section 1, the attorney general may require the person under investigation or any other person to answer questions or otherwise furnish information relevant to the investigation; require the production of any documents that appear to the attorney general to relate to the matter under investigation, and to take copies of such documents or request the person producing them to furnish an explanation of the documents.

- Under CJICL Section 4, the attorney general may require any person to attend and give evidence in proceedings before the court in relation to the request, to provide the attorney general or the court any documents or other articles as specified in the notice, and to attend and give evidence in proceedings before the court or the viscount in relation to the evidence produced. The provision also allows for the production of documents or evidence otherwise covered by banking confidentiality.

C.3. Access to Information Covered by Banking or Professional Secrecy

- Apart from legal professional privilege (see below), there is no banking or professional secrecy in Guernsey. A common law principle of confidentiality applies to financial institutions, but it cannot prevent the Guernsey authorities from providing MLA because the legislation governing the obtaining of evidence or information contains provisions that specifically override duties of confidentiality, as follows:
  - POCL Sections 45 (9) (b), 48(10), 48F, and 48L.
  - DTL Sections 63(9) (b), 67(10), 67F, and 67L.
  - Tl Schedule 5 section 5(4)(b), Schedule 6 section 1(3), and Schedule 7 section 5 (2).
  - FOML Sections 23 (2), 33, 39, 45(5), 47(5), and 52(4).
  - CJICL Schedule 1, Para 5, applying the Bankers Books Law.
  - FIL Section 2.
  - IDL Section 11(5).
- Guernsey laws do not allow for the compelled production of documents or evidence covered by legal professional privilege unless there is a suspicion that the lawyer himself committed a criminal offense.

Provisional Measures (Freezing, Seizing, and Restraint Orders)

C.4. Direct Enforcement of Foreign Freezing and Seizing Orders

- Foreign seizing or freezing orders cannot be implemented directly in Guernsey.

C.5. Issuance of Domestic Provisional Measures upon Request by a Foreign Jurisdiction

- **Legal basis:** Primary legislation: POCL Section 35, DTL Section 35 DTL, and TL Section 18/Schedule 2. Subordinate legislation: the PCLOCO, the DTDCTO, and the TLEO.
- **Procedures:** The subordinate legislation contains provisions to facilitate the admissibility of foreign documents and evidence, and modifies the relevant domestic powers in the primary legislation as necessary so that seizing orders may be obtained at the request of designated jurisdictions. Effectively the regime for enforcing overseas orders mirrors the regime for domestic orders. For nondesignated jurisdictions, civil powers of seizure in respect of cash at TL

Section 19/Schedule 3, and of seizure of cash and freezing of money in bank accounts at FOML Sections 6, 10, and 13, can be invoked in the absence of criminal proceedings at the request of any other country in the same way as in domestic cases.

- **Evidentiary requirements:** Orders under the POCL, the DTL, and the TL may be issued if the request of the foreign jurisdiction relates to, respectively, an "offense triable under indictment" under Guernsey law, drug trafficking in line with the definitions in the Vienna Convention, or terrorism as defined in the TL in line with the definition in the UN Terrorist Financing Convention; if proceedings have been instituted or are about to be instituted in the requesting country; and if an external confiscation order has been made or there is reasonable grounds to believe that such an order will be made in the course of those proceedings and the request comes from a "designated country." The restraint order may extend to any property specified in the external confiscation order or, where such an order has not yet been made, to any property held by the defendant, by a person to whom the defendant has directly or indirectly made a gift, or to any property to which the defendant is beneficially entitled. The civil seizure and freezing powers in the TL may be used at the request of a foreign jurisdiction if the relevant property relates to terrorism as described above. The civil seizure and freezing powers in the FOML may be used at the request of a foreign jurisdiction if the relevant property relates to conduct that is unlawful under the criminal law of both Guernsey and the requesting jurisdiction.
- **Time limit:** Restraint orders under the POCL, DTL, and TL are not ordinarily subject to any time limits. Civil orders under the TL and the FOML are subject to an initial time limit of 48 hours, extendable by court order for up to a maximum of two years.

Confiscation

C.6. Enforcement of Foreign Confiscation Orders

- **Legal basis:** Primary legislation: POCL and DTL Sections 35 and 36, and TL Section 18/Schedule 2. Subordinate legislation: the PCLOCO, the DTDCTO, and the TLEO.
- **Procedures:** The subordinate legislation contains provisions to facilitate the admissibility of foreign documents and evidence and modifies the relevant domestic powers in the primary legislation as necessary so that confiscation orders may be obtained at the request of jurisdictions that are designated in the ordinances. The effect is to put in place a regime for enforcing overseas orders that mirrors the regime for domestic orders. This means that once an external confiscation order has been registered, the court may issue a restraint order and, upon application of the attorney general, empower the authorities to realize the restrained property and to satisfy the external confiscation order.
- **Evidentiary requirements:** External confiscation orders may be implemented if at the time of the application for registration the order is in force and not subject to appeal; in cases where the person against whom the order was made

did not appear in the proceedings and the person received notice of the proceedings in sufficient time to enable him or her to defend them; enforcing the order in Guernsey would not be contrary to the interests of justice; and the case relates to "an offense triable under indictment" under Guernsey law, drug trafficking in line with the definition in the Vienna Convention, or terrorism as defined in the TL in line with the definition in the UN Terrorist Financing Convention.

C.7. Applicability of Non-Conviction Based Asset Forfeiture Orders

- Overseas forfeiture orders from designated countries can be given effect under section 49 of the Civil Forfeiture Law.

C.8. Confiscation of Legitimate Assets Equivalent in Value to Illicit Proceeds

- Based on the definitions of "confiscation" and "realizable property" under Guernsey law, the provisions of the POCL and the DTL also allow for the seizing of legitimate assets equivalent to the value of illegitimate property or instrumentalities.

D. Types of Informal Assistance

- Informal assistance may be provided by the Guernsey Financial Services Commission (GFSC) (http://www.gfsc.gg/AML-CFT/Pages/Home.aspx); the Income Tax authority; and the police and customs authorities, including the financial investigation unit, which is a branch of the customs service (http://guernsey-live-fiu.runtime-collective.com/ccm/portal/).
- MOUs are not required by any of these authorities to provide decentralized types of assistance, except for certain types of information regarding tax information, which can be shared with other jurisdictions only under DTAs and TEIAs.

Hong Kong SAR, China

A. MLA Legal Framework and Preconditions to Cooperation (General)

A.1. Relevant Laws, Treaties, and Conventions Dealing with or Including a Component Relevant for MLA and Asset Recovery

- The *Mutual Legal Assistance in Criminal Matters Ordinance* (MLAO) regulates the provision and receipt of assistance in criminal matters (excluding other parts of China) and gives effect to multilateral and bilateral MLA agreements (http://www.hklii.org/hk/legis/ord/525/index.html#s26).
- The *Drug Trafficking (Recovery of Proceeds) Ordinance* (DTROP) enables mutual legal assistance in the restraint and confiscation of proceeds and instrumentalities of drug trafficking. Under the *Drug Trafficking (Recovery of Proceeds) (Designated Countries and Territories) Order (DTROP Or)*, confiscation orders made in relation to proceeds of drug trafficking in designated countries and territories may be registered and enforced in Hong Kong SAR, China (http://www.hklii.hk/hk/legis/en/ord/405/).
- Hong Kong SAR, China, may provide MLA directly based only on the MLAO, the DTROP, or the Evidence Ordinance, but not based on international agreements.
- The *Evidence Ordinance* (EO) enables courts to provide assistance to foreign courts in obtaining evidence in criminal cases that have been or are likely to be instituted (http://www.hklii.org/hk/legis/ord/8/index.html#s77c). Limited types of assistance are available pursuant to the EO and based on letters rogatory.
- As of September 2009, Hong Kong SAR, China, has entered into bilateral MLA Agreements with Australia, Belgium, Canada, Denmark, France, Germany, Israel, Japan, Republic of Korea, Malaysia, Netherlands, New Zealand, the Philippines, Portugal, Poland, Singapore, Switzerland, Ukraine, United Kingdom, and United States. Agreements have been signed but have not yet come into force with Finland, Indonesia, India, Ireland, Italy, South Africa, and Sri Lanka. Furthermore, the Merida, Vienna, Palermo, and Terrorist Financing Conventions apply to Hong Kong SAR, China.

A.2. Legal Preconditions for the Provision of MLA

- All requests for assistance pursuant to the MLAO have to meet dual criminality. Certain types of assistance (search and seizing warrants, compelled production of evidence, issuance of restraint orders, and enforcement and registration of foreign confiscation orders) require not only dual criminality but involvement of a "serious offense" (an offense punishable under the law of the requesting country with imprisonment for not less than 24 months).
- Assistance with public record searches, interviews of witnesses, or the release of information on a consensual basis may be rendered outside the ambit of MLA, and dual criminality is therefore not required.

- Reciprocity is required in all cases, either pursuant to bilateral or multilateral agreements on MLA or through an ad hoc arrangement for a specific request.

A.3. Grounds for Refusal of MLA

Pursuant to MLAO Section 5, a request for MLA *must* be refused if

- The granting of the request would impair the sovereignty, the security, or public order of China (for further details see B.2. and B.3.).
- The request relates to the prosecution of a person for an offense of a political character or is, by reason of the circumstances in which it is alleged to have been committed or was committed, an offense of a political character.
- The request relates to the prosecution or punishment of a person for an act or omission that, if it had occurred in Hong Kong SAR, China, would have constituted an offense under the military law applicable in there but not also under the ordinary criminal law.
- There are substantial grounds for believing that the request was made for the purpose of prosecuting, punishing, or otherwise causing prejudice to a person because of the person's race, religion, nationality, or political opinions.
- The request relates to the prosecution of a person for an offense in a case where the person has been convicted, acquitted, or pardoned by a competent court or other authority in the place, or has undergone the punishment provided by the law of that place, for that offense or of another offense constituted by the same act or omission as that offense.
- The granting of the request would seriously impair the essential interests of Hong Kong SAR, China.
- The request relates to an act or omission that, if it had occurred in Hong Kong SAR, China, would not have constituted an offense against its laws.
- The requesting place is not a prescribed place and fails to provide an undertaking of reciprocity for future requests by Hong Kong SAR, China, for assistance in criminal matters.
- The requesting place is not a prescribed place and the request relates to an investigation into a taxation offense, unless the primary purpose of the request is not the assessment or collection of tax.

Pursuant to MLAO Section 5 (43), a request *may* be refused if

- The requesting jurisdiction is not a prescribed place.
- The requesting jurisdiction is a prescribed place pursuant to the terms of the prescribed arrangement concerned.
- The request relates to an offense punishable with the death penalty and the act, if it had occurred in Hong Kong SAR, China, would not have constituted a serious offense punishable with death or would have constituted a serious offense punishable with death in respect of which the punishment was not normally carried out, and the requesting place fails to assure that the death penalty will not be imposed or carried out.

B. MLA General Procedures

B.1. Central Authority Competent to Receive, Process, and Implement MLA Requests in Criminal Matters

- The secretary for justice is the central authority to make and receive MLA requests in criminal matters. Requests do not have to be sent through the consular or diplomatic channel but may be sent directly to the central authority.
- In practice, MLA requests are processed by an MLA unit within the Department of Justice. The MLA unit acts as a central coordination hub that liaises with both external agencies and the requesting jurisdiction to expedite the request.
- The central authority to receive requests through letters rogatory based on the EO is the chief secretary for administration, who will forward the letters rogatory to the registrar of the High Court.

B.2. Language Requirements

- Foreign requests and their enclosures shall be submitted in English or Chinese.

C. Asset Recovery Specific

C.1. Stage of Proceedings at Which Assistance may be Requested

- Most forms of assistance pursuant to the MLAO may be provided during the investigation stage. Requests for application of provisional measures, however, may be implemented only if proceedings (in which an "external confiscation order" may have been made) have been or are to be instituted in the requesting jurisdiction and the conduct to which the confiscation order relates is a "serious offense."
- Pursuant to the DTROP, assistance may be rendered to restrain proceeds of drug trafficking and to register or enforce confiscation orders relating to drug trafficking offenses.
- Assistance pursuant to the EO is limited to the obtaining of oral and documentary evidence and may be granted only if it is sought for the purpose of proceedings that have been or are likely to be instituted or whose institution is likely if the evidence is obtained.

Tracing

C.2. Available Tracing Mechanisms

- Taking of evidence by a magistrate (MLAO Section 10): This provision includes taking evidence under oath or by live TV link and transmission of the evidence to the requesting country as well as the production of things and the transmission of those things to the requesting jurisdiction.

- Obtaining of evidence (EO Section 76): Evidence may be obtained through examination of witnesses and the production of documents.
- Search and seizures for evidentiary purposes (MLAO Section 12): Search warrants relating to persons, land, and any premises, including the seizing of anything found in the course of the search that is reasonably believed to be relevant, may be issued if the request relates to a serious offense and there are reasonable grounds to believe that a thing relevant to the case is located in Hong Kong SAR, China. A search and seizing warrant may be issued with respect to any "thing" including books, documents, or other records and any articles or substances. The "things," however, do not include any item subject to legal privilege or, if the request relates to an investigation into taxation offenses, any "tax documents" that belong to a tax adviser or auditor and are (in specified ways) connected with the giving or obtaining of advice about the tax affairs of the client.
- Production Orders (MLAO Section 15): Assistance may be sought if the request relates to a serious offense and there are reasonable grounds to believe that the material for which the order is sought is located or likely to be located in Hong Kong SAR, China. The "things," however, do not include any item subject to legal privilege or, if the request relates to an investigation into taxation offenses, any "tax documents" that belong to a tax adviser or auditor and are (in specified ways) connected with the giving or obtaining of advice about the tax affairs of the client.
- Serving of Documents (MLAO Section 31): A person's failure to comply with any foreign process served is not an offense under Hong Kong SAR, China, law.
- Monitoring orders are not available under the MLAO and the DTROP.

C.3. Access to Information Covered by Banking or Professional Secrecy

- Pursuant to MLAO Section 15, the production of items or information covered by other secrecy obligations (including banking secrecy) may be compelled if the secretary for justice is satisfied that it is in the public interest of Hong Kong to do so; items may not be compelled if they are subject to legal privilege or, if the request relates to an investigation into taxation offenses and the production order relates to a tax advisor or a relevant auditor, "tax documents" that belong to a tax advisor or auditor and are (in specified ways) connected with the giving or obtaining of advice about the tax affairs of the client.

Provisional Measures (Freezing, Seizing, and Restraint Orders)

C.4. Direct Enforcement of Foreign Freezing and Seizing Orders

- The MLAO and the DTROP do not provide for direct application of foreign restraint or seizing orders. Rather, requesting countries through the secretary of justice have to apply for issuance of a domestic restraint order pursuant to MLAO Section 27 MLAO or DTROP Section 10 (as modified by DTROP Or) as outlined below. The DTROP is confined to proceeds relating to drug trafficking offenses.

C.5. Issuance of Domestic Provisional Measures upon Request by a Foreign Jurisdiction

- **Legal basis:** MLAO Section 27 in combination with Sections 6 and 7 of Schedule 2; DTROP Section 10 P (as modified by DTROP Or). The DTROP is confined to proceeds relating to drug trafficking offenses.
- **Procedure:** A foreign country through the secretary of justice may apply to the Court of First Instance for a restraining order if the proceedings (in which an "external confiscation order" may be made) have been or may be instituted in the requesting country, and if the offense to which the confiscation order relates is a "serious offense."
- **Evidentiary requirements:** Restraint orders may be issued if an external confiscation order has been made in judicial proceedings or if there are reasonable grounds for believing that such an order may be made in those proceedings, the proceedings have not yet been concluded, and the property is reasonably believed to be located in Hong Kong SAR, China; or if the court is satisfied that judicial proceedings are to be instituted in a prescribed foreign country and there are reasonable grounds for believing that an external confiscation order may be made. Restraint orders may be applied to all realizable property held by or subject to the control of the defendant, including property transferred to him after the making of the restraint order, as well as property held by a person to whom the defendant has made a gift.
- **Time limit:** If, after such a time as is considered "reasonable" by the Court of First Instance, the proceedings have not yet been instituted in the requesting country, the court will discharge the restraining order. Proceedings are considered to be instituted in the requesting country if a case is pending before a court or tribunal.

Confiscation

C.6. Enforcement of Foreign Confiscation Orders

- **Legal basis:** MLAO Section 28 and DTROP Section 28. The DTROP is confined to drug trafficking offenses.
- **Procedure:** External confiscation orders made in relation to "serious offenses" may be registered and consequently directly enforced in Hong Kong SAR, China, by the court of first instance. Once the confiscation order is registered, application may be made to the court to appoint a receiver to enforce the order.
- **Evidentiary requirements:** The court of first instance may register an external confiscation order if the order is in force and not subject to further appeal in the foreign country; the persons affected by the order that did not appear in the proceedings received notice of the proceedings in sufficient time to defend themselves; and enforcing the order in Hong Kong SAR, China, would not be contrary to the interests of justice.

C.7. Applicability of Non-Conviction Based Asset Forfeiture Orders

- The definition of "external confiscation order" encompasses both civil forfeiture and conviction based confiscation orders, and foreign civil forfeiture orders are thus enforceable in Hong Kong SAR, China.

C.8. Confiscation of Legitimate Assets Equivalent in Value to Illicit Proceeds

- The equivalent value of payments, rewards, and instrumentalities of criminal offenses may be confiscated under Hong Kong SAR, China, law.

D. Types of Informal Assistance

- Assistance may be provided by the Joint Financial Intelligence Unit (http://www.jfiu.gov.hk/), the police and customs authorities, as well as the Hong Kong Monetary Authority (HKMA) (http://www.info.gov.hk/hkma/), subject to the provisions laid down in the Banking Ordinance, Cap. 155, Laws of Hong Kong SAR, China.
- MOUs are not required by any of these authorities to provide decentralized types of assistance.

Japan

A. MLA Legal Framework and Preconditions to Cooperation (General)

A.1. Relevant Laws, Treaties, and Conventions Dealing with or Including a Component Relevant for MLA and Asset Recovery

- *The Law for International Assistance in Investigation and other Related Matters (LIAI)* (http://www.moj.go.jp/ENGLISH/information/liai-01.html) regulates MLA for all offenses under Japanese law.
- *The Act on the Punishment of Organized Crime, Control of Crime Proceeds and Other Matters (APOC)* and the *Anti-Drug Special Provisions Law (ADSPL)* contain provisions for the identification, seizing or preserving of assets or instrumentalities, and the execution of foreign confiscation orders for all serious offenses upon request by a foreign state.
- *The Law for Judicial Assistance in Foreign Countries* allows for the serving of foreign judicial documents in Japan and for providing assistance by a Japanese court in taking evidence.
- Japan has concluded bilateral MLA treaties with China; Hong Kong SAR, China; the Republic of Korea, and the United States. Treaties with the Russian Federation and the European Union have been signed and are under parliamentary consideration.
- Japan has signed but not yet ratified the Merida Convention and is a party to the Vienna and the Terrorism Financing Conventions as well as to the Suppression of the Financing of Terrorism Convention and the OECD's Convention on Combating Bribery of Foreign Public Officials in International Business Transactions. Japan provides MLA based on domestic laws while MLA treaties modify the specific conditions under domestic laws.

A.2. Legal Preconditions for the Provision of MLA

- Reciprocity is required in all cases (LIAI Article 4) when a request is made that is not based on a treaty. Countries that are members to applicable multilateral conventions are considered to have met the reciprocity requirement if a specific provision regarding reciprocity is included. In other cases, reciprocity has to be guaranteed by the requesting country every time a request is made.
- Unless an applicable treaty provides otherwise, dual criminality is required in all cases and for all forms of assistance pursuant to LIAI Article 2.2.
- Japan reserves the right to attach certain conditions to the use of information or evidence provided on the basis of a MLA request (principle of specialty).

A.3. Grounds for Refusal of MLA
Pursuant to LIAI Article 2, requests may be refused:

- When the offense for which assistance is requested is a political offense, or when the request for assistance is deemed to have been made with a view to investigating a political offense.

- Unless otherwise provided by a treaty, when the act constituting the offense for which assistance is requested would not constitute an offense under the laws, regulations, or ordinances of Japan were it committed in Japan.
- With respect to a request for an examination of a witness or a submission of material evidence, unless otherwise provided by a treaty, when the requesting country does not clearly demonstrate in writing that the evidence is essential to the investigation.
- Dual criminality is a discretionary refusal in all MLATs and is required for only coercive measures by the Japan-U.S. MLAT. Essentiality is not required in all MLATs.

B. MLA General Procedures

B.1. Central Authority Competent to Receive, Process, and Implement MLA Requests in Criminal Matters

- Without an MLAT: The Ministry of Foreign Affairs (MOFA) is the central authority to receive all requests for MLA pursuant to LIAI Article 3. The MOFA forwards requests to the Ministry of Justice (MOJ), whose International Affairs Division determines whether the request is to be granted and, if so, forwards the request to the competent authority for execution.
- With MLAT: The Ministry of Justice is the central authority to receive all requests for MLA.

B.2. Language Requirements

- Requests have to be submitted in writing and be accompanied by Japanese translations (including supplemental documents).

C. Asset Recovery Specific

C.1. Stage of Proceedings at Which Assistance may be Requested

- All measures pursuant to the LIAI are available during the investigative stage.

Tracing

C.2. Available Tracing Mechanisms

- Serve court documents using the Judicial Assistance Law.
- LIAI Article 8(1) provides for the collection of evidence necessary for the investigation in the foreign country by a prosecutor or judicial officer by asking any person to appear before the authorities for interrogation and by asking the owner, possessor, or custodian of a document or other material to submit it. In addition, the following measures are available: requesting an expert opinion; making an

inspection; and asking a public office or a public or private organization to make reports on necessary matters. There is no specific evidentiary standard, and all the requests are examined on a case-by-case basis.

- Where a person does not comply with a request pursuant to Article 8(1) (that is, noncompulsory measures), the prosecutor or officer may apply to the court for issuance of a warrant.
- LIAI Article 8(2) allows for the competent authority to conduct compulsory measures, upon the court warrant, such as for search and seizure or compulsory inspection of evidence. There is no specific evidentiary standard.
- LIAI Article 10 provides that where a person has refused to make a statement pursuant to Article 8 (1) or where an MLA request is for compulsory examination of a witness by the court, the prosecutor may apply for the compulsory examination of the witness by the judge. In such cases, the requesting country has to clearly demonstrate in writing that the evidence is essential to the investigation, unless otherwise provided by a treaty. Japan cannot conduct the interception of telecommunications (wiretap) under an LIAI request.
- Japan cannot conduct account monitoring under an LIAI request.

C.3. Access to Information Covered by Banking or Professional Secrecy

- Japanese law does not provide for a bank secrecy restriction on the provision of mutual legal assistance. The authorities may therefore obtain and share any information held by financial institutions with the requesting country. However, the MOJ could impose restrictions on the use of such information by the requesting country pursuant to LIAI Articles 14.5 and 14.6.
- Article 105 of the Code of Criminal Procedure, which applies *mutatis mutandis* to MLA requests, exempts information covered by professional legal privilege from the disclosure requirement or from any seizing measures. Nonetheless, under certain conditions, just as in domestic cases, a court order pursuant to LIAI Article 13 may waive professional privilege in the context of MLA.

Provisional Measures (Freezing, Seizing, and Restraint Orders)

C.4. Direct Enforcement of Foreign Freezing and Seizing Orders

- Foreign freezing and seizing orders may not be directly enforced in Japan. Rather, countries may request assistance in securing the asset pursuant to APOC Articles 66–73 or ADSPL Articles 21–23.

C.5. Issuance of Domestic Provisional Measures upon Request by a Foreign Jurisdiction

- **Legal basis:** APOC Articles 59–74 and ADSPL Articles 21 and 22.
- **Procedure:** Without MLAT, the minister of foreign affairs receives the case and forwards it to the minister of justice for consideration. With MLAT, the minister of justice receives the case directly. The justice minister passes the case to a chief

prosecutor, who then appoints a prosecutor who is responsible for the case. The prosecutor in charge applies to the District Court for examination, and once the court order is issued, the crime proceeds can be seized.

- **Evidentiary requirements:** Assistance can be provided if dual criminality is met, the offense for which the measure is requested is an offense covered by APOC Article 59 or the ADSPL as outlined below, the case for which assistance is requested is not pending before Japanese courts, there is reasonable grounds to suspect that the act for which the request is made has been committed, and the property is subject to confiscation under Japanese law.
- **Time limit:** None.

Confiscation

C.6. Enforcement of Foreign Confiscation Orders

- **Legal basis:** APOC Articles 59–74 and ADSPL Articles 21 and 22.
- **Procedure:** Without MLAT, the minister of foreign affairs receives the case and forwards it to the minister of justice for consideration. With MLAT, the minister of justice receives the case directly. The justice minister passes the case to a chief prosecutor, who then appoints a prosecutor who is responsible for the case. The prosecutor in charge applies to the District Court for examination, and once the court order is issued, the crime proceeds can be confiscated.
- **Evidentiary requirements:** Assistance can be provided only if dual criminality is met, the offense for which the measure is requested is an offense covered by APOC Article 59 or ADSPL Articles 21–23, the case for which assistance is requested is not pending before Japanese courts, the confiscation order is final and binding in the requesting jurisdiction, the property is subject to confiscation under Japanese law, and interested persons had an opportunity to present their defenses in the proceeding in the requesting jurisdiction.

C.7. Applicability of Non-Conviction Based Asset Forfeiture Orders

- Non-conviction based asset forfeiture orders are not enforceable in Japan.

C.8. Confiscation of Legitimate Assets Equivalent in Value to Illicit Proceeds

- APOC Articles 59–74 and ADSPL Articles 21 and 22 apply to the restraint and confiscation of legitimate assets equivalent in value to the criminal property or the instrumentalities of the crime.

D. Types of Informal Assistance

- Informal assistance may be provided by the Japanese Financial Intelligence Center (FIU) (http://www.npa.go.jp/sosikihanzai/jafic/jaficenglishpage/jaficenglish .html), the Financial Services Agency (supervisor) (http://www.fsa.go.jp/en/ index.html), as well as the police and customs authorities.

- Statements of Cooperation or MOUs are not required by any of these authorities to provide informal assistance. However, they stipulate certain conditions and facilitate cooperation and information exchange.
- Japan maintains and uses attaché offices and Interpol liaison officers in certain jurisdictions.[96]

---

96. Practitioners should contact the nearest Japanese embassy to determine the appropriate attaché office.

Jersey

A. MLA Legal Framework & Preconditions to Cooperation (General)

A.1. Relevant Laws, Treaties, and Conventions Dealing with or Including a Component Relevant for MLA and Asset Recovery

- The *Criminal Justice (International Cooperation)(Jersey) Law* (CJICL) (http://www.jerseylaw.je/Law/LawsInForce/default.aspx) allows for a wide range of MLA to any country.
- The *Investigation of Fraud (Jersey) Law* serves as a legal basis to granted MLA in cases involving serious fraud.
- The *Proceeds of Crime (Enforcement of Confiscation Orders)(Jersey) Regulations* (POCR) and *Drug Trafficking Offenses (Enforcement of Confiscation Orders) (Jersey) Regulations* (DTOR) (both at http://www.jerseylaw.je/Law/LawsInForce/default.aspx) govern the issuance of seizing orders and the registration and enforcement of external confiscation orders relating to serious offenses.
- The *Evidence (Proceedings in other Jurisdictions)(Jersey) Order* (EO) (http://www.jerseylaw.je/Law/LawsInForce/default.aspx) enables the Royal Court to provide assistance to foreign courts in obtaining evidence in criminal and civil cases.
- The United Kingdom's ratification of the Merida Convention has not yet been extended to Jersey. Ratification of the Vienna Convention, the Terrorism Financing Convention and the European Convention on Mutual Legal Assistance in Criminal Matters 1959 has been extended to Jersey. Jersey is able to provide MLA, notwithstanding the absence of international treaties.

A.2. Legal Preconditions for the Provision of MLA

- Mutual legal assistance does not necessarily require reciprocity. The provision of assistance is at the attorney general's discretion.
- Entry by force, search, and seizure pursuant to CJICL Article 6 may be undertaken only where there is dual criminality. The position under Article 2 of the Investigation of Fraud (Jersey) Law is different (there is no requirement for dual criminality).
- Seizing and confiscation measures pursuant to the POCR require not only that dual criminality is met but that the request relates to conduct that would constitute a "serious offense" under Jersey law (that is, an offense—not drug trafficking—for which a person may receive a custodial sentence of a year or more). Under DTOR there is no requirement for dual criminality or that the conduct would constitute a "serious offense" in Jersey.

A.3. Grounds for Refusal of MLA

- All assistance provided by Jersey is within the discretion of the attorney general. There are no binding guidelines on grounds for refusal of MLA requests but Jersey's MLA policy is to grant all requests unless the request is not proportional or does not fit within the legislative frame work that empowers the attorney general to assist. As a matter of policy, Jersey does not provide assistance in cases where Jersey itself would not request the help of another country in the same circumstances on grounds of costs and/or seriousness. The authorities would be hesitant to provide assistance in cases involving less than £10,000 (or equivalent) or, in the case of serious or complex fraud, less than £2,000,000 (or equivalent). However, this policy does not exclude the provision of MLA based on public policy grounds in cases where the threshold is not met. Reciprocity is not an absolute requirement but will be taken into account when consideration is given to whether or not assistance may be provided.

- There is no requirement to involve the U.K. Foreign Office in any request to Jersey for MLA, although as part of his enquiries the attorney general will in some circumstances take soundings from that office as well as from other agencies before reaching a view.
- Consideration is also given to human rights and the nature of the trial process in the requesting country before a request is granted.

B. MLA General Procedures

B.1. Central Authority Competent to Receive, Process, and Implement MLA Requests in Criminal Matters

- The attorney general is the central authority for all MLA requests.
- In practice, requests are handled in the initial stages by an assistant legal adviser, who reports to and obtains advice from a legal adviser or senior legal adviser on how to proceed with the specific request.

B.2. Language Requirements

- All requests have to be submitted in English or with English translation.

C. Asset Recovery Specific

C.1. Stage of Proceedings at Which Assistance may be Requested

- Most measures pursuant to the CJICL and the *Investigation of Fraud (Jersey) Law* may be taken as soon as an investigation for an offense has been initiated in the requesting country.
- Under CJICL coercive measures such as entry by force, search and seizing warrants, as well as seizing orders pursuant to the POCR and DTOR may be taken only if criminal proceedings have been instituted or there are reasonable grounds to believe that proceedings will be instituted in the requesting country (or in the case of CJICL if a person has been arrested in connection with an investigation or is to be arrested). Proceedings are considered to be instituted in the requesting country once the defendant has been notified in writing that proceedings have

begun relating to a specific offense or an application has been made to a court in the relevant country for an external confiscation order.

Tracing

C.2. Available Tracing Mechanisms

- CJICL Article 5: The attorney general, upon request by a foreign country, may require any person to attend and give evidence in proceedings before the court or the viscount in relation to the request, to provide to the attorney general, the court, or the viscount any documents, or other articles as specified in the notice, and/or to attend and give evidence in proceedings before the court or the viscount in relation to the evidence produced. The provision also allows for the production of documents or evidence otherwise covered by banking confidentiality.
- CJICL Article 6: Upon request by the attorney general, the bailiff may issue a warrant for the search premises for the purpose of discovering evidence and to seize any evidence found on the searched premises if criminal proceedings have been instituted or an arrest has been made or if there are reasonable grounds to believe that proceedings will be instituted or an arrest be made in the requesting country; the conduct in question would constitute a "serious offense" had it been committed in Jersey; and there are reasonable grounds to suspect that there is evidence on premises in Jersey relating to the offense. Any evidence seized by the police has to be transmitted by the attorney general to the requesting country.
- Article 2 *Investigation of Fraud (Jersey) Law*: The attorney general may exercise investigatory powers where there is a suspected offense, wherever committed, involving "serious or complex fraud." Under the law, the attorney general has the power to issue a notice requiring the person under investigation or any other person to answer questions or otherwise furnish information relevant to the investigation, and/or requiring the production of any documents that appear to the attorney general to relate to the matter under investigation. The attorney general may make copies of such documents or request the person producing them to furnish an explanation of the documents.
- EO: Where proceedings have been instituted the attorney general may apply to the Royal Court on behalf of a court or tribunal in the requesting country for an order for the production of documents and witness statements in Jersey.

C.3. Access to Information Covered by Banking or Professional Secrecy

- Article 6 of the *Bankers' Books Evidence (Jersey) Law 1986* grants access to information and documents otherwise covered by banking secrecy based on a court order.
- For mutual legal assistance under the *Investigation of Fraud (Jersey) Law 1991*, Article 2 (9) provides that the attorney general may require disclosure of information covered by banking confidentiality.

- Jersey laws do not allow for the compelled production of documents or evidence covered by legal professional privilege unless there is a suspicion that the lawyer himself committed a criminal offense.

Provisional Measures (Freezing, Seizing, and Restraint orders)

C.4. Direct Enforcement of Foreign Freezing or Seizing Orders

- Foreign seizing or freezing orders cannot be implemented directly in Jersey.

C.5. Issuance of Domestic Provisional Measures upon Request by a Foreign Jurisdiction

- **Legal basis:** POCR Articles 15 and 16 and DTOR Articles 15 and 16.
- **Procedures:** The attorney general may apply for issuance of seizing order (*saisie judiciaire)* to the Royal Court on behalf of a requesting jurisdiction.
- **Evidentiary requirements:** An order may be issued if the request of the foreign jurisdiction relates to a "serious offense" under Jersey law; proceedings have been instituted or are about to be instituted in the requesting country; and an external confiscation has been made or there are reasonable grounds to believe that such an order will be made in the course of those proceedings. Under the POCR, the seizing order may extend to any property specified in the external restraint order or to any realizable property held by the defendant. The DTOR also allows the same action against a person to whom the defendant has directly or indirectly made a gift or to any property to which the defendant is beneficially entitled.
- **Time limit:** Where proceedings have not been instituted, the court may discharge the *saisie judiciaire* if proceedings are not instituted within a time period the court considers reasonable.

Confiscation

C.6. Enforcement of Foreign Confiscation Orders

- **Legal basis:** POCR Section 39; DTOR Section 39.
- **Procedures:** After obtaining a *saisie judiciaire,* the attorney general may apply to the court (following a request from an overseas country) to register an external confiscation order. Once an external confiscation order has been registered, the court may empower the viscount to realize the seized property to satisfy the external confiscation order and pay the confiscated assets into the Criminal Offenses Confiscation Fund or the Drug Trafficking Confiscation Fund (subject to any asset-sharing agreement).
- **Evidentiary requirements:** External confiscation orders may be implemented if at the time of the application for registration the order is in force and not subject to appeal; where the person against whom the order was made did not appear in

the proceedings, and the person received notice of the proceedings in sufficient time to enable him or her to defend them; and enforcing the order in Jersey would not be contrary to the interests of justice.

C.7. Applicability of Non-Conviction Based Asset Forfeiture Orders

- The *Civil Asset Recovery (International Co-operation)(Jersey) Law 2007* allows for the obtaining of evidence and property restraint orders, as well as registration of external civil asset recovery orders.

C.8. Confiscation of Legitimate Assets Equivalent in Value to Illicit Proceeds

- Based on the definitions of "confiscation" and "realizable property" under Jersey law, the provisions of the POCR and DTOR also allow for the seizing of legitimate assets equivalent to the value of illegitimate property or instrumentalities.

D. Types of Informal Assistance

- Informal assistance may be provided by the JFCU (FIU) (http://www.jersey.police .uk/about/departments/JFCU/index.html), the Financial Services Commission (FSC) (http://www.jerseyfsc.org/), and the police and customs authorities.

Liechtenstein

A. MLA Legal Framework and Preconditions to Cooperation (General)

A.1. Relevant Laws, Treaties, and Conventions Dealing with or Including a Component Relevant for MLA and Asset Recovery

- Liechtenstein may provide MLA directly based on international conventions, including the European Convention on Mutual Assistance in Criminal Matters (ECMA), Council of Europe Convention on Laundering, Search, Seizure, and Confiscation of the Proceeds from Crime, the Palermo, Vienna, and Suppression of the Financing of Terrorism (SFT) Conventions, and a bilateral MLA treaty with the United States. Liechtenstein has ratified the Merida Convention.
- For countries with which Liechtenstein does not have an applicable treaty, MLA may be provided based on the *Law on International Mutual Legal Assistance in Criminal Matters* (RHG) (http://www.gesetze.li/Seite1.jsp?LGBlm=2000215). The RHG provides for all kinds of assistance regarding criminal matters, including provisional measures such as the freezing and restraining of assets and the enforcement of foreign judgments, including forfeiture orders (money judgments).

A.2. Legal Preconditions for the Provision of MLA

- All requests are subject to the principle of reciprocity, but reciprocity is assumed for treaty countries.
- With the exception of the serving of foreign documents, all requests based on the RHG have to meet dual criminality. All other cases are determined based on the provisions of the relevant and applicable treaty.

A.3. Grounds for Refusal of MLA
RHG Article 51 provides that MLA is not permissible if

- A request violates the public order or other essential interests of Liechtenstein.
- It cannot be guaranteed that the state making the request would comply with an identical request made by Liechtenstein.
- The offense underlying the request is not sanctioned with legal punishment under Liechtenstein law.
- Special requirements of the Code of Criminal Procedure for coercive measures like wire tapping or search and seizure are not met.
- The request relates to confidential information but the secrecy obligation cannot be lifted even by a Liechtenstein court decision (legal professional privilege, for example). Banking secrecy does not fall under this category.
- Banking secrecy does not fall under any of these categories. If the general conditions for granting MLA are met, account and banking information can be obtained and exchanged with the requesting authority.

B. MLA General Procedures

B.1. Central Authority Competent to Receive, Process, and Implement MLA Requests in Criminal Matters

- The central authority to receive and process all requests related to MLA is the Ministry of Justice (MOJ). Only requests based on the RHG have to be sent through diplomatic channels. Requests based on MLA treaties may be sent directly to the ministry.
- Requests are forwarded by the MOJ to a judge at the Court of Justice who rules whether the assistance will be granted. All MLA requests are also copied to the Office of the Public Prosecutor (OPP) for commenting. The OPP may instigate a domestic investigation based on the facts described in the request. In the MLA proceeding, the OPP is a party and may challenge decisions of the judge. The court examines the request to determine whether the basic legal conditions are met, whether grounds for refusal exist, and whether the request contains sufficient information to be executed.
- Once the court deems the request admissible, it is executed. When the legal assistance proceedings are concluded, the materials to be surrendered are transferred to the MOJ, who forwards them to the requesting foreign authority directly or through diplomatic channels.

B.2. Language Requirements

- Requests have to be made in German or be accompanied by a German translation. Requests based on the Palermo and Merida Conventions may also be sent in English.

C. Asset Recovery Specific

C.1. Stage of Proceedings at Which Assistance may be Requested

- All measures as outlined below are available once a criminal investigation or prosecution has been instituted by the competent authority, which may be an investigating judge; a public prosecutor; or the police, if under the laws of the requesting state the policy are competent to undertake such investigations and the investigation will lead into a judicial investigation. It is not required that proceedings already be pending before a court.

Tracing

C.2. Available Tracing Mechanisms

Liechtenstein may take any measures on behalf of a foreign country that would be available in the context of domestic cases (RHG Article 9), namely:

- *Strafprozessordnung* (StPO) (Criminal Procedure Code) Articles 105–124 provide for the questioning of witnesses in court.

- StPO Article 92 allows for the searches of houses or of persons if there is a suspicion that objects whose possession or inspection could be of importance for a criminal investigation are located in the premises or possessed by that person. StPO Article 96 provides for the seizing of objects and documents found in the course of a search as outlined below.
- Pursuant to StPO Article 98a, banks and finance companies may be required through a court order to disclose client data and provide information and documentation on existing and past business relationships if this disclosure is "necessary to solve" a criminal case or there is an assumption of a relation with criminal proceeds.
- Subject to a court order, StPO Article 103 allows for the surveillance of electronic communications in cases where an investigation relates to an act punishable with imprisonment of one year or more.
- Orders to monitor accounts are not explicitly ruled in law. In practice, it is common that judges order banks to monitor accounts and report certain transactions or carry out transactions only after consent by the court.

C.3. Access to Information Covered by Banking or Professional Secrecy

- Banking secrecy does not apply in domestic criminal investigations or MLA proceedings. Based on an MLA request that outlines the grounds for suspicion that a criminal act was committed in the requesting country and provided that this activity is also punishable under Liechtenstein laws, the judge will order the bank to submit the requested documents or information. Coercive measures may be used if the bank does not comply. A "simple" suspicion is sufficient. The MLA request must include the order of the competent judicial authority of the requesting state ordering the seizure of the banking documentation. If under the law of the requesting state such an order cannot be made (for example, because the documents are held by a bank outside the jurisdiction of the requesting state), the request must enclose a declaration, that under the laws of the requesting state such an order cannot be issued.

Provisional Measures (Freezing, Seizing, and Restraint Orders)

C.4. Direct Enforcement of Foreign Freezing and Seizing Orders

- **Legal basis:** RHG Article 56 and StPO Section 97.
- **Procedures:** Foreign freezing, seizure, or restraint orders are never enforced directly. Foreign countries must send an MLA request. The competent court will then order the freezing, restraint, or seizure order. See C.3.
- **Evidentiary requirements:** A "simple" suspicion is sufficient. For further requirements see C.3.

C.5. Issuance of Domestic Provisional Measures upon Request by a Foreign Jurisdiction

- **Legal basis:** StPO Article 97a.
- **Procedure:** Foreign freezing, seizure, or restraint orders are never enforced directly. Foreign countries must send an MLA request. The competent court will

then order the freezing, restraint, or seizure order. See C.4. The procedure is the same as for any MLA request as described in B.1.

- **Evidentiary requirements:** Seizing orders for criminal proceeds may be issued if there is a suspicion of unjust enrichment or that the proceeds originate from criminal activity; it must be assumed that the enrichment or the assets will be subject to forfeiture. Anything that may be subject to confiscation can be seized pursuant to StPO Article 97a. A "simple" suspicion, which is sufficient to open a preliminary investigation, is sufficient.
- **Time limit:** Seizing orders are issued for a limited time only but may be extended. After two years, extension may be granted only under approval by the Court of Appeals. In practice, provisional orders are usually limited to one year. This time limit can be prolonged for another year and in exceptional cases for further periods of time. However requesting states must provide the court, in due time before the expiration of the time limit, with information about the development of the proceedings and the reasons why the case has not been completed. Otherwise the provisional order will expire.

Confiscation

C.6. Enforcement of Foreign Confiscation Orders

- **Legal basis:** RHG Article 64.
- **Procedure:** Requests for the enforcement of decisions taken by foreign criminal courts received by the MOJ are transmitted to the Court of Justice, which will determine whether there are any circumstances prohibiting the enforcement of the order. Supplementary documents may be requested from the foreign jurisdiction, if necessary for enforcement of the order. If the court is satisfied that all requirements of the RHG are met, it will issue a ruling, adapting the foreign order, and thus making it enforceable in Liechtenstein.
- **Evidentiary requirements:** Foreign confiscation orders may be executed if the decision has been taken in a trial that complies with the basic principles of Article 6 of the Convention for the Protection of Human Rights and Fundamental Freedoms; dual criminality is met and the offense does not constitute a political, military, or fiscal criminal offense; the statute of limitation has not expired; and a prosecution for the same offense is not pending in Liechtenstein or the person has been acquitted or convicted by a Liechtenstein court for the same offense. Foreign confiscation or forfeiture orders may be enforced only if a corresponding domestic order has not yet been issued and if the assets or objects of the order are located in Liechtenstein.

C.7. Applicability of Non-Conviction Based Asset Forfeiture Orders

- Non-conviction based (*in rem*) forfeiture orders fall within the scope of RHG Article 64 and can hence be executed. The Liechtenstein Criminal Code allows non-conviction based forfeiture in domestic proceedings. This concept is well established in the law and practice of Liechtenstein. Problems may arise with the enforcement of "civil" forfeiture orders from common law jurisdictions. Whether the respective "civil" forfeiture order was obtained in a proceeding that can be considered "criminal" pursuant to the RHG is established on a case-by-case basis.

C.8. Confiscation of Legitimate Assets Equivalent in Value to Illicit Proceeds

- Liechtenstein law generally provides for confiscation by an order to pay an amount equal to the proceeds generated by criminal activity, which can also be the basis for the execution of foreign equivalent-value orders.
- Seizure of all assets, tainted or not, can be ordered on the principle that anything that may be subject to confiscation can be seized (StPO Article 96).

D. Types of Informal Assistance

- Informal assistance may be provided by the Liechtenstein FIU (http://www.llv.li/llv-sfiu-home.htm), the Financial Market Authority (http://www.fma-li.li/?l=2&page_id=8), the Liechtenstein Tax Authority, and the police.
- MOUs are not required by any of these authorities to provide assistance. Assistance is granted on the basis of the mentioned treaties or based on domestic law and reciprocity.
- Liechtenstein does not maintain attaché offices abroad, and foreign countries do not maintain such offices in Liechtenstein. Liechtenstein uses attaché offices of foreign countries based in Switzerland or Germany, which are also competent for Liechtenstein.

Singapore

A. MLA Legal Framework and Preconditions to Cooperation (General)

A.1. Relevant Laws, Treaties, and Conventions Dealing with or Including a Component Relevant for MLA and Asset Recovery

- *Mutual Assistance in Criminal Matters Act* (MACMA) (http://statutes.agc.gov.sg/ non_version/cgi-bin/cgi_retrieve.pl?actno=REVED-190A&doctitle= MUTUAL%20ASSISTANCE%20IN%20CRIMINAL%20MATTERS%20 ACT&date=latest&method=part).
- Bilateral MLA treaties with Hong Kong SAR, China, and India.
- Bilateral MLA treaty for drug offenses with the United States.
- Multilateral MLA treaty with the 10 ASEAN (Association of Southeast Asian Nations) countries.
- Singapore has ratified the Vienna, Palermo, Terrorism Financing, and Merida Conventions. MLA may not be granted directly based on the conventions but based only on the provisions of the *MACMA* or an applicable multilateral or bilateral MLA treaty.

A.2. Legal Preconditions for the Provision of MLA

- All requests for assistance under MACMA have to meet dual criminality, but technical differences in the categorization of offenses do not pose an impediment because the underlying conduct is considered and not the label or elements of the offense used by the requesting jurisdiction.
- Reciprocity is required, and this requirement can be met either through an undertaking under MACMA Section 16(2) for an ad hoc arrangement for a specific request (either in the request itself or a separate document) and relating to a specific offense or through an applicable bilateral or multilateral MLA agreement with Singapore.

A.3. Grounds for Refusal of MLA

Pursuant to MACMA Article 20, requests for MLA *must* be refused if, in the opinion of the attorney general,

- The requesting jurisdiction failed to comply with the terms of an applicable MOU or bilateral or multilateral agreement.
- The request relates to the investigation, prosecution, or punishment of a person for a political offense.
- The request relates to the investigation, prosecution, or punishment of a person for an offense under military law only.
- There are substantial grounds to believe that the request was made for the purpose of investigating, prosecuting, punishing, or otherwise causing prejudice to a

person on account of the person's race, religion, sex, ethnic origin, nationality, or political opinions.

- The request relates to the investigation, prosecution, or punishment of a person for an offense in a case where the person has been convicted, acquitted, or pardoned by a competent court or other authority in that country; or has undergone the punishment provided by the law of that country applicable to that offense or of another offense constituted by the same act or omission as the first-mentioned offense.
- Lack of dual criminality.
- The offense to which the request relates is not an offense of sufficient gravity.
- The evidence requested is of insufficient importance to the investigation or could reasonably be obtained by other means.
- It would be contrary to public interest to provide the assistance.
- The appropriate authority of the requesting jurisdiction fails to undertake that the item or information requested will not be used for a matter other than the criminal matter in respect of which the request was made, except with the consent of the attorney general.
- The appropriate authority of the requesting jurisdiction fails to undertake that it will return anything obtained pursuant to a request to take evidence or for search and seizure at the conclusion of the criminal matter in the requesting jurisdiction.
- Provision of the assistance could prejudice a criminal matter in Singapore.

A request for assistance under this part *may* be refused by the attorney general, if pursuant to the terms of the treaty MOU or other arrangements between Singapore and the requesting jurisdiction,

- The assistance would, or would be likely to, prejudice the safety of any person.
- The provision of the assistance would impose an excessive burden on the resources of Singapore.
- The requesting jurisdiction is not declared as a prescribed foreign country under MACMA Section 17 and the appropriate authority of that country fails to give an undertaking of reciprocity under MACMA section 16(2).

B. MLA General Procedures

B.1. Central Authority Competent to Receive, Process and Implement MLA Requests in Criminal Matters

- The attorney general is the designated central authority for all requests for MLA in criminal matters. The attorney general has a set of standard operating procedures, including a set of standard forms, to deal with and facilitate such requests. These documents are available to officials from other countries (http://www.agc .gov.sg/criminal/mutual_legal_asst.htm).
- Requests need not be sent through the consular or diplomatic channel but may be sent directly by the central authority of the requesting State.

B.2. Language Requirements

- Requests and their enclosures shall be submitted in Mandarin, Malay, Tamil, and English or be accompanied by a translation. All requests have to be received in writing.

C. Asset Recovery Specific

C.1. Stage of Proceedings at Which Assistance may be Requested

- Most forms of assistance pursuant to the MACMA may be provided in the investigative stage.
- Restraining orders may be issued only if criminal judicial proceedings have been or are to be initiated. Proceedings are considered to be instituted in the requesting country once criminal charges have been brought against a defendant. If, after three months of issuance of the restraint order, proceedings have not yet been instituted in the requesting country, the order will be lifted.

Tracing

C.2. Available Tracing Mechanisms

- Taking of evidence before a Singapore magistrate for use in criminal proceedings pending in the court of a foreign country pursuant to MACMA Section 21.
- Production orders relating to information, documents, or evidence (including financial records) from financial institutions, other entities, or natural persons (MACMA Section 22) may be issued if there are reasonable grounds for suspecting that a specified person has carried out or benefited from a foreign offense; the thing to which the application relates is likely to be of substantial value (whether by itself or together with another thing) to the criminal matter in respect of which the application was made and does not consist of or include items subject to legal privilege; and it is not contrary to the public interest for the thing to be produced or access to it be given.
- The execution of searches and seizures for evidentiary purposes (MACMA Section 33) may be issued if a request relates to a criminal matter and there are reasonable grounds for believing that the thing to which the request relates is relevant to the criminal matter and is located in Singapore.
- Obtaining of voluntary statements from witnesses.

C.3. Access to Information Covered by Banking or Professional Secrecy

- Financial information can be provided to foreign jurisdictions based only on an order by the High Court in accordance with MACMA Sections 22 (2) and 33.
- Items subject to legal privilege may not be accessed based on the MACMA, including, for example, communications between an advocate or solicitor and client made in connection with the giving of legal advice or in connection with judicial proceedings.

Provisional Measures (Freezing, Seizing, and Restraint Orders)

C.4. Direct Enforcement of Foreign Freezing and Seizing Orders

- MACMA does not provide for direct application of foreign restraint orders. Rather, requesting countries have to apply for issuance of a domestic restraint order through the attorney general pursuant to MACMA Section 29, as outlined below.

C.5. Issuance of Domestic Provisional Measures upon Request by a Foreign Jurisdiction

- **Legal basis:** MACMA Section 29.
- **Procedure:** The attorney general, on behalf of the requesting country, applies to the High Court for a restraining order of property. Restraint orders may be applied to all realizable property held by a specified person, including property transferred to him after the making of the restraint order.
- **Evidentiary requirements:** The High Court may issue the order if a foreign confiscation order has been made in judicial proceedings that have been instituted in that country or it appears that there are reasonable grounds for believing that such an order may be made in those proceedings, the proceedings have not yet been concluded, and the property is reasonably believed to be located in Singapore; or if judicial proceedings are to be instituted in a prescribed foreign country and there are reasonable grounds for believing that a foreign confiscation order may be made in them.
- **Time limit:** If, after three months, proceedings have not yet been instituted in the requesting country, the High Court will lift the restraining order. Proceedings are considered to be instituted in the requesting country once criminal charges have been brought against a defendant.

Confiscation

C.6. Enforcement of Foreign Confiscation Orders

- **Legal basis:** MACMA Section 30.
- **Procedure:** External confiscation orders may be registered and enforced in Singapore by the High Court based upon a request by the attorney general and against property that is reasonably believed to be located in Singapore. A foreign confiscation order is defined as an order by a court in a foreign country for the recovery, forfeiture, or confiscation of payments or other rewards received in connection with an offense against the law of the country or the value of such payments or rewards; or property derived or realized, directly or indirectly, from payments or other rewards received in connection with such an offense, or the value of such property.
- **Evidentiary requirements:** The High Court may register the foreign confiscation order if the order is in force and not subject to further appeal in the foreign

country; if persons affected by the order that did not appear in the proceedings received notice of the proceedings in sufficient time to enable them to mount a defense; and enforcing the order in Singapore would not be contrary to the interests of justice.

C.7. Applicability of Non-Conviction Based Asset Forfeiture Orders

- The definition of "foreign confiscation order" as contained in MACMA Section 2(1) is broad enough to encompass both civil forfeiture and conviction-based confiscation orders. Thus, foreign non-conviction based forfeiture orders are enforceable in Singapore pursuant to MACMA Section 29.

C.8. Confiscation of Legitimate Assets Equivalent in Value to Illicit Proceeds

- As indicated above, a foreign confiscation order is defined in MACMA section 2(1) to cover direct and indirect payments, rewards, or property received in connection with such an offense, or the value of such property. Equivalent-value confiscation is thus possible for proceeds from but not for instrumentalities used or intended to be used in the commission of the relevant offense.

D. Types of Informal Assistance

- Informal assistance may be provided by the Suspicious Transaction Reporting Office (FIU) (http://www.cad.gov.sg/amlcft/STRO.htm/), the Monetary Authority of Singapore (MAS) (http://www.mas.gov.sg/), and the police and customs authorities.
- MOUs are required only by the STRO. The MAS, police, and customs authorities may provide certain types of assistance even in the absence of an applicable MOU.

Spain

A. MLA Legal Framework and Preconditions to Cooperation (General)

A.1. Relevant Laws, Treaties, and Conventions Dealing with or Including a Component Relevant for MLA and Asset Recovery

Spain may provide MLA based on:

- Multilateral agreements, such as the Merida, Palermo, and Vienna Conventions, the Schengen Convention, and the 1959 Council of Europe Convention on MLA in Criminal Matters, the 1990 Council of Europe Convention on Money Laundering, and the EU mutual legal assistance convention and its protocol.
- A number of bilateral agreements with countries in the Americas, North Africa and Asia (Algeria, Argentina, Australia, Bolivia, Brazil, Cabo Verde, Canada, Chile, China, Colombia, Cuba, Dominican Republic, El Salvador, Guatemala, India, Japan, Liberia, Mauritania, Morocco, Mexico, Panama, Paraguay, Peru, the Philippines, Tunisia, United States, Uruguay, República de Bolivariana Venezuela).
- Reciprocity and through letters rogatory pursuant to Article 278 of the Organic Law of the Judiciary.

A.2. Legal Preconditions for the Provision of MLA

- MLA may be rendered based on a treaty or subject to the principle of reciprocity, whereby reciprocity is assumed without a need for guarantees.
- Dual criminality is required for search or seizure of goods. All other measures may be rendered even in the absence of dual criminality. Spanish judges can execute orders freezing property or evidence and confiscation orders within the scope of European Union without verification of dual criminality in a number of cases, provided that the order is issued by a judge of member state and the case involves certain kinds of offenses listed in Law 18/2006, 5th June (seizure), and Law 4/2010, 10th March (confiscation). The offense must also be punishable in the issuing state by a custodial sentence of a maximum of at least three years.
- Where dual criminality is required, the judicial authorities evaluate the acts underlying the offense, regardless of their legal specification.

A.3. Grounds for Refusal of MLA

- Requests based on treaties may be refused based on the grounds provided for in the applicable treaties, such as Article 18 (21) of the Palermo Convention and Article 7 (15) of the Vienna Convention.
- Requests based on letters rogatory pursuant to Law of the Judiciary (Principle of Reciprocity) Article 278 may be refused if the request relates to a case that is within the exclusive jurisdiction of Spain; the requested action is not within the scope of competencies of the judicial authority; the request is not written in Spanish or does not meet all the requirements of authenticity; or the matter of the request is contrary to the public order of Spain.

B. MLA General Procedures

B.1. Central Authority Competent to Receive, Process, and Implement MLA Requests in Criminal Matters

- Spain does not have a central authority to receive and deal with MLA requests. Rather, both the public prosecutor and the judges are involved in and may order the execution of MLA requests. However, only the latter may order measures that could affect the exercise of fundamental rights, such as provisional measures with respect to property.
- When signing or ratifying MLA treaties, Spain has appointed the Ministry of Justice (Ministerio de Justicia, Dirección General de Cooperación Jurídica Internacional. C/ San Bernardo n° 45, Madrid, España) as a central authority. The Ministry of Justice forwards the letter of request to the judge or the prosecutor. There are some exceptions that allow letters of request to be sent directly to the judge or the prosecutor without intervention of the Ministry of Justice—requests under the Schengen Convention and EU MLA Treaty (2000), as a rule. According to the 1959 Council of Europe Convention on MLA in Criminal Matters, the request can be sent directly to the judge in case of emergency (although the request must be sent back through central authority).

B.2. Language Requirements

- Requests must be submitted in Spanish (as a rule). A bilateral agreement with Portugal (1997) permits requests to be submitted in Portuguese.

C. Asset Recovery Specific

C.1. Stage of Proceedings at Which Assistance may be Requested

- All forms of MLA may be provided once a criminal investigation has been initiated in the requesting country.

Tracing

C.2. Available Tracing Mechanisms

- Spain may provide any type of assistance set out in a multilateral or bilateral agreement applicable to a specific case, including those tracing mechanisms set out in Article 46 of the Merida Convention, Article 7 of the Vienna Convention, and Article 18 of the Palermo Convention.
- In the absence of an applicable treaty, Spain may provide mutual legal assistance based on Criminal Procedural Code (Organic Law of the Judiciary) Articles 276 and 278, including any type of measure that is not incompatible with Spanish legislation and case law. Pursuant to the provision, investigating judges therefore have the power to request all information and take (ex officio or on request of the

parties) any measure they consider relevant to the investigation conducted in a foreign country to the same extent they could take such measures in the context of domestic proceedings.

- For "tracing" assets, judges can resort to public registries (land registry, registrar of companies, movable registry), Tax Agency bank accounts database, and the notary registry. A judge can issue search and seizing warrants and adopt phone interceptions in relation to serious crimes if there are sound grounds. There is no evidentiary threshold, but a measure affecting fundamental rights must be fully justified.

C.3. Access to Information Covered by Banking or Professional Secrecy

- Banking or professional secrecy may not be invoked against providing mutual legal assistance under Spanish law. In Spain recipients of a judicial order, including financial institutions, are obliged, without exception, to provide the court with any kind of data maintained by the recipient of such an order. No confidentiality clause of any type can be invoked as a reason for refusing to satisfy such an order.
- Refusing to provide information to a judge or court acting within its area of responsibility is a criminal offense pursuant to Criminal Code Article 410 (civil servants) or Article 556 (particular persons, such as bank clerks).
- In addition, some treaties, such as the European Convention state that in the context of international assistance, states shall empower their courts to order the production or seizure of bank, financial, or commercial records, regardless of bank secrecy laws. Equal provisions are contained in the Merida Convention Article 46 (8), Article 4.1 of the 1990 Council of Europe convention on money laundering, Article 7 of the protocol to the EU mutual legal assistance Convention, Article 12 (6) of the Palermo Convention, and Article 5 of the Vienna Convention.

Provisional Measures (Freezing, Seizing, and Restraint Orders)

C.4. Direct Enforcement of Foreign Freezing and Seizing Orders

- Spanish law does not provide for direct enforceability of foreign restraint or seizing orders. Restraint of property may be conducted only through application of domestic measures. Within the European Union, Spain recognizes the direct enforcement of member state orders, although the order must be executed according to Spanish law. See Law 18/2006, 5th June (for seizures), and Law 4/2010, 10th March (for confiscations).

C.5. Issuance of Domestic Provisional Measures upon Request by a Foreign Jurisdiction

- **Legal basis:** Criminal Procedural Code (main rule) and the Civil Procedural Code (supplementary rule).
- **Procedure:** Spanish law allows for the application of provisional measures to guarantee effectiveness of a future conviction. The provision extends to any

instrumentalities used or intended for use in the commission of an offense, and direct and indirect profits derived from the commission of the offense.

- **Evidentiary requirements:** There is no specific evidential threshold to execute the request apart from treaties, conventions, and Spanish law. A provisional measure affecting fundamental rights must be fully justified.
- **Time limit:** Restraint orders regarding buildings (that is, lands, plots, flats) must be registered in the land registry to become effective and must be renewed every four years, or else they will expire.

Confiscation

C.6. Enforcement of Foreign Confiscation Orders

- **Legal basis:** Spanish law does not provide for direct enforceability of foreign confiscation orders except as set out below. Foreign confiscation orders may be implemented only through application of domestic seizing measures as outlined above. Within the European Union, Spain recognizes the direct enforcement of member states orders, although the order must be executed according to the Spanish law. See Law 4/2010, 10th March (for confiscations).
- **Procedures:**
- **Evidentiary requirements:** No specific evidentiary requirements.

C.7. Applicability of Non-Conviction Based Asset Forfeiture Orders

- No mechanism available.

C.8. Confiscation of Legitimate Assets Equivalent in Value to Illicit Proceeds

- This is possible according to the Criminal Code Article 127.

D. Types of Informal Assistance

- Informal assistance may be provided by the SEPBLAC (Ejecutivo de la Comisión de Prevención del Blanqueo de Capitales e Infracciones Monetarias) (FIU), Bank of Spain, the CNMV(Comisión Nacional del Mercado de Valores), the DGFSP (Dirreción General de Seguros y Fondos de Pensiones) (supervisory authorities), and the police.

Switzerland

A. MLA Legal Framework and Preconditions to Cooperation (General)

A.1. Relevant Laws, Treaties, and Conventions Dealing with or Including a Component Relevant for MLA and Asset Recovery

- All requests for MLA are executed based on the Federal Act on International Mutual Assistance in Criminal Matters (IMAC) (http://www.rhf.admin.ch/etc/medialib/data/rhf/recht.Par.0016.File.tmp/sr351-1-e.pdf) and the Ordinance on International Mutual Assistance in Criminal Matters (O-IMAC) (http://www.rhf.admin.ch/etc/medialib/data/rhf/recht.Par.0012.File.tmp/sr351-11-e.pdf).
- Switzerland has entered into bilateral and multilateral MLA treaties with a large number of countries and has ratified numerous international treaties that include MLA provisions (including the UNCAC). The full list of treaties relevant for MLA can be found on http://www.rhf.admin.ch/rhf/fr/home/straf/recht/multilateral.html.

A.2. Legal Preconditions for the Provision of MLA

- Reciprocity applies to all MLA requests (IMAC Article 8). In case of a treaty relationship or an ad hoc agreement with a requesting state, reciprocity is met. In other cases, a reciprocity guarantee is required. Reciprocity may be waived for the serving of documents or if the execution of a request seems advisable given the type of offense involved.
- Dual criminality is mandatory with respect to coercive measures, including the gathering of evidence, searches, seizures, or confiscation of assets. Noncoercive forms of assistance may be granted in the absence of dual criminality. Whether dual criminality is met is determined based on the law at the time the assistance is given, not at the time the offense was committed or the request was received.
- IMAC Article 67 provides for the principle of specialty, according to which MLA may be granted only under the condition that the documents and information provided are not used for investigative purposes or as formal evidence in court for political offenses, military offenses, and fiscal offenses other than tax fraud. Where an offense for which MLA is requested has a component relating to any of these offenses, the information or documents received from Switzerland may be used only to investigate and prosecute the "ordinary" but not the offense pursuant to Article 3.

A.3. Grounds for Refusal of MLA
Pursuant to IMAC Articles 2, 3, and 4, requests may not be granted if:

- The foreign proceeding does not meet the procedural requirements of the European Convention of Human Rights and Fundamental Freedoms or the International Covenant on Civil and Political Rights.

- The foreign proceeding is carried out so as to prosecute or punish a person because of his political opinions; his belonging to a certain social group; his race, religion, or nationality.
- The foreign proceeding could result in aggravating the situation of the person pursued for any of the reasons mentioned above.
- The foreign proceeding is tainted with other grave defects.
- The subject of the proceeding is an act that has a predominantly political character, constitutes a violation of the obligation to perform military or similar service, or appears to be directed against the national defense or military strength of the requesting state.
- The subject of the proceeding is an offense that appears to be aimed at reducing fiscal duties or taxes or that violates regulations concerning currency, trade, or economic policy.
- The importance of the offense does not justify the carrying out of the proceedings.
- A judge in Switzerland or the requesting state acquitted the defendants, or the sanction was executed or cannot be executed.
- Reciprocity is not granted by the requesting state.

B. MLA General Procedures

B.1. Central Authority Competent to Receive, Process, and Implement MLA Requests in Criminal Matters

- The Swiss Federal Office of Justice is the centralized authority to receive and disseminate the majority of formal MLA requests. After conducting a summary examination pursuant to IMAC Article 78 (whether the request meets the form requirements), requests are generally forwarded to the examining magistrate of a Swiss canton, who will conduct a preliminary examination of the request pursuant to IMAC Article 80 and execute the request.
- Austria, France, Germany, and Italy may send MLA requests directly to the cantonal or federal executing authority in Switzerland based on bilateral agreements; Schengen countries may also make direct contacts.
- For MLA requests received from Italy or the United States, or if a request relates to more than one canton, the request relates to a complex case, or the competent canton is unable to respond to the request within an appropriate time, the Federal Office of Justice, and not the cantonal judicial authorities, is competent to process and implement requests.

B.2. Language Requirements

- Foreign requests and their enclosures may be submitted in German, French, or Italian or be accompanied by an officially certified translation into one of these languages (IMAC Article 28.5). Requests have to be in written form (IMAC Article 28.1).

C. Asset Recovery Specific

C.1. Stage of Proceedings at Which Assistance may be Requested

- Measures pursuant to the IMAC may generally be taken once a criminal investigation has been initiated in the requesting country. For administrative procedures aiming at identifying whether a criminal investigation must be opened (Article 63 IMAC), assistance may be granted even before an investigation has been opened.

Tracing

C.2. Available Tracing Mechanisms

Pursuant to IMAC Article 63, transmission of information as well as procedural acts permitted under Swiss law may be taken if they appear necessary for the proceedings abroad. The measures listed below do not require a court order but can be ordered by an examining judge:

- The serving of documents or of summons by personal delivery to the recipient or by mail (IMAC Article 68).
- The obtaining of evidence, in particular searches of persons and rooms, seizure, order to produce, expert opinion, hearing and confrontation of persons (IMAC Article 18).
- The production of documents and papers.
- The handing over or surrender of objects or assets subject to precautionary seizure with a view to forfeit or restitution to the entitled person (IMAC Articles 74, 74a).
- IMAC Article 18a allows for the temporary surveillance of mail and telecommunication services.
- IMAC Article 64 further provides that if any of the measures outlined above require the use of compulsion (house search, wiretapping, document search, account freezing), dual criminality is required, and the measure requested needs to be proportionate to the importance of the offense. Offenses listed in IMAC Article 3, such as political and tax offenses, may not serve as a basis to request coercive measures.

C.3. Access to Information Covered by Banking or Professional Secrecy

- Swiss banking secrecy is enshrined in Article 47 of the Federal Law on Banks and Savings Banks. However, banking secrecy can be lifted based on a judicial order in the context of MLA in criminal matters. In cases where a lawyer is acting as an asset manager, a financial intermediary, a trustee, or a nominee, legal privilege does not apply.

Provisional Measures (Freezing, Seizing, and Restraint Orders)

C.4. Direct Enforcement of Foreign Freezing and Seizing Orders

- The IMAC does not contain provisions relating to the direct enforceability of foreign seizing and freezing orders. Countries may obtain assistance in restraining property in Switzerland through application for domestic orders pursuant to IMAC Article 18, as outlined below.

C.5. Issuance of Domestic Provisional Measures upon Request by a Foreign Jurisdiction

- **Legal basis:** IMAC Article 18.
- **Procedure:** The request submitted by the foreign authority has to describe the provisional measures requested to be taken and the context of the case in which the request is made. Based on this information, the Swiss authorities may obtain an order from the examining magistrate.
- **Evidentiary requirements:** Upon request by a foreign authority, the Swiss authorities, based on a standard of reasonable grounds for a criminal suspicion, may take measures to preserve existing situations, to safeguard legal interests, or to protect jeopardized evidence. Article 18 does not specify the types of property to which the measure may be applied. However, Article 74 specifies that instruments used in the commission of an offense, the products or profits of the offense, their replacement value and any illicit advantage, and any gifts and other contributions that served to instigate the offense or recompense the offender as well as their replacement value may be subject to provisional measures.
- **Time limit:** As a rule, precautionary measures are valid until the end of the MLA proceeding.

Confiscation

C.6. Enforcement of Foreign Confiscation Orders

- **Legal basis:** IMAC Article 74a.
- **Procedure:** Assets traceable to the crime (that is, the value of products or profits of the offense, any illicit advantage, and any gifts and other contributions that served to instigate the offense or recompense the offender) may be transferred to the requesting State, if the requesting State provides a final and executable order of confiscation.
- **Evidentiary requirements:** A certified final and enforceable confiscation order, supporting the conclusion that the assets located in Switzerland are traceable to the crime, has to be provided. Swiss authorities will also check whether the fair trial clauses were respected in the foreign procedure.

C.7. Applicability of Non-Conviction Based Asset Forfeiture Orders
The Swiss legal system permits non-conviction based forfeiture (Swiss Penal Code Article 70) and the enforcement of foreign NCB orders.

C.8. Confiscation of Legitimate Assets Equivalent in Value to Illicit Proceeds
According to jurisprudence, confiscation of legitimate assets equivalent in value to illicit proceeds seems to be possible under IMAC Article 74a when the order is affecting

non-Swiss residents. For Swiss residents, the execution is possible under IMAC Article 94ss (*exequatur* of the judgment before a Swiss Court).

D. Types of Informal Assistance

- Assistance may be provided by the Money Laundering Reporting Office Switzerland (FIU) (www.fedpol.admin.ch/fedpol/en/home/themen/kriminali-taet/geldwaescherei.html), the Swiss Financial Market Supervisory Authority (http://www.finma.ch/e/Pages/default.aspx), and Swiss law enforcement authorities.

United Kingdom

A. MLA Legal Framework and Preconditions to Cooperation (General)

A.1. Relevant Laws, Treaties, and Conventions Dealing with or Including a Component Relevant for MLA and Asset Recovery

- The *Crime (International Co-operation) Act* (CICA) (http://www.statutelaw.gov.uk/SearchResults.aspx?TYPE=QS&Title=Crime&Year=&Number=&LegType=Act+%28UK+Public+General%29) allows for the provision of mutual legal assistance to any country.
- The *Proceeds of Crime Act 2002 (External Requests and Orders) Order 2005* (POC) (http://www.opsi.gov.uk/si/si2008/uksi_20080302_en_1) allows for the issuance of restraint warrants and the confiscation of assets upon request or based on an order issued by a foreign country in both conviction based and non-conviction based proceedings.
- The *Criminal Justice (International Cooperation) Act 1990 (Enforcement of Overseas Forfeitures) Order* (CRIJICA) (http://www.opsi.gov.uk/Acts/acts1990/ukpga_19900005_en_1) regulates the restraining and forfeiture of the instrumentalities of crime upon request or based on an order issued by a foreign country.
- The United Kingdom has entered into 32 bilateral MLA agreements with Antigua and Barbuda; Argentina; Australia; Bahamas; Bahrain; Barbados; Bolivia; Canada; Chile; Colombia; Ecuador; Grenada; Guyana; Hong Kong SAR, China; India, Ireland; Italy; Malaysia; Mexico; Netherlands; Nigeria; Panama; Paraguay; Romania; Saudi Arabia; Spain; Sweden; Thailand, Trinidad and Tobago; Ukraine; United States; and Uruguay.
- The United Kingdom is a party to the following multilateral agreements, which include provisions on mutual legal assistance: the Merida, Vienna, and Palermo conventions; the European Convention on Mutual Legal Assistance in Criminal Matters and Additional Protocol; the Council of Europe Convention on Laundering, Search, Seizure and Confiscation of the Proceeds of Crime; the Convention on Mutual Assistance in Criminal Matters between the Member States of the European Union and Protocol to the Convention on Mutual Assistance in Criminal Matters between Member States of the European Union; and the Harare Scheme. However, the United Kingdom may provide MLA directly based only on domestic law and not on international treaties.

A.2. Legal Preconditions for the Provision of MLA

- Reciprocity is generally not required for the provision of MLA.
- Dual criminality is not required for most measures under the CICA. However, requests for search and seizure for evidentiary reasons as well as restraint and confiscation of assets are subject to dual criminality; that is, they cannot be executed unless the underlying criminal conduct would be an offense under U.K. law.

A.3. Grounds for Refusal of MLA

- Requests involving double jeopardy will not be executed.
- Requests relating to offenses punishable with the death penalty or relating to trivial offense may be refused.
- Requests that affect the U.K. national security or other U.K. essential interests may be declined.

B. MLA General Procedures

B.1. Central Authority Competent to Receive, Process, and Implement MLA Requests in Criminal Matters

- For assistance in England, Wales, and Northern Ireland, the U.K. Home Office, Judicial Cooperation Unit, is the central authority to receive all requests for MLA.
- For assistance in Scotland, the Crown Office, International Cooperation Unit, is the central authority to receive MLA requests.
- The central authorities ensure that requests meet the form requirements and the requirements under U.K. law and subsequently disseminate requests to the relevant domestic authorities for implementation.

B.2. Language Requirements

- Requests must be made in writing in English or be submitted with an English translation. If no translation is provided, the central authorities will ask for one, and the request will remain unexecuted until the translation is received.

C. Asset Recovery Specific

C.1. Stage of Proceedings at Which Assistance may be Requested

- Measures pursuant to CICA Sections 13–15 as well as account and customer information orders may be issued as soon as an investigation for an offense has been initiated in the requesting country.
- In Scotland, search and seizing warrants may be issued as soon as there are reasonable grounds to suspect that an offense under the law of the requesting country has been committed.
- Search and seizing orders in England, Wales, and Northern Ireland (CICA Section 17) may be taken only if criminal proceedings have been instituted or an arrest been made in the requesting country.

Tracing

C.2. Available Tracing Mechanisms

- Obtaining of Evidence (CICA Sections 13–15): Evidence gathering orders may be issued if a request is made in connection with criminal proceedings or a criminal investigation in the requesting state. In England, Wales, and Northern Ireland, suspects cannot be compelled to attend court or be coerced to provide evidence under oath for the purposes of MLA. In Scotland, both suspects and witnesses can be compelled to attend the court, but suspects cannot be compelled to provide evidence.

- CICA Section 17: Search and seizing warrants for England, Wales, and Northern Ireland may be issued if criminal proceedings have been instituted or an arrest has been made in the requesting country; if the conduct in question would constitute an arrestable offense had it been committed in the United Kingdom; and if there are reasonable grounds to suspect that evidence is in the United Kingdom relating to the offense. In Scotland, such warrants may be issued if there are reasonable grounds to suspect that an offense under the law of the requesting country has been committed and if the offense would be punishable with imprisonment under Scottish law had the conduct occurred domestically. Warrants may not be issued with respect to items or documents subject to professional legal privilege.
- Customer Information Orders (CICA Sections 32 and 37): Orders may be issued requiring a financial institution to provide any customer information it has relating to the person specified in the order if the specified person is subject to an investigation in the requesting country, if the investigation concerns serious criminal conduct, if the conduct meets dual criminality, and if the order is sought for the purposes of the investigation. A customer information order has effect regardless of any restrictions on the disclosure of information that would otherwise apply.
- Account Monitoring Orders (CICA Sections 35 and 40): Orders may be issued requiring a financial institution specified in the application to provide account information of the description specified in the order and at the time and in the manner specified if there is a criminal investigation in the requesting country and if the order is sought for the purposes of the investigation. It is an offense under U.K. law to tip off customers that an account monitoring order has been received by a financial institution. The monitoring period may not exceed 90 days.
- Interception of Telecommunication: This measure is available only to parties of the EU Convention on Mutual Legal Assistance in Criminal Matters.

C.3. Access to Information Covered by Banking or Professional Secrecy

- Customer or account information orders pursuant to CICA Sections 32, 37, 35, and 40 have effect regardless of any restrictions on the disclosure of information that would otherwise apply. Therefore, they may also be used to obtain information covered by banking secrecy.
- Information covered by legal privilege is protected and may not be subject to search and seizing warrants.

Provisional Measures (Freezing, Seizing, and Restraint Orders)

C.4. Direct Enforcement of Foreign Freezing and Seizing Orders

- **Legal basis:** Foreign freezing orders are executed through CICA Sections 17 and 18.

- **Procedure:** Direct application of foreign freezing orders through a decision by the territorial authority for the part of the United Kingdom in which the evidence to which the order relates is situated. Only orders relating to criminal proceedings or investigations for an offense listed in the CICA may be directly applicable. The court may decide not to give effect to a foreign freezing order that would be incompatible with the rights under the Human Rights Act 1998 or if the person whose conduct is in question, if he was charged under the law of the requesting state or the United Kingdom, would be entitled to be discharged based on a previous acquittal or conviction.

C.5. Issuance of Domestic Provisional Measures upon Request by a Foreign Jurisdiction

- **Legal basis:** POC Articles 8, 58, and 95.
- **Procedure:** Countries may apply for issuance of a restraint order by the Crown Court.
- **Evidentiary requirements:** An order may be issued if a criminal investigation has been started in the requesting country or proceedings for an offense have been initiated and not concluded in the requesting country and if there is reasonable cause to believe that the alleged offender named in the request has benefited from his criminal conduct. The POC provides for the seizing order to extend to any "realizable property," which is defined to include any free property held by the defendant or by the recipient of a tainted gift.
- **Time limit:** A restraint order remains in force until it is discharged by a further order of the court on the application of either the U.K. authorities or any person affected by the order. The court must discharge the order if at the conclusion of the foreign proceedings no external confiscation order is made or if the external order is not registered for enforcement within a reasonable time.

Confiscation

C.6. Enforcement of Foreign Confiscation Orders

- **Legal basis:** POC Articles 21, 68, and 107.
- **Procedure:** Foreign conviction-based confiscation orders may be registered and subsequently directly enforced in the United Kingdom if the Crown Court is satisfied that the conditions of the POC are met.
- **Evidentiary requirements:** A foreign confiscation order may be executed if it was made based on a conviction, if it is in force and final, if giving effect to the order will not violate any rights of the Human Rights Act of 1998, and if the property specified in the order is not subject to a charge under U.K. law.

C.7. Applicability of Non-Conviction Based Asset Forfeiture Orders

- POC Articles 143 ff. allow for the registration and implementation of (civil) forfeiture orders. Article 147 permits an application for a property freezing order to preserve property so that it is available to satisfy an external order enforced in the United Kingdom by means of civil recovery.

C.8. Confiscation of Legitimate Assets Equivalent in Value to Illicit Proceeds

- Criminal confiscation in the United Kingdom is value-based, that is, the defendant's proceeds of crime are calculated as a value and the defendant is then ordered to pay that amount. Therefore, equivalent-value confiscation is possible.

D. Types of Informal Assistance

- Informal assistance may be provided by the police; the Serious Organized Crime Agency (FIU) (http://www.soca.gov.uk/), and the Financial Services Authority (http://www.fsa.gov.uk/).
- The United Kingdom has attaché offices in France, Italy, Pakistan, Spain, and the United States.[97]

---

97. Practitioners should inquire with the nearest British High Commission to determine the nearest attaché.

United States

A. MLA Legal Framework and Preconditions to Cooperation (General)

A.1. Relevant Laws, Treaties, and Conventions Dealing with or Including a Component Relevant for MLA and Asset Recovery

- The United States provides assistance directly based on bilateral and multilateral treaties, letters of request, and letters rogatory. The types of assistance available are very broad but, with regard to asset recovery, depend on the provisions of the applicable treaty or convention to a specific case.
- The United States has entered into bilateral MLA treaties with more than 70 jurisdictions, namely: Anguilla; Antigua and Barbuda; Argentina; Aruba; Australia; Austria; the Bahamas; Barbados; Belgium; Belize; Brazil; British Virgin Islands; Bulgaria; Canada; Cayman Islands; China; Colombia, Cyprus; Czech Republic; Denmark; Dominica; Arab Republic of Egypt; Estonia; Finland; France; Germany; Greece; Grenada; Guadeloupe; Hong Kong SAR, China; Hungary; India; Ireland; Israel; Italy; Jamaica; Japan; Republic of Korea; Latvia; Liechtenstein; Lithuania; Luxembourg; Malaysia; Malta; Martinique; Montserrat; Mexico; Morocco; Netherlands; Netherlands Antilles; Nigeria; Panama; the Philippines; Poland; Romania; Russian Federation; Singapore; Slovak Republic; St. Kitts and Nevis; St. Lucia; St. Vincent and the Grenadines; Slovenia; South Africa; Spain; Sweden; Switzerland; Thailand; Trinidad and Tobago; Turkey; Turks and Caicos Islands; Ukraine; United Kingdom; Uruguay; and República de Bolivariana Venezuela. An agreement was also entered into on June 25, 2003, between the United States and the European Union concerning mutual legal assistance that, among other things, provides a mechanism for more quickly exchanging information regarding bank accounts held by suspects in criminal investigations.
- The United States has ratified the Merida Convention and may therefore grant MLA directly based on the provisions of the convention. The United States has also ratified the Inter-American Convention on Mutual Legal Assistance of the Organization of American States; the Vienna, Palermo, and the Financing of Terrorism conventions; the Inter-American Convention against Terrorism; the Inter-American Convention on Letters Rogatory and the Additional Protocol to the Convention; the OECD Convention on Combating Bribery of Foreign Public Officials in International Business Transactions; and the Inter-American Convention against Corruption.
- The United States responds to requests in the form of letters of requests and letters rogatory, as well as to MLA requests, pursuant to US Code Title 28 Section 1782 and US Code Title 18 Section 3512 even in the absence of a treaty relationship. The United States is able to provide broad assistance in response to requests from foreign authorities.

A.2. Legal Preconditions for the Provision of MLA

- Most bilateral MLA treaties do not generally require dual criminality. Some but not all of them require dual criminality with respect to coercive measures. When dual criminality is required, technical differences between the categorization of the crime in the United States and requesting state do not affect the provision of the requested assistance because the qualification of the offense is irrelevant, as long as the underlying acts are punishable in both states.

- Many forms of assistance based on letters of request or letters rogatory, including the issuance of compulsory measures, do not require dual criminality.

A.3. Grounds for Refusal of MLA

- Grounds for refusals are set out in the applicable bilateral and multilateral agreements, such as Article 7 of the Vienna Convention, Article 18 of the Palermo Convention, and Article 46 of the Merida Convention.

B. MLA General Procedures

B.1. Central Authority Competent to Receive, Process, and Implement MLA Requests in Criminal Matters

- The Office of International Affairs of the Department of Justice (OIA) is the U.S. central authority for all requests for MLA and coordinates all international evidence gathering.
- OIA has attorneys and support staff with responsibilities and expertise in various parts of the world and in different substantive areas. The OIA executes MLA requests through competent law enforcement authorities, such as the United States Attorney's Offices, ICE (Immigration and Customs Enforcement), USSS (United States Secret Service), FBI (Federal Bureau of Investigation), the USMS (United States Marshall's Service), Interpol, and others. Requests for freezing, seizing, or confiscation of assets are executed in close cooperation with the Department of Justice's Asset Forfeiture Money Laundering Section.

B.2. Language Requirements

- English is the preferred language for requests. Requesting jurisdictions could incur translation costs if the request is submitted in any other language.

C. Asset Recovery Specific

C.1. Stage of Proceedings at Which Assistance may be Requested

- Most bilateral treaties allow for the provision of MLA during the investigative stage. Equally, OIA may apply to the courts for a production order or a search, freezing, or seizing warrant once an investigation has commenced in the requesting country, depending on the provisions of the MLA treaty or convention at issue.

Tracing

C.2. Available Tracing Mechanisms

- The types of measures available with respect to MLA requests by a specific country and with respect to a specific offense depend on the provisions of the applicable multilateral and bilateral treaties. In general, bilateral treaties allow for a substantial range of measures, including taking the testimony or statements of persons; providing documents, records, and other items; locating or identifying persons or items; serving documents; transferring persons in custody for testimony or other purposes; executing searches and seizures; assisting in proceedings related to immobilization and forfeiture of assets and restitution; collection of fines; and any other form of assistance not prohibited by the laws of the requested state.
- For requests based on letters of request or letters rogatory, OIA, based on US Code Title 18 Section 3512 or Title 28 Section 1782, may request the district court to order any person to give a testimony or statement or to produce a document or other thing for use in proceedings in a foreign tribunal, including in the course of criminal investigations conducted before the filing of formal accusations. Furthermore, OIA may apply to a federal judge for issuance of search warrants and other compulsory measures.

C.3. Access to Information Covered by Banking or Professional Secrecy

- Information covered by financial secrecy may be provided, if necessary by a court order.
- Information subject to professional legal privilege is protected from disclosure.

Provisional Measures (Freezing, Seizing, and Restraint Orders)

C.4. Direct Enforcement of Foreign Freezing and Seizing Orders

- For requests based on a treaty or agreement that provides for assistance in forfeiture (for example, the Merida Convention), US Code Title 28 Section 2467 allows for the registration and subsequent direct enforcement of foreign restraining orders to preserve property that is or may become subject to forfeiture or confiscation. Recent case law has called into question the viability of this option in the prejudgment context, and the Department of Justice is considering the need for a statutory amendment to clarify the congressional intent to enforce foreign prejudgment restraining orders.
- Requests for enforcement of foreign orders have to be submitted, along with a certified copy of the foreign order, to the U.S. attorney general, who will make a final decision on whether to grant the request.

C.5. Issuance of Domestic Provisional Measures upon Request by a Foreign Jurisdiction

- **Legal basis:** US Code Title 28 Section 2467
- **Procedure:** OIA, often in conjunction with the Asset Forfeiture and Money Laundering Section, may apply to the courts for issuance of a restraining order on behalf of the requesting country.
- **Evidentiary requirements:** The United States may initiate domestic seizing proceedings if the requesting country can establish through written affidavit that an investigation or proceeding is under way and that there are reasonable grounds to believe that the property to be restrained will be confiscated at the conclusion of such proceedings. The request has to be made pursuant to a treaty or agreement that provides for mutual assistance in forfeiture, and the foreign offenses that give rise to confiscation also have to give rise to confiscation under U.S. federal law.
- **Time limit:** None, if a permanent restraining order was issued in foreign state. If the requesting country has arrested or charged somebody, property that might become subject to confiscation may be restrained for 30 days even without the requirement to establish probable cause, but upon the expectation the United States will file its own *in rem* confiscation action against the proceeds or instrumentalities of foreign crime based upon probable cause evidence that will be provided by the requesting state at a later date. This 30-day order can be extended for cause shown, for example, a delay in gathering or translating the foreign evidence.

Confiscation

C.6. Enforcement of Foreign Confiscation Orders

- **Legal basis:** US Code Title 28 Section 2467.
- **Procedure:** Requests for enforcement of foreign orders, including a copy of the foreign order, have to be submitted to the U.S. attorney general, who will in turn make a final decision on whether the request should be granted. If the request is granted, the attorney general may apply to the district court for enforcement.
- **Evidentiary requirements:** The requested state must provide a certified copy of the judgment and submit an affidavit or sworn statement by a person familiar with the underlying confiscation proceedings setting forth a summary of the facts of the case and a description of the proceedings that resulted in the confiscation judgment, as well as showing that the jurisdiction in question, in accordance with the principles of due process, provided notice to all persons with an interest in the property in sufficient time to enable such persons to defend against the confiscation and that the judgment rendered is in force and is not subject to appeal.

C.7. Applicability of Non-Conviction Based Asset Forfeiture Orders

- The United States can seek the registration and enforcement of a foreign forfeiture judgment whether it is for specific property or an order to pay a sum of money, whether conviction based or non-conviction based.

C.8. Confiscation of Legitimate Assets Equivalent in Value to Illicit Proceeds

- Both domestic and foreign confiscation orders may be executed toward legitimate assets of equivalent value to proceeds or instrumentalities of crime.

D. Types of Informal Assistance

- Assistance may be provided by the Financial Crimes Enforcement Network (Fin-CEN) (http://www.fincen.gov/), as well as U.S. regulatory, supervisory, and law enforcement authorities. However, all requests have to be channeled through Fin-CEN, which serves as the primary portal through which information may be shared.
- The United States does maintain and use law enforcement attaché offices in foreign jurisdictions primarily by the FBI, ICE, and DEA. The FBI has over 75 offices serving 200 countries. For details, visit http://www.fbi.gov/contact/legat/legat .htm. ICE has offices serving over 40 countries: Argentina; Austria; Brazil; Canada; Caribbean; China; Colombia; Denmark; Dominican Republic; Ecuador; Arab Republic of Egypt; El Salvador; France; Germany; Greece; Guatemala; Honduras; Hong Kong SAR, China; India; Italy; Jamaica; Japan; Jordan; Republic of Korea; Mexico; Morocco; Netherlands; Pakistan; Panama; the Philippines; Russian Federation; Saudi Arabia; Singapore; South Africa; Spain; Switzerland; Thailand; United Arab Emirates, United Kingdom; República Bolivariana de Venezuela; and Vietnam. For details, see http://www.ice.gov/international-affairs/.[98]

---

98. Practitioners should contact the nearest United States embassy to determine the appropriate attaché office.

Glossary

Asset confiscation. The permanent deprivation of property by order of a court or other competent authority. The term is used interchangeably with forfeiture. Confiscation takes place through a judicial or administrative procedure that transfers the ownership of specified funds or assets to the state. The persons or entities that held an interest in the specified funds or other assets at the time of the confiscation or forfeiture lose all rights, in principle, to the confiscated or forfeited funds or other assets.[99]

Beneficial owner(s). The natural person(s) who ultimately owns or controls a customer and/or the person on whose behalf a transaction is being conducted. The term also incorporates those persons who exercise ultimate effective control over a legal person (such as a corporation) or arrangement.

Central authorities. The entity designated by a jurisdiction to receive requests for mutual legal assistance from other jurisdictions. The central authority may deal with these requests itself or forward them to the appropriate authority.

Egmont Group of Financial Intelligence Units. An informal gathering of financial intelligence units formed in 1995. Now known as the Egmont Group of Financial Intelligence Units, these FIUs meet regularly to find ways to cooperate, especially in the areas of information exchange, training, and the sharing of expertise.[100]

***Exequatur* ruling.** A judgment by a domestic court that a foreign order may be enforced in the jurisdiction in which the court operates.

***Ex parte* proceedings.** Legal proceedings brought by one person in the absence of, and without representation or notification of, other parties.

Financial intelligence unit (FIU). "A central, national agency responsible for receiving (and as permitted, requesting), analyzing and disseminating to the competent authorities, disclosures of financial information: (i) concerning suspected proceeds of crime and potential financing of terrorism, or (ii) required by national legislation or regulation, in order to combat money laundering and terrorism financing."[101]

Focal point. A single, readily accessible office or official with designated authority to communicate with other jurisdictions with respect to mutual legal assistance requests and other related matters and whose contact details are provided through the Internet and/or other media.

---

99. FATF Interpretive Note to Special Recommendation III: Freezing and Confiscating Terrorist Assets, para. 7(c), http://www.fatf-gafi.org/dataoecd/53/32/34262136.pdf.
100. http://www.egmontgroup.org/about
101. Definition adopted at the plenary meeting of the Egmont Group in Rome in November 1996, as amended at the Egmont Plenary Meeting in Guernsey in June 2004.

Freeze of assets. A temporary prohibition on the transfer, conversion, disposition, or movement of property or temporary assumption of custody or control of property on the basis of an order issued by a court or other competent authority.[102] The term is used interchangeably with seizure and restraining.

In personam. Latin for "directed toward a particular person." In the context of asset confiscation or a lawsuit, it is a legal action directed against a specific person.

In rem. Latin for "against a thing." In the context of asset confiscation, it is a legal action against a specific thing or property.

Legal persons. Refers to bodies corporate, foundations, anstalts, partnerships, or associations, or any similar bodies that can establish a permanent customer relationship with a financial institution or otherwise own property.

Letters rogatory. A formal request from a court to a foreign court for some type of judicial assistance. It permits formal communication between a judge, a prosecutor, or law enforcement official of one jurisdiction, and his or her counterpart in another jurisdiction. A particular form of mutual legal assistance.

Merida Convention. The United Nations Convention against Corruption.

Mutual legal assistance. Assistance provided by one jurisdiction to another jurisdiction in order to enforce laws, including identifying people and things, as well as providing assistance to freeze, restrain, or confiscate the proceeds or instrumentalities of crime.

Mutual legal assistance treaty (MLAT). A bilateral treaty that creates clear and binding obligations between two jurisdictions for cooperation on mutual legal assistance and sets out efficient and comprehensive procedures to be applied. These treaties are typically not limited in scope to a range of offenses but apply to any criminal activity that falls within their scope of application. MLATs typically create a closer relationship between the signatory states than multilateral conventions and are customized to fit that relationship.

Originating jurisdiction. A jurisdiction that asks for the assistance of another jurisdiction for the purpose of assisting an investigation or prosecution or enforcing a judgment.

Palermo Convention. The United Nations Convention against Transnational Organized Crime.

Politically exposed person (PEP). "Individuals who are, or have been, entrusted with prominent public functions, for example, Heads of State or of government, senior politicians, senior government, judicial or military officials, senior executives of state owned corporations, important party officials. Business relationships with family members or close associates of PEPs involve reputational risks similar to those with PEPs

---

102. UNCAC, Article 2(d).

themselves. The definition is not intended to cover middle ranking or more junior individuals in the foregoing categories."[103]

Requested jurisdiction. A jurisdiction that is asked to provide assistance to another jurisdiction for the purpose of assisting an investigation or prosecution, or enforcing a judgment.

Restraint of assets. See freeze of assets.

Seizure. See freeze of assets.

States parties. A country that has ratified or acceded to a particular treaty, and is therefore legally bound by the provisions in the instrument.

Suspicious transaction report (STR). A report filed by a financial institution or other reporting entity about a suspicious or potentially suspicious transaction or activity. The report is filed with the country's FIU; also, known as a **Suspicious Activity Report (SAR).**

Vienna Convention. United Nations Convention against Illicit Traffic in Narcotic Drugs and Psychotropic Substances.

---

103. FATF Forty Recommendations, Glossary. http://www.fatf-gafi.org/glossary/0,3414,en_322503079_3 2236889_35433764_1_1_!_!,00.html#34285860.

www.ingramcontent.com/pod-product-compliance
Lightning Source LLC
Chambersburg PA
CBHW080547220326
41599CB00032B/6387